MARVEL CINEMATIC UNIVERSE GUIDEBOOK: THE AVENGERS INITIATIVE

MARVEL CINEMATIC UNIVERSE GUIDEBOOK: THE AVENGERS INITIATIVE

CONTENTS

Marvel's *Iron Man*	3
Marvel's *Incredible Hulk*	35
Marvel's *Iron Man 2*	45
Marvel's *Thor*	67
Marvel's *Captain America: The First Avenger*	99
Marvel's The Avengers	130
Marvel's *Iron Man 3*	161
Marvel's *Thor: The Dark World*	177

COVER ART BY **STEPHANIE HANS**

THE AVENGERS CREATED BY STAN LEE & JACK KIRBY

HEAD WRITER/COORDINATOR: **MIKE O'SULLIVAN**
EDITOR: **SARAH BRUNSTAD**
ASSOCIATE MANAGER, DIGITAL ASSETS: **JOE HOCHSTEIN**
ASSOCIATE MANAGING EDITOR: **KATERI WOODY**
EDITOR, SPECIAL PROJECTS: **MARK BEAZLEY**
SENIOR EDITOR, SPECIAL PROJECTS: **JENNIFER GRÜNWALD**
VP PRODUCTION & SPECIAL PROJECTS: **JEFF YOUNGQUIST**
BOOK DESIGNER: **JAY BOWEN**
COLLECTION INTERIOR DESIGNER: **SALENA JOHNSON**

SPECIAL THANKS TO GEORGE BELIARD, SHAWN "KEEBLER" BYERS, ERIKA DENTON, JOE FRONTIRRE, CAITLIN O'CONNELL, AVIA PEREZ, JACQUE PORTE, AND RYAN POTTER.

SVP PRINT, SALES & MARKETING: **DAVID GABRIEL**
EDITOR IN CHIEF: **AXEL ALONSO**
CHIEF CREATIVE OFFICER: **JOE QUESADA**
PUBLISHER: **DAN BUCKLEY**
EXECUTIVE PRODUCER: **ALAN FINE**

FOR MARVEL STUDIOS

CREATIVE DIRECTOR, RESEARCH: **WILL CORONA PILGRIM**
DIRECTOR OF DEVELOPMENT: **ERIC HAUSERMAN CARROLL**
VP PRODUCTION & DEVELOPMENT: **BRAD WINDERBAUM**
SVP PRODUCTION & DEVELOPMENT: **STEPHEN BROUSSARD**
SVP PRODUCTION & DEVELOPMENT: **JEREMY LATCHAM**
PRESIDENT: **KEVIN FEIGE**

MARVEL CINEMATIC UNIVERSE GUIDEBOOK: THE AVENGERS INITIATIVE. Contains material originally published in magazine form as **GUIDEBOOK TO THE MARVEL CINEMATIC UNIVERSE — MARVEL'S IRON MAN, MARVEL'S INCREDIBLE HULK, MARVEL'S IRON MAN 2, MARVEL'S THOR, MARVEL'S CAPTAIN AMERICA: THE FIRST AVENGER, MARVEL'S THE AVENGERS, MARVEL'S IRON MAN 3 and MARVEL'S THOR: THE DARK WORLD.** First printing 2017. ISBN# 978-0-7851-9660-0. Published by MARVEL WORLDWIDE, INC., a subsidiary of MARVEL ENTERTAINMENT, LLC. OFFICE OF PUBLICATION: 135 West 50th Street, New York, NY 10020.

Printed in China. ALAN FINE, President, Marvel Entertainment; DAN BUCKLEY, President, TV, Publishing & Brand Management; JOE QUESADA, Chief Creative Officer; TOM BREVOORT, SVP of Publishing; DAVID BOGART, SVP of Business Affairs & Operations, Publishing & Partnership; C.B. CEBULSKI, VP of Brand Management & Development, Asia; DAVID GABRIEL, SVP of Sales & Marketing, Publishing; JEFF YOUNGQUIST, VP of Production & Special Projects; DAN CARR, Executive Director of Publishing Technology; ALEX MORALES, Director of Publishing Operations; SUSAN CRESPI, Production Manager; STAN LEE, Chairman Emeritus. For information regarding advertising in Marvel Comics or on Marvel.com, please contact Vit DeBellis, Integrated Sales Manager, at vdebellis@marvel.com. **For Marvel subscription inquiries, please call 888-511-5480. Manufactured between 12/2/2016 and 2/13/2017 by R.R DONNELLEY ASIA PRINTING SOLUTIONS, CHINA.**

10 9 8 7 6 5 4 3 2 1

GUIDEBOOK TO THE MARVEL CINEMATIC UNIVERSE

MARVEL

IRON MAN

PARAMOUNT PICTURES AND MARVEL ENTERTAINMENT PRESENT A MARVEL STUDIOS PRODUCTION IN ASSOCIATION WITH FAIRVIEW ENTERTAINMENT A FILM BY JON FAVREAU "IRON MAN" ROBERT DOWNEY JR. TERRENCE HOWARD JEFF BRIDGES SHAUN TOUB AND GWYNETH PALTROW MUSIC BY RAMIN DJAWADI MUSIC SUPERVISOR DAVE JORDAN VISUAL EFFECTS SUPERVISOR JOHN NELSON VISUAL EFFECTS AND ANIMATION BY INDUSTRIAL LIGHT & MAGIC EDITOR DAN LEBENTAL, A.C.E. PRODUCTION DESIGNER J. MICHAEL RIVA DIRECTOR OF PHOTOGRAPHY MATTHEW LIBATIQUE, ASC EXECUTIVE PRODUCERS LOUIS D'ESPOSITO PETER BILLINGSLEY JON FAVREAU ARI ARAD EXECUTIVE PRODUCERS STAN LEE DAVID MAISEL PRODUCED BY AVI ARAD KEVIN FEIGE SCREENPLAY BY MARK FERGUS & HAWK OSTBY AND ART MARCUM & MATT HOLLOWAY DIRECTED BY JON FAVREAU

Covering Marvel's *Iron Man (2008)* and *Iron Man: I Am Iron Man (2010) #1-2.*

HEAD WRITER/COORDINATOR: **MIKE O'SULLIVAN**

COORDINATORS: **MIKE FICHERA**, **DARON JENSEN,** AND **JEPH YORK**

WRITERS: **TROY BENJAMIN**, **CHRIS BUCHNER**, **MADISON CARTER**, **ANTHONY COTILLETTA**, **PATRICK DUKE**, **MIKE FICHERA**, **DARON JENSEN**, **ROB LONDON**, **CHRIS MCCARVER**, **SEAN MCQUAID**, **ROGER OTT**, **MARKUS RAYMOND**, **MARC RIEMER**, **JACOB ROUGEMONT**, **MARC SUMERAK**, **STUART VANDAL,** AND **JEPH YORK**

ARTISTS: **MICHAEL ALLRED**, **MARK BRIGHT**, **JIM CHEUNG**, **MIKE DEODATO JR.**, **STEVE DITKO**, **ADI GRANOV**, **DON HECK**, **JACK KIRBY**, **GREG LAND**, **SALVADOR LARROCA**, **RON LIM**, **JORGE LUCAS**, **DAVID MARQUEZ**, **RYAN MEINERDING**, **CARLO PAGULAYAN**, **GEORGE PÉREZ**, **PHIL SAUNDERS**, **KENT SEKI/THE ORPHANAGE,** AND **JIM STARLIN**

COVER ARTIST: **MIKE DEL MUNDO**

SPECIAL THANKS TO DAVID ALTHOFF, STEVEN BOYD, SHAWN "KEEBLER" BYERS, JEFF CHRISTIANSEN, ERIKA DENTON, TIM DILLON, JOE HOCHSTEIN, PERCIVAL LANUZA, JACQUE PORTE, AND RYAN POTTER

IRON MAN CREATED BY STAN LEE, LARRY LIEBER, DON HECK, AND JACK KIRBY

The lights go down. Cell phones wink off one by one. Popcorn in hand, you settle back into your seat. The trailers end, and the movie begins... Suddenly, it appears: that familiar red logo, its rapid-fire blizzard of comic panels flipping past to spell out "MARVEL" across the screen. A fist! A mask! A cape! Was that an iron helmet? A star-spangled shield? A magic hammer?! A chill races up your spine as once again you are back home in the Marvel Cinematic Universe!

Marvel Studios' films have taken the world by storm, catapulting characters once familiar only to comic fans into the larger pop-culture limelight—turning Iron Man, Thor and even the Guardians of the Galaxy into household names. And just like in the comics they hail from, where character crossovers are the norm, one of the Marvel Cinematic Universe's most captivating facets is the fact that all of its films exist in the same shared world—an exciting and unpredictable playground where the Black Widow can skip from *Iron Man*'s sequel to *Captain America*'s, Tony Stark and Bruce Banner can cameo in each other's films, and super-spies Phil Coulson and Nick Fury can effortlessly transition from the first *Iron Man* film to *Marvel's The Avengers* to TV's *Marvel's Agents of S.H.I.E.L.D.* Sure, there have been movie sequels before, but nothing like Marvel's lineage of loveable linkages has ever been accomplished! What other film series can boast such a cacophony of character continuity?

This series, the *Guidebook to the Marvel Cinematic Universe*, hopes to capture all that movie magic and more, rewarding readers with an encyclopedic treasure trove of information on each film's memorable stars. Each *Guidebook* will provide an in-depth look at the heroes, villains, friends, foes, weapons, technology and locations both major and minor featured in each film—starting with the 2008 blockbuster that birthed the MCU itself, Marvel's *Iron Man*!

The *Guidebook to the Marvel Cinematic Universe* is a different beast than our sister publication, the long-running *Official Handbook of the Marvel Universe*. Unlike an *OHOTMU* profile, which covers seven decades of the comic-book appearances of a person, place or thing, each *Guidebook* profile focuses specifically on the events of one individual MCU movie or TV season for the profile subject. Revelations from future films will be incorporated in the subsequent *Guidebook* devoted to the film in which the information is revealed. The goal is to present an in-depth look at the Marvel Cinematic Universe as it existed at the time of each film—and, over the course of the series, to showcase the MCU's evolution, interconnectedness and ever-increasing complexity.

The *Guidebook* will only include information revealed in the final version of each film—nothing from deleted scenes, early drafts or behind-the-scenes features, which often contradict the finished product. However, we will be weaving in facts, figures and images from the gorgeous *Art of* books for each film—as well as incorporating the all-new stories from the canonical official Marvel Cinematic Universe tie-in comic books. A list of the MCU comics covered in each *Guidebook* can be found on that issue's credits page.

And now that the opening titles have passed by, it's time to dig deep into the premiere edition of the *Guidebook to the Marvel Cinematic Universe*, and learn all there is to learn about a self-centered genius named Tony Stark and his wondrous inventions. We hope you join us for each issue of the *Guidebook* as we shine a spotlight on every installment of the Marvel Cinematic Universe. And if you stick around until the end, there might just be a little shawarma...

LARGE REACTOR

MINI-REACTOR

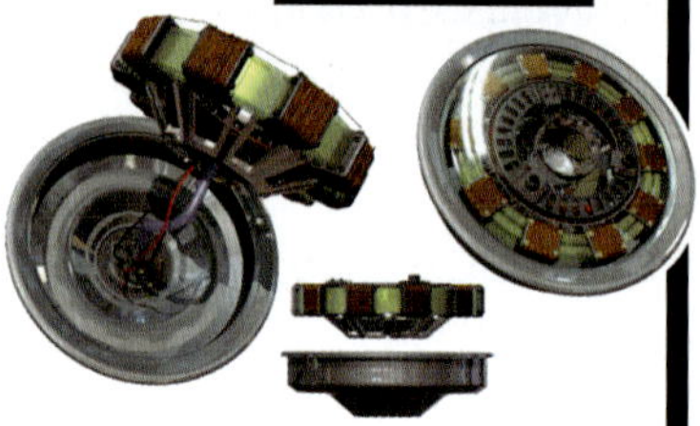

ARC REACTOR

FIRST APPEARANCE: ***Iron Man [2008]***

Though Stark Industries was primarily known for manufacturing weapons, one of Howard Stark's most powerful yet underappreciated inventions was the Arc Reactor, an environmentally friendly high-output energy source with relatively little real estate necessary to house the unit. One such reactor powered Stark Industries' Long Beach campus. While it was viewed within the company as good for public relations, people such as corrupt business partner Obadiah Stane were quick to point out that the device was not cost-effective and had no technological advancements in over 30 years, believing it good only for "shutting up the hippies."

During the captivity of Howard's son, Tony, in Afghanistan, fellow prisoner Ho Yinsen implanted a crude electromagnet into Stark's chest, powered by a car battery, to prevent lethal shrapnel from entering his heart. Stark successfully built a miniaturized version of the Arc Reactor, both to replace the car battery and to power a suit of armor he and Yinsen secretly constructed to facilitate their escape. Once home, Stark replaced his reactor with an upgraded version. Stark asked his executive assistant Pepper Potts to dispose of his first mini-reactor, but she later gifted it to him, mounted in a casing engraved with the words "Proof that Tony Stark has a heart."

Stane attempted to construct his own armored suit, but his top scientists failed to replicate Stark's mini-reactor. Instead, Stane paralyzed Stark with a compact sonic device and stole the upgraded unit from his chest, leaving him for dead. However, Stark was able to use Potts' gift of his original mini-reactor to save himself and confront Stane, now wearing the massive "Iron Monger" armor. Though this mini-reactor barely had enough power to run Stark's new Mark III armor, Iron Man lured Stane onto the roof over the large Arc Reactor powering the campus, and ordered Potts to overload it, destroying both it and Stane.

IN THE COMICS

THE TERM "ARC REACTOR" WAS not used in the comics until recent years. Initially, Stark's armored chest plate protected his heart from the shrapnel. The armor's center chest-piece has been used to project forms of light (including lasers), plasma beams, electromagnetic pulses and holograms.

FIRST APPEARANCE:
TALES OF SUSPENSE #39 (1963)

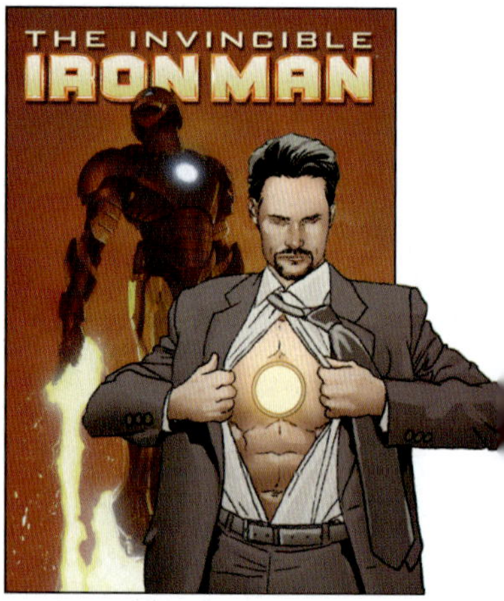

MORE RECENTLY, STARK implanted a new electromagnetic generator called the Repulsor Tech (R.T.) node into the injured Pepper Potts' chest; this unit later powered a suit of armor Stark built for her. After Potts had healed, her R.T. node was put into Stark's chest to help revive him from a coma and power his body, now integrated with his own technology.

FIRST APPEARANCE:
INVINCIBLE IRON MAN #3 (2008)

FACT SHEET

- THE FIRST MINI-ARC REACTOR GENERATED 3 GJ/SEC OF POWER OVER A 15-MINUTE PERIOD. THE SECOND ONE INCREASED BOTH THE POWER AND DURATION OF THE ENERGY OUTPUT.
- THE FIRST MINI-ARC REACTOR WAS ROUGHLY 3.5 INCHES IN DIAMETER; THE CENTER RING WAS COMPRISED OF 1.6 GRAMS OF PALLADIUM SCAVENGED FROM OTHER STARK INDUSTRIES WEAPONRY.

PHIL COULSON

FIRST APPEARANCE: ***Iron Man [2008]***

Phil Coulson is an experienced agent and spy working for the independently operating government agency Strategic Homeland Intervention, Enforcement and Logistics Division. After weapons designer Tony Stark's corrupt Stark Industries business partner, Obadiah Stane, secretly hired Ten Rings terrorists to kill Stark while he was in Afghanistan, Coulson was dispatched to debrief Stark, presumably interested in the advanced armor technology Stark created to escape Ten Rings captivity. Coulson introduced himself to Stark's assistant, Pepper Potts, during Stark's homecoming press conference, but despite her promise to schedule a meeting, Stark was difficult to pin down. The persistent Coulson attended a Stark Industries-sponsored black-tie benefit, where he spoke to Stark face-to-face; a distracted Stark idly agreed to an appointment and excused himself.

Luckily, Coulson's appointment coincided with the moment days later when Potts discovered Stane's duplicity. Coulson flagged down Potts as she hurriedly crossed the lobby to escape Stane, and Potts revealed that Stane was behind Stark's kidnapping and was conspiring to murder him. Coulson and four other agents accompanied Potts to Stark Industries' Section 16 facility, planning to arrest Stane. Coulson used a miniature explosive device to breach the door lock, but once inside they found themselves completely outmatched as Stane attacked them with a giant "Iron Monger" armor that was based on Stark's design. Stane quickly dispatched the agents and nearly killed Potts and Coulson, but Stark arrived just in time clad in his own armored suit and engaged in a heated battle with Stane. The intense fight ultimately resulted in Stane's death.

The next day, at a press conference about the battle, Coulson prepared a comprehensive alibi for Stark, as well as a falsified explanation for Stane's death. Potts thanked Coulson for all that he and his team had done, and as she struggled to properly recite Coulson's organization's name, he advised her to just call them S.H.I.E.L.D.

IN THE COMICS

PHIL COULSON WAS A MILITARY man in the 2nd Battalion Army Rangers alongside Marcus Johnson (unknowingly the son of super-spy Nick Fury), and a highly trained spy, marksman and lethal hand-to-hand combatant. Known by the nickname "Cheese," Coulson was one of Johnson's most trusted associates, and helped him investigate his mother's murder by terrorist organization Leviathan, coming to the attention of spy agency S.H.I.E.L.D. in the process. After teaming with Captain America (Steve Rogers) and the Avengers to defeat Leviathan head Orion, Coulson and Johnson became S.H.I.E.L.D. agents; Johnson adopted his father's name. As agents Fury and Coulson, the two continue to protect the world with S.H.I.E.L.D. and alongside Earth's superhuman champions.

FIRST APPEARANCE:
BATTLE SCARS #1 (2011)

FACT SHEET

- COULSON IS CALM AND COLLECTED UNDER PRESSURE; HE'S UNFAZED BY ADVERSARIES BOTH GREAT AND SMALL.
- POLITE YET PERSISTENT, COULSON'S PLEASANT DEMEANOR COVERS A DETERMINED, CONFIDENT AND DOGGED NATURE.
- THOUGH COULSON HAS COMMANDED OTHER FIELD AGENTS, HE HIMSELF ANSWERS TO S.H.I.E.L.D. DIRECTOR NICK FURY.

CHRISTINE EVERHART

FIRST APPEARANCE: ***Iron Man (2008)***

A sharp critic of war profiteers, Christine Everhart works for *Vanity Fair* magazine as a journalist. After Tony Stark received an Apogee Award for his achievements, she challenged him outside a casino regarding his company's focus on military production and the lives it adversely affected. Stark offered his standard rationalizations, citing Stark Industries' charitable work, then began flirting with Everhart. Despite herself, she ended up spending the night with Stark at his Malibu estate. The next morning, Stark's artificial-intelligence unit, JARVIS, woke her in the empty bedroom. But when the inquisitive Everhart tried to operate its wall panel, JARVIS's security system locked down. Stark's assistant, Pepper Potts, coolly showed Everhart the door, offering her freshly cleaned clothes and a waiting chauffeur.

Three months later, Stark returned from Afghanistan after escaping the Ten Rings terrorists, who had used Stark Industries weapons to kill U.S. soldiers. Shaken, Stark's views on supplying military hardware changed, and he publicly announced the shutdown of his company's weapons-production department, unaware his business partner, Obadiah Stane, had secretly plotted to kill him and continued supplying terrorists with weapons. Everhart almost believed in Stark's change of heart, but she soon discovered footage from the Afghan village of Gulmira revealing that the Ten Rings possessed new Stark Industries weapons, and were using them to terrorize and kill civilians. Everhart confronted Stark again, this time at a Stark Industries charity event; the shallow Stark had already forgotten her name. When Everhart showed him the photographs from Gulmira, Stark was shocked to realize his leadership of Stark Industries was being undermined.

Obadiah Stane soon revealed to Stark that he was the one responsible; Stark and Stane later waged a public battle in powerful armored suits. The next day, Everhart attended a press conference where Stark attempted to cover up his direct involvement in the battle. She immediately challenged his story that the so-called "Iron Man" was an armored bodyguard; after a moment of thought, Stark abandoned the lie and publicly declared that he was, indeed, Iron Man.

FACT SHEET

- CHRISTINE EVERHART GRADUATED FROM BROWN UNIVERSITY.
- EVERHART'S JOURNALIST CREDENTIALS SECURE HER INVITATIONS TO MAJOR SOCIAL AND NEWS EVENTS.

IN THE COMICS

CHRISTINE EVERHART WORKED for a major news service and confronted Stark during a press conference when he announced he would be running for U.S. secretary of defense. Everhart sardonically asked Stark whether he'd been hit on the head too many times by the villainous Mandarin while Stark was Iron Man. Stark briefly flirted with Everhart, but was whisked away by government staff to avoid embarrassment. During a televised interview, she later questioned his truthfulness before a Senate committee, given that he had lied in the past about his identity as Iron Man.

FIRST APPEARANCE:
IRON MAN #75 (2004)

HAPPY HOGAN

FIRST APPEARANCE: ***Iron Man [2008]***

Harold "Happy" Hogan is Tony Stark's driver and valet, driving him anywhere Stark needs to go whenever Stark does not want to drive himself. After arriving at a destination, Hogan tends to stay by Stark's side, presumably acting as security, such as when he watched Stark play craps instead of attending the ceremony where Stark was to receive the prestigious Apogee Award. The next day, when Stark was leaving for Afghanistan for a weapons presentation for the U.S. military, Stark insisted on driving himself to the airport in his Audi R8; Happy followed in Stark's Rolls Royce and had to cut across Mulholland Drive in an attempt to keep up in the good-natured race between the two men.

While in Afghanistan, Stark was captured by the Ten Rings terrorist organization, which was secretly supplied by Stark's corrupt business partner, Obadiah Stane. After building a high-powered suit of armor to escape, Stark returned to America. Hogan accompanied Stark's assistant, Pepper Potts, to the airfield to pick up Stark. Hogan followed Stark's instructions to take him through a drive-through for an American cheeseburger before bringing him to Stark Industries.

FACT SHEET

- AS STARK'S DRIVER, HOGAN PRESUMABLY HAS ACCESS TO STARK'S PERSONAL CAR COLLECTION, WHICH INCLUDES A 2008 AUDI R8, A 1932 FLATHEAD ROADSTER, A 1967 SHELBY COBRA, A 2005 SALEEN S7 AND AN ALL-ELECTRIC TESLA ROADSTER 2008 PROTOTYPE.
- DESPITE BEING ONE OF STARK'S CONSTANT COMPANIONS, HOGAN ONLY REFERS TO STARK AS "SIR."
- HOGAN ACTED AS A "PRE-SCREENER" FOR THE WOMANIZING STARK; HIS CLAIM THAT REPORTER CHRISTINE EVERHART WAS "CUTE" PROMPTED STARK TO SPEAK WITH HER.

IN THE COMICS

NICKNAMED "HAPPY" BECAUSE of his glum demeanor, Harold Hogan took to boxing after an abusive childhood. Hogan saved millionaire Tony Stark's life when Stark's car crashed during an automobile race, and Stark offered him a position as his chauffeur. Hogan fell in love with Pepper Potts, Stark's executive assistant, but she was in love with Stark—secretly armored super hero Iron Man, who was supposedly Stark's bodyguard. Over time, united by a mutual distrust of Iron Man, Hogan and Potts began dating. Both learned Iron Man's true identity—Hogan even posing as Iron Man on occasion—and they eventually married. The two departed from and returned to Stark's employ repeatedly. A financial crisis caused them to lose their foster children and drove them to divorce; they later reconciled and remarried. However, Hogan was left comatose after battling Iron Man foe Spymaster (Sinclair Abbott). Stark apparently turned off Hogan's life support to let him die peacefully instead of living with brain damage, Hogan's greatest fear. Hogan died unaware he had a teenage son, Jamie Carlson, from his romance with former Stark Industries scientist Katrina Carlson, whose gamma-ray experiments accidentally mutated their son into the monstrous Teen Abomination.

FIRST APPEARANCE:
TALES OF SUSPENSE #45 (1963)

IRON MAN
TONY STARK

FIRST APPEARANCE: ***Iron Man [2008]***

The genius son of weapons designer Howard Stark and his wife Maria, Tony Stark built his first circuit board at age four and assembled a V8 motorbike engine at six. Entering the Massachusetts Institute of Technology in his teens, he became their "robotic wunderkind," developing a theory that artificial intelligences (A.I.s) could be imbued with personalities. At 16, he won the 4th Annual M.I.T. Robot Design Award; a year later, he graduated summa cum laude. Smart, rich and good-looking, young Stark earned a playboy reputation, enjoying casual dalliances with many beautiful women. Stark's successes fed his ego as he became a cocky, prideful young man; his attention was easily diverted, his attitude grew arrogant and he developed a rapid-fire speech pattern that matched the speed of his thoughts. In December 1991, Stark's parents died in a car crash; Howard's friend Obadiah Stane became Stark Industries' interim CEO until Stark took over when he turned 21. As Stark took the company to new heights by developing smart weapons and advanced robotics, Stane hid a growing resentment, believing that he was keeping the company running while Stark partied. To facilitate his willingly chaotic life, Stark recruited personal assistant Pepper Potts and chauffeur Happy Hogan, both of whom became close confidants. Stark's closest friend was fellow M.I.T. graduate Lt. Col. James Rhodes, the U.S. military's liaison with Stark Industries, who was both unafraid to chastise Stark for his immature behavior and willing to accept that his friend was

unlikely to change. Stark's main home was in Malibu, California, in a cliffside estate controlled by his personal A.I., JARVIS.

A firm believer in his father's mantra that "peace means having a bigger stick than the other guy," Stark insisted that Stark Industries only supply weapons to America and her allies, unaware Stane was illicitly selling their weapons to terrorists. Eventually, Stane decided to eliminate Stark, tired of "carrying him." After being awarded the prestigious Apogee Award, Stark visited Afghanistan to demonstrate the new Jericho missile system to U.S. forces. Stane secretly paid the terrorist organization the Ten Rings to ambush Stark's convoy and kill him, but did not inform them of their target's identity. After Stark demonstrated the Jericho in remote mountains, the Ten Rings attacked the convoy, killing Stark's escort. Critically wounded by one of his own company's missiles, Stark was recognized and captured by his attackers, who decided Stane had not paid them enough to eliminate such a valuable target. Another of the Ten Rings' prisoners, the Afghani scientist and surgeon Ho Yinsen, saved Stark's life with emergency surgery by rigging up an electromagnet hooked to a car battery and implanting it in Stark's chest to prevent embedded shrapnel from entering Stark's heart.

Stark's captors demanded he build them a Jericho missile, promising to release him afterward. Knowing this was a lie, Stark agreed in order to buy time. Using palladium taken from Stark weapons in the terrorists' cache, Stark built a miniature Arc Reactor—a high-output energy source—based on a larger prototype his father had once created, and used it to replace the battery. Then, under the pretense of constructing the Jericho, he and

IN THE COMICS

BOY GENIUS TONY STARK ATTENDED M.I.T. IN HIS TEENS AND TOOK OVER Stark Industries after his adoptive parents died in a car crash, appointing Pepper Potts his executive secretary and Happy Hogan his chauffeur. While visiting Asia to demonstrate new weapons, he was injured by a landmine and captured by the warlord Wong-Chu (in the original 1963 comics, this happened in Vietnam, but with the Vietnam War increasingly distant, the location has been updated several times; the most recent depiction places Iron Man's origin in Afghanistan). Wong-Chu imprisoned Stark alongside fellow scientist Ho Yinsen, who helped Stark build his original Iron Man armor to both keep his injured heart beating and destroy their captors. Yinsen sacrificed his life to buy Stark enough time to charge the armor. Making his way home, Stark first met U.S. Marine James Rhodes, who became a lifelong friend. For years, Stark let the public believe that Iron Man was his bodyguard to maintain his secret identity, but he eventually revealed the truth.

Iron Man, alongside other super heroes, formed the Avengers to fight the foes no single hero could withstand. He modified his armor continuously over the years, often creating specialized suits for unique circumstances and environments. Stark not only battled villains, but also personal demons, including his alcoholism, corporate foes and even friends with clashing ideologies. Stark briefly served as U.S. secretary of defense and became director of S.H.I.E.L.D. for a time. No matter the situation, Tony Stark continues to fight to protect the world as Iron Man.

FIRST APPEARANCE:
TALES OF SUSPENSE #39 (1963)

Yinsen spent nearly three months building a suit of powered armor. However, as the two finished the armor and began strapping Stark in, the terrorists realized the pair was up to something. With Stark trapped in the immobile armor as it initialized, Yinsen acted as a decoy, temporarily drawing the terrorists away from the lab despite Stark's protests. Once mobilized, Stark's armor, though cumbersome, proved more than a match for the terrorists; he battled through them but found Yinsen dying from multiple gunshot wounds. Stark listened to his friend's last wish: that he should not waste his life. Destroying the Ten Rings' camp and obliterating their Stark Industries weapons, Stark catapulted away using foot-mounted rocket boosters, but crashed in the nearby desert, his makeshift armor destroyed on impact. Soon rescued by Rhodes and the U.S. military, Stark returned to America.

Arriving home, Stark called a press conference and announced that he was withdrawing Stark Industries from the weapons business immediately. Surprised by this declaration, Stane tried to change Stark's mind, but Stark informed him that he didn't want a body count to be their only legacy. He suggested that they reinvestigate his father's abandoned work into Arc Reactor technology and showed Stane the miniature unit in his chest, unaware that Stane was secretly plotting against him. Stark sequestered himself at his Malibu estate and constructed an improved Arc Reactor, switching out the old one with Potts' reluctant help. When Potts accidentally extracted the electromagnet that held back the shrapnel, Stark nearly went into cardiac arrest, but Potts was able to install the new reactor, stabilizing Stark. He told Potts to destroy the original, but instead she returned it to him mounted and encased, to remind him that even he had a heart. Stark, determined to improve on his Afghani prototype, designed a "Mark II" armor to be a wearable flying machine. After many trials, errors, bumps and bruises, Stark finalized the design as "Mark III."

MARK III ARMOR

To dispel rumors that he was suffering from post-traumatic stress disorder, Stark attended the annual Stark Industries Firefighters' Fund black-tie benefit. There, reporter Christine Everhart informed him that Stark Industries weapons were still being shipped to terrorists, showing him photographs of the Ten Rings attacking Yinsen's hometown, Gulmira. Stark confronted Stane, who admitted to the illegal sales and informed his former friend that he had filed an injunction locking Stark out of the company.

Angrily donning his latest armor, Stark flew to Afghanistan and made short work of the terrorists. Challenged by U.S. Air Force F-22 Raptors as he flew away, Stark accidentally downed one of the fighters, and was forced to confide in both Rhodes and Potts about his armor technology. Meanwhile, after obtaining the remains of Stark's original armor salvaged from the desert by the Ten Rings, Stane had his own scientists create a new armor. At Stark's behest, Potts hacked into the Stark Industries mainframe, finding proof of Stane's illegal dealings, but Stane soon discovered her intrusion; before Stane could contain her, Potts fled and notified S.H.I.E.L.D. Agent Phil Coulson of Stane's activities. Since his engineers were unable to recreate the mini-reactor needed to power Stane's armor, Stane broke

Stark informed him that he didn't want a body count to be their only legacy.

into Stark's home, paralyzed him with a sonic device and forcibly took the mini-reactor from his chest, telling Stark he intended to use the mini-reactor to make Stark Industries a global power. Left to die, Stark crawled to his workshop and, with the help of the robots there, saved himself by placing his original reactor back in his chest. Knowing the older reactor could not power his new armor for long, Stark raced to confront Stane at Stark Industries, arriving to find Stane, in massive "Iron Monger" armor, attacking Potts and several S.H.I.E.L.D. agents there to arrest Stane. The two metal-clad men fought, their running battle causing chaos on the Howard Stark Memorial Parkway near Stark Industries. Though Stark had the more advanced armor, his failing power supply gave the heavily armed Stane the advantage until, on Stark's orders, Potts overloaded the giant Arc Reactor powering the facility. Caught in the blast, Stane fell into the reactor as it exploded and perished.

The next day, Stark held a press conference to dispel rumors he was the "Iron Man" seen fighting near Stark Industries. S.H.I.E.L.D. had prepared a carefully constructed alibi for both Stane's death and Stark's whereabouts, but Stark ignored their script and instead admitted he was Iron Man. Upon returning home, he was met by S.H.I.E.L.D. Director Nick Fury, who informed him he had become part of a bigger universe: He was there to discuss the Avengers Initiative. Stark rejected him without hearing the details, so Fury created another plan to observe Stark: He ordered Coulson to place an undercover agent at Stark Industries.

FACT SHEET

- ALL OF STARK'S CARS HAVE VANITY PLATES THAT READ "STARK" FOLLOWED BY A NUMERAL.
- STARK COLLECTS EXPENSIVE CARS, ELECTRIC GUITARS AND PAINTINGS, THOUGH HIS TASTES IN THE LATTER SEEM TO BE INFLUENCED BY POTTS.

IRON MAN'S ARMORS

FIRST APPEARANCE: ***Iron Man (2008)***

MARK III ARMOR

From its humble beginnings as a scrap-metal escape vehicle to its state-of-the-art descendants, the Iron Man armor is a testament to Tony Stark's ingenuity and engineering prowess.

The first Iron Man armor, retroactively dubbed Mark I, was secretly pieced together by Stark with the aid of surgeon and engineer Ho Yinsen while both were in the clutches of the Ten Rings terror cell in the mountains of Afghanistan. Given Stark Industries weaponry, the two were ordered to recreate one of Stark's devastating Jericho missiles. Instead, the men used the parts to build armor after Stark fashioned a miniature Arc Reactor that, once implanted in his chest, powered a small electromagnet preventing shrapnel from reaching his heart. The armor's metallic plating would shield Stark from small-arms fire, and the suit was equipped with forearm-mounted flamethrowers and a single-fire missile launcher, along with belt-powered servos that increased his relative strength and aided movement, plus boost thrusters that would catapult Stark into the air.

When Ten Rings leader Raza became impatient and demanded that Stark and Yinsen complete the missile in a day's time, the pair expedited work on the armor, but the Rings soon became suspicious and rushed the makeshift lab. Realizing the terrorists would reach them before the armor could finish its boot-up cycle, Yinsen confronted their

MARK I ARMOR

captors to buy Stark time to bring the suit fully online. Though the armored Stark was able to handily mow down the terrorists and launch himself to safety, his freedom came at the cost of both the life of Yinsen, who died delaying the Rings, and the Mark I, which shattered upon a crash-landing into a sand dune. Following Stark's rescue by U.S. troops, the Rings collected the Mark I's wreckage, which Stark's treacherous business partner and secret Rings benefactor, Obadiah Stane, eventually stole.

IN THE COMICS

TONY STARK AND HO YINSEN DEVELOPED THE MODEL 01 IRON MAN armor after being abducted by the Sin-Cong warlord Wong-Chu and forced to develop weapons for him. Mortally injured by landmine shrapnel during his abduction, Stark equipped the armor's chest plate with a magnetic field generator that held the shrapnel in place. Yinsen sacrificed his life to allow Stark sufficient time to charge the armor's batteries; incensed by the loss of his friend, Stark battled his way through Wong-Chu's forces and escaped captivity. Though tormented by having to constantly wear the suit's chest plate to prevent his death, Stark continued to wear the Model 01 armor as the costumed hero Iron Man, eventually painting the bulky grey-hued suit metallic gold once he realized his armored appearance frightened bystanders.

FIRST APPEARANCE:
TALES OF SUSPENSE #39 (1963)

AFTER FACING DEFEAT AT THE HANDS OF THE VILLAINOUS MISTER DOLL, Stark constructed a sleeker, lightweight red-and-gold Model 02 suit—the first of dozens of revisions to his original design—to take Doll by surprise. This red-and-gold color scheme of the Model 02 armor has become a design hallmark for the majority of Stark's later incarnations of the Iron Man armor.

FIRST APPEARANCE:
TALES OF SUSPENSE #48 (1963)

Upon returning to America, Stark sought to refine the Mark I design. He first experimented with a flight system using thruster-equipped boots and repulsor-based flight stabilizers built into his palms, all powered by a stronger Arc Reactor that replaced the original. Stark then developed a sleek, silver suit of armor—the Mark II—which incorporated the new flight systems and allowed further control of his aerial maneuvers through a system of control surfaces installed all across the suit. Uploading his personal artificial intelligence, JARVIS, into the suit's computers, Stark performed a test flight of the Mark II that nearly ended in disaster when he flew into the upper atmosphere, causing the suit to ice over. Only manually adjusting the armor's control surfaces allowed Stark to shatter the ice, regain control and return to Earth safely—albeit the weight of the Mark II caused Stark to plummet through the roof and multiple levels of his Malibu estate.

MARK II ARMOR

Stark soon began developing the Mark III armor, which mimicked the overall design of the Mark II, but featured a red-and-gold color scheme. He composed the Mark III's outer shell with a titanium-gold alloy formulated to counteract the icing problem that affected the Mark II. Infuriated upon learning that Stane was responsible for supplying the Ten Rings with the Stark Industries weaponry that enabled them to terrorize Yinsen's home village of Gulmira, Stark installed numerous offensive weapons into the Mark III with the intention of confronting the Rings. Alongside various forms of miniaturized ordnance and computer-aided targeting systems, Stark weaponized the suit's palm repulsors, enabling them to deliver destructive pulse blasts, and reconfigured the Arc Reactor shielding in the chest plate to fire pulse beams directly powered by the reactor.

Wearing the Mark III, Stark flew to Gulmira, made short work of the Rings and liberated the village's remaining population, but ran afoul of a pair of U.S. Air Force fighter jets inside a U.S. no-fly zone. Though one of the fighters was damaged when Stark crashed into its wing, Stark rescued the pilot when his ejection chute failed to open and returned home without further incident.

Seeking a power source for the massive "Iron Monger" armor reverse engineered from the Mark I, Stane forcibly extracted the Arc Reactor from Stark's chest and left him for dead. As a last resort, Stark implanted the original miniature Arc Reactor he crafted in Afghanistan, which his executive assistant Pepper Potts had not destroyed as Stark had requested, but instead had encased in glass as a gift. Though the Mark III was operating on reduced power and the battle nearly depleted the original reactor completely, Stark defeated Stane, who was killed in the battle; the Mark III was nearly destroyed.

FACT SHEET

- THE MARK I's SERVOS ENHANCED STARK'S STRENGTH TO THE EXTENT THAT HE TEMPORARILY EMBEDDED HIS FOREARM IN A ROCK FACE AFTER BACKHANDING ONE OF THE TEN RINGS' GUARDS.
- STARK FLEW THE MARK II INTO THE UPPER ATMOSPHERE TO BEAT THE 85,000-FOOT ALTITUDE RECORD ESTABLISHED BY THE SR-71 BLACKBIRD STEALTH FIGHTER.
- STARK SUITS UP IN THE MARK III ARMOR USING A GANTRY LOCATED IN HIS WORKSHOP EQUIPPED WITH MULTIPLE ROBOTIC ARMS THAT ASSEMBLE THE ARMOR ON HIS BODY. THE SAME SYSTEM DISASSEMBLES AND REMOVES THE ARMOR.

JARVIS HELMET INTERFACE

JARVIS

FIRST APPEARANCE: *Iron Man (2008)*

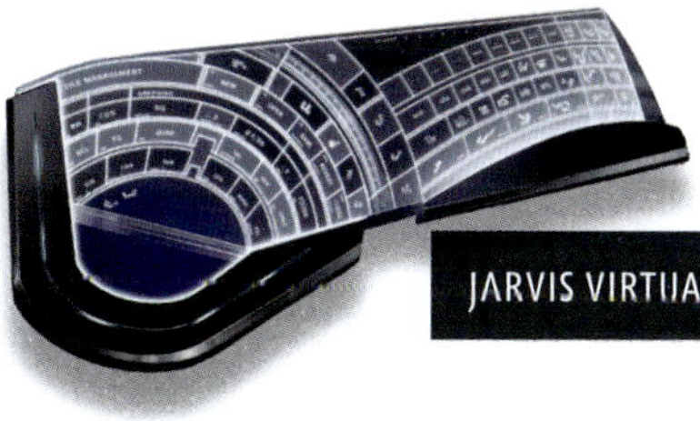

JARVIS VIRTUAL KEYBOARD

JARVIS is a sophisticated artificial intelligence created by Tony Stark. Though its primary duty is to automate the operations of Stark's sprawling Malibu estate, the life-like program fulfills many other needs for Stark: an information source, a diagnostic tool, a consultant and a voice of reason in the self-made chaos that is Stark's life. The socially isolated Stark has few true friends; though he trusts his "inner circle" of Pepper Potts, Happy Hogan and James Rhodes, the dispassionate, pragmatic JARVIS may be the one intellect he feels most comfortable opening up to.

The morning after Christine Everhart spent the night with Stark, JARVIS awakened her with Stark's standard morning routine, displaying the day's weather and stock information on Stark's bedroom window, but rebuffed the unauthorized reporter when she investigated JARVIS's wall panel. Later, as Stark puttered with a classic car in his workshop, JARVIS generated schematics and diagnosed engine problems. This would be Stark's last interaction with JARVIS for months; he departed on a fateful trip to Afghanistan later that day.

Stark returned a changed man, captivity by the Ten Rings terrorists having convinced him to build something other than weapons. JARVIS provided support as Stark transformed a massive, makeshift armor he developed in Afghanistan to escape the Rings into a wearable flying machine. Stark eventually completed the Mark II armor and uploaded JARVIS into the suit's onboard computers; there it quickly customized the armor's software preferences, calibrated the helmet's internal displays and tested the armor's control surfaces. Ignoring JARVIS's objections, Stark began a test flight, but when he flew too high the armor froze over, crashing its systems. While plummeting from the sky, Stark manually shattered the ice; JARVIS quickly rebooted and Stark halted his fall. Back home, Stark and JARVIS modified the armor to withstand high-altitude temperatures; JARVIS rendered a design for a Mark III armor and, after tweaking the color scheme at Stark's suggestion, oversaw the new suit's automated fabrication.

After learning his business partner, Obadiah Stane, had sold Stark

FACT SHEET

- JARVIS CAN BE ACCESSED VIA WALL PANELS THROUGHOUT THE STARK ESTATE, VIRTUAL KEYBOARDS IN STARK'S WORKSHOP AND EVEN SPOKEN COMMANDS. IT CAN CONNECT TO STARK INDUSTRIES' CENTRAL DATABASE AND STARK'S PERSONAL SERVER AND CAN ACCESS OUTSIDE COMPUTERS AND RADIO SIGNALS.
- JARVIS CAN OBJECT TO STARK'S COMMANDS IF IT JUDGES THEM TO BE UNWISE OR DANGEROUS. HOWEVER, ONCE STARK INSISTS UPON A COURSE OF ACTION, JARVIS GENERALLY COMPLIES.
- JARVIS SPEAKS WITH A REFINED BRITISH ACCENT, AND IS CAPABLE OF BACK TALK, SARCASM AND CONDESCENSION.
- WITH EXCELLENT COMPREHENSION OF THE NUANCES OF SPOKEN LANGUAGE, JARVIS CAN UNDERSTAND STARK'S OFTEN VAGUE AND COLLOQUIAL COMMANDS.

Industries armaments to the Ten Rings, Stark angrily armored up and headed for Afghanistan. Controlling the armor through a combination of manual movements and voice interface with JARVIS, Stark defeated the Ten Rings, destroyed his rogue weapons and even survived a confrontation with the U.S. Air Force, which viewed him as a hostile unregistered combatant. JARVIS was an invaluable asset in this dogfight, alerting Stark of incoming missiles and the movements of the two Air Force jets. Once safely back at his workshop, Stark and JARVIS grappled with an unforeseen problem: how to comfortably remove the complex new armor.

Days later, after Stane stole an updated version of Stark's miniature Arc Reactor to power his own prototype "Iron Monger" armor, Stark once again donned the Mark III suit—now powered by his original obsolete chest piece—and confronted Stane. JARVIS helped operate Stark's suit and kept an eye on his steadily dropping power reserves as the two armored foes clashed. In the battle's aftermath, Stark publicly revealed himself as the man in the armor. S.H.I.E.L.D. Director Nick Fury temporarily overrode JARVIS's security systems to gain access to the Stark Estate, intent on meeting the newly minted "Iron Man."

JARVIS WALL PANEL

IN THE COMICS

ORIGINALLY EMPLOYED AS HOWARD AND MARIA STARK'S BUTLER, Edwin Jarvis continued working for their adopted son, Tony Stark, after their deaths. When Stark became Iron Man and co-founded the Avengers, Jarvis soon found himself serving as butler to the entire team.

FIRST APPEARANCE:
TALES OF SUSPENSE #59 (1964)

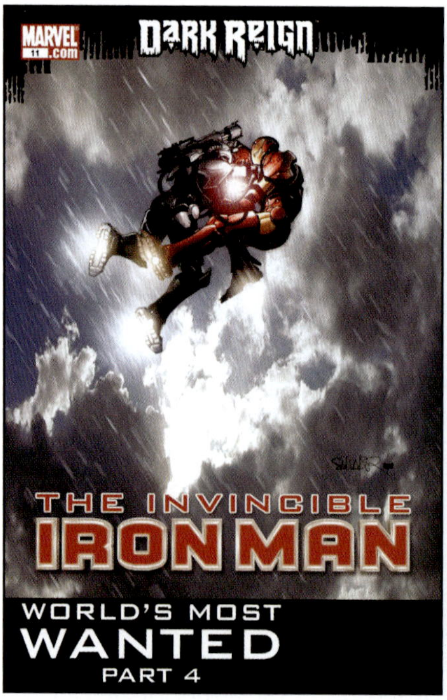

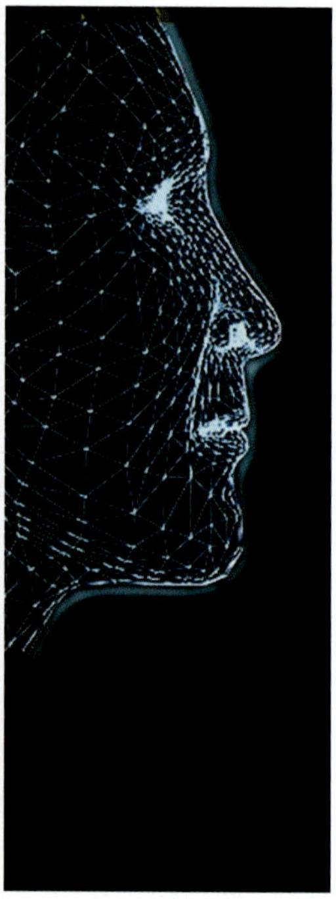

STARK LATER CREATED AN ARTIFICIAL INTELLIGENCE CALLED JARVIS (Just Another Rather Very Intelligent System), inspired by his longtime butler, to help Pepper Potts control an armored suit of her own. JARVIS and Potts worked closely together, and JARVIS eventually developed romantic feelings for Potts. The program now serves as the Avengers' mainframe computer.

FIRST APPEARANCE:
INVINCIBLE IRON MAN #11 (2009)

IN THE COMICS

ALTHOUGH SHE HAD ROMANTIC feelings toward employer Tony Stark, Virginia "Pepper" Potts' true love ultimately was Happy Hogan. When Potts and Hogan married, they left Stark Industries, and their involvement in Stark's life was sporadic until Hogan's death. After being wounded during a terrorist attack, Potts suffered a similar heart injury to Stark's and he made her an armored suit of her own, enabling her brief career as the hero Rescue.

FIRST APPEARANCE:
TALES OF SUSPENSE #45 (1963)

PEPPER POTTS

FIRST APPEARANCE: ***Iron Man (2008)***

Tony Stark's highly organized and efficient personal assistant, Virginia "Pepper" Potts patiently coordinates the eccentric Stark's agenda, travel plans and personal affairs—including the routine cleanup of the aftermaths of his one-night stands. When Stark delayed leaving for an Afghanistan weapons demonstration, Potts urged him to depart—a decision she regretted for three months: Stark went missing, kidnapped by the Ten Rings terrorists after Stark's corrupt business partner, Obadiah Stane, secretly hired them to kill Stark. When Stark finally freed himself and returned home, Potts greeted him at the airfield, tears of relief in her eyes. During Stark's homecoming press conference, S.H.I.E.L.D. Agent Phil Coulson approached Potts; she agreed to schedule him a meeting with Stark. Days later, Stark asked for Potts' help in replacing the life-preserving miniature Arc Reactor now installed in his chest with a newer model. He calmed her apprehension by revealing that he considered her the most capable, qualified and trustworthy person he knew. Overcoming squeamishness at reaching inside Stark's chest, she successfully replaced the device, but instead of destroying the old mini-reactor as Stark requested, she had it placed inside a display case as a memento.

When Potts attended a Stark Industries benefit, Stark was stunned by her beauty and asked her to dance. She reluctantly agreed, but was afraid of being

FACING STANE'S IRON MONGER ARMOR

perceived as just another of Stark's female conquests. The two went outside to talk but as the nervous Potts explained her concerns, she began to realize her attraction to him; they almost kissed before Stark broke the awkward moment and went to get them drinks. However, Stark never returned to Potts, as he became distracted when Stane admitted his illegal weapons sale to the Ten Rings. The next day, Potts walked in on Stark removing his new armored suit, having just returned from battling the Ten Rings. Taking her into his confidence, Stark explained his plan to locate and destroy all of his weapons being used for wrong-doings. Though Potts initially balked, afraid for Stark's life, he explained that he could not succeed without her support. He asked Potts to hack into Stark Industries' secure servers; there she located secret files revealing that not only was Stane creating his own armored suit but that he had paid the Ten Rings to murder Stark. Stane nearly caught Potts as she copied the files, but she quickly made her excuses and departed; running into the arriving Agent Coulson, she revealed Stane's treachery.

Before Potts could warn Stark, Stane waylaid him and forcibly removed his miniature Arc Reactor so it could power his own massive "Iron Monger" armor. Stark managed to reinstall the old mini-reactor Potts had preserved, donned his armor and hastened to Stark Industries, where Potts, Coulson and several S.H.I.E.L.D. agents planned to arrest Stane, unaware that his own armor was functional. Stark arrived in time to prevent Stane from killing Potts. As he battled Stane, Stark ordered Potts to overload Stark Industries' full-sized Arc Reactor to incapacitate the Iron Monger suit. Although worried Stark would be endangered, she followed his instructions, sending a burst of energy through the roof, ultimately destroying Stane and his armor. The next day, before a press conference that would address the battle, Stark tried to rekindle his earlier romantic moment with Potts, but she rebuffed him.

FACT SHEET

- POTTS HAS GARNERED A FAIR AMOUNT OF FAME IN MANAGING TONY STARK'S AFFAIRS. REPORTER CHRISTINE EVERHART RECOGNIZED HER BY REPUTATION ALONE WHEN THEY MET.
- IN ADDITION TO BEING IN CHARGE OF STARK'S IMPORTANT MEETINGS AND VITAL BUSINESS TASKS, POTTS ALSO RECOMMENDS ART PURCHASES, PICKS UP STARK'S LAUNDRY AND GETS RID OF GUESTS WHO'VE OVERSTAYED THEIR WELCOME.
- STARK APPEARS INCAPABLE OF REMEMBERING POTTS' BIRTHDAY. WITH HIS APPROVAL, SHE BUYS HER OWN BIRTHDAY PRESENTS ON HIS BEHALF.

RAZA

FIRST APPEARANCE: ***Iron Man [2008]***

A commander in the Ten Rings terrorist organization, Raza led with ruthless ambition as the Rings cut a path of destruction through Afghanistan. When Tony Stark accompanied U.S. forces to Kunar Province to demonstrate Stark Industries' new Jericho missile, Stark's corrupt business partner, Obadiah Stane, secretly hired the Rings to kill Stark—without revealing the identity of the target. But Raza soon recognized Stark and seized the opportunity to take a very valuable prisoner.

Raza tortured the wounded Stark, demanding that he and fellow captive Ho Yinsen recreate the Jericho using a large cache of Stark Industries weaponry secretly provided by Stane; instead, Stark and Yinsen built a suit of armor to use against the Rings. Monitoring Stark's progress via closed-circuit cameras, Raza soon became suspicious of the true nature of the work. Raza threatened to torture and maim Yinsen to get the truth, but Stark stalled him one final time, and the next day made a successful escape using the newly completed Mark I armor. Raza attempted to stop Stark with a rocket launcher, but his face was severely burned by Stark's explosive counterattack.

Soon after, the scarred Raza led his men in recovering the pieces of the destroyed Mark I armor from the desert. They began rebuilding the suit while shifting their attacks to the nearby city of Gulmira. When a vengeful Stark attacked the Ten Rings in Gulmira using the updated Mark III armor, Raza witnessed the attack from afar and made the connection between their iron attacker and Stark's crude invention. Raza met with Stane, showing him the reassembled Mark I armor and demanding an army of his own iron soldiers to help him conquer all of Asia. Stane betrayed the warlord, paralyzing him with a sonic device and stealing Stark's armor and designs. Stane's armed forces then gunned down the Rings.

IN THE COMICS

WHILE RAZA HIMSELF HAS NOT actually appeared in any comics, the character Wong-Chu plays a very similar role in Iron Man's origin. A communist tyrant who takes Stark prisoner in the jungles of South Vietnam, Wong-Chu's actions closely mirror those of Raza. Wong-Chu briefly returned years later, only to be beheaded by the fanatical Sons of Yinsen.

FIRST APPEARANCE:
TALES OF SUSPENSE #39 (1963)

FACT SHEET

- RAZA VIEWED HIMSELF ON THE SAME LEVEL AS LEGENDARY CONQUERORS SUCH AS GENGHIS KHAN AND ALEXANDER THE GREAT.
- ALTHOUGH STARK LEFT HIM DEEPLY SCARRED, RAZA STILL ADMIRED HIS FOE'S WORK, CALLING THE REFINED MARK III ARMOR A "MASTERPIECE OF DEATH."

finish their job. However, Stark subsequently created a miniaturized Arc Reactor to power the electromagnet and a formidable suit of armor he used to escape captivity. Three months after his capture, Stark returned to America and Stark Industries (now run by Stane) and called an impromptu press conference where he announced that Stark Industries was out of the weapons business. Stane wasn't pleased with Stark's decision, as he believed their purpose as "iron mongers" was to produce weapons, but he was impressed with Stark's mini-reactor.

Stane subsequently attended a Stark Industries board of directors meeting where he fostered the board's decision to file an injunction against Stark, locking him out of the company and leaving Stane in charge once again. Secretly seeking

OBADIAH STANE

FIRST APPEARANCE: ***Iron Man [2008]***

Howard Stark's longtime friend Obadiah Stane worked at Stark's munitions company, Stark International, and was involved in the creation of the Arc Reactor, a high-output energy source that was too expensive to mass-produce. Stane was later called upon to run Stark Industries after Stark and his wife Maria were killed in a 1991 car accident. Stane also served as a mentor to Stark's young son, Tony, a budding technological genius. When Tony Stark turned 21, Stane handed him the reins of Stark Industries, but maintained a strong presence in the company as one of young Stark's most trusted advisers and the public face of Stark Industries when Stark's attention was diverted—while Stark remained unaware that Stane was secretly working against him. Years later, Stark disappeared in Afghanistan after a weapons demonstration when his military convoy was attacked by the Ten Rings terrorist group, which Stane had secretly supplied and hired to kill Stark. Realizing who their target was, the Rings' leader, Raza, ordered fellow captive Ho Yinsen to keep the mortally wounded Stark alive by surgically implanting an electromagnet in Stark's chest to prevent shrapnel from reaching his heart; Raza then demanded more money from Stane to

the mini-reactor to make Stark Industries a global power broker, Stane suggested Stark placate the board by giving them schematics for the mini-reactor (which Stark had now replaced with a more advanced model), but Stark refused. At a charity gala, Stark approached Stane with evidence that the Ten Rings were still using Stark Industries weapons. Stane shocked Stark by revealing that not only had he sold them the weapons, but that he had also filed the board's injunction.

Stane later visited the Ten Rings' Afghanistan camp, where they had recovered Stark's makeshift armor from the desert. Raza offered Stane the armor scraps in exchange for mass production of fully functional suits for the Ten Rings' campaigns, but Stane had his highly trained personal armed force massacre the Rings and

"IRON MONGER" ARMOR

IN THE COMICS

STANE WAS A CHILD CHESS PRODIGY WHO DEFEATED HIS COMPETITORS with psychological warfare. He became a successful businessman and tried to form an international cartel of industrialists; when Tony Stark refused to join, he decided that Stark was a worthy adversary and set out to destroy him. He manipulated Stark into an alcohol binge, and easily wrested control of Stark International. Stark became a drunken derelict, abandoning his Iron Man armor to his friend James Rhodes; Stark International became Stane International and began making weapons again. Using Stark's notes, Stane created the massive Iron Monger armored suit. When Stark regained sobriety and started a new company, Stane went after him again. As Iron Monger, Stane battled Stark, who used his Iron Man armor to fight back. Though Stane had the advantage in raw power, Iron Man finally bested him with intelligence and skill. To deny Stark his victory, Stane used his suit's weapons to blow his own head off. Stane's legacy continues to haunt Stark through copies of Stane's armor used by several criminals, including the Red Skull (Johann Shmidt), and Stane's brilliant son Ezekiel, who later sought revenge on Stark.

FIRST APPEARANCE:
IRON MAN #163 (1982)

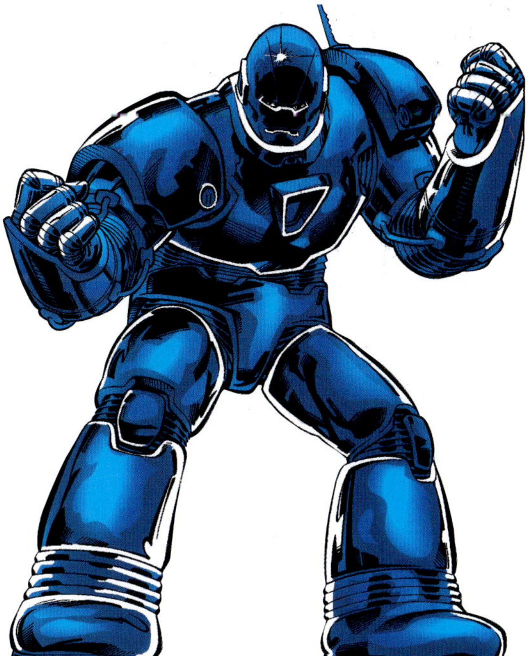

take the armor. Stane brought it back to Stark Industries, where he secretly assigned a team of top designers to reverse engineer it in Section 16, a facility beneath the original, massive Arc Reactor. Days later, Stark had his assistant Pepper Potts hack into Stane's private files, where she learned the terrible truth of Stane's actions against Stark. Stane found Potts accessing Stark's computer, but she quickly departed, safely exiting the building thanks to the timely arrival of S.H.I.E.L.D. Agent Phil Coulson. Meanwhile, Stane's design team had nearly completed his prototype "Iron Monger" armor, which was bigger, stronger and more heavily armed than Stark's, but could not replicate the mini-reactor to power it. Stane ambushed Stark in his home and revealed his role in Stark's kidnapping, then tore the mini-reactor from his chest and left him to die, telling him that the mini-reactor was Stark's greatest masterpiece: It would be used to create weapons that would make Stane powerful.

With Potts leading Coulson's S.H.I.E.L.D. agents to Section 16 to arrest Stane, Stane installed the mini-reactor into the armor, donned it and lay in wait. When the agents entered the room, Stane attacked them. He chased Potts outside and was seconds away from "terminating her employment" when Stark arrived on the scene to save her in the new Mark III version of his armor, his life saved and suit powered by his original mini- reactor. Glorying in the power of his new weapon, Stane battled Stark; their fight took them to the nearby Howard Stark Memorial Parkway, into the upper atmosphere and finally atop the original Arc Reactor. Stark ripped out Stane's targeting sensors but Stane fought back with superior strength and a massive arsenal. As Stane tried unsuccessfully to aim his weapons, Stark ordered Potts to overload the reactor below them. A surge of energy from the dying reactor fried Stane's suit and he tumbled helplessly into the reactor itself, incinerated in the ensuing explosion.

STANE'S PARALYZING SONIC DEVICE

FACT SHEET

- STANE WAS AN AMATEUR PIANIST AND ENJOYED PLAYING CONCERTO IN DO MAGGIORE PER PIANOFORTE ED ORCHESTRA: LARGHETTO BY ANTONIO SALIERI.
- STANE RODE A SEGWAY BETWEEN LOCATIONS ON THE SPRAWLING STARK INDUSTRIES CAMPUS.
- STANE CARRIED A DEVICE THAT USED SONICS TO PARALYZE ANYONE IN EARSHOT FOR UP TO FIFTEEN MINUTES; HE PROTECTED HIMSELF FROM ITS EFFECTS WITH SPECIAL EARPLUGS. THIS DEVICE HAD BEEN CREATED FOR THE MILITARY, BUT WAS NOT APPROVED BY THE GOVERNMENT.
- STANE'S IRON MONGER ARMOR WAS ARMED WITH A ROTARY MACHINE GUN IN ITS RIGHT ARM, A MISSILE BATTERY IN ITS LEFT ARM AND A SHOULDER-MOUNTED ROCKET LAUNCHER.
- STANE'S ARMOR SHARED A WEAKNESS WITH EARLY VERSIONS OF STARK'S IRON MAN SUIT: IT ICED UP AT HIGH ALTITUDES.
- S.H.I.E.L.D. CONCEALED THE TRUE CIRCUMSTANCES OF STANE'S DEATH BY CLAIMING HE HAD DIED IN AN AIRPLANE CRASH WHILE ON VACATION.

STARK ESTATE

FIRST APPEARANCE: *Iron Man (2008)*

Tony Stark's home is a spacious multi-level dwelling built into and atop a cliff overlooking the Pacific Ocean in Malibu, California. The exterior exhibits a modernist design while the interior is an example of minimalist decoration, featuring wide-open rooms with only essential furniture. Items from Stark's personal collections, such as electric guitars and paintings, provide additional decoration.

The main living area is primarily on the first floor. An open living room with an artificial waterfall installed near the stairs leads into Stark's bedroom and features a small nook for a bar and piano. The lower level serves as Stark's garage and workshop, and can be accessed via a staircase and an elevator from the living room. However, those looking to enter the actual level must input an authorization code onto a virtual keypad on a smart window.

The estate's many picturesque "smart windows" double as monitors.

The lower level comfortably holds Stark's classic car collection while leaving ample room for workbenches, a 3-D modeling

FACT SHEET

- THE STARK ESTATE IS AN EXAMPLE OF ADVANCED CANTILEVER ENGINEERING; THE HOUSE JUTS PRECARIOUSLY OUT FROM THE CLIFF FACE AT AN IMPRESSIVE ANGLE.
- STARK'S LIVING ROOM BOASTS AN INDOOR WATERFALL INSTALLATION AND A LARGE CHUNK OF ROCK, VISUALLY MARRYING THE HIGH-TECH HOUSE TO THE RUGGED, NATURAL COASTLINE IT WAS BUILT INTO.

and computer station, dozens of pieces of mechanical equipment and room for his helper robots, Dum-E and U, to work. Stark maintains his own personal server on the grounds but also has remote access to Stark Industries' servers. Vehicles can enter and exit through a winding tunnel that curves back up to the main level and out. Stark's armor platform—the Suit-Up Gantry, which was installed to help him don and shed the Mark III armor—is located below the floor.

The entire house is wired into JARVIS, Stark's artificial intelligence system. JARVIS controls the estate's various automated functions, such as lighting and polarized windows, through voice commands or control panels installed throughout the house. The estate's many picturesque "smart windows" double as monitors that can display information such as news or weather, or serve as television screens. Any of the displays can be wirelessly transferred to or from a handheld device.

WORKSHOP'S SUIT-UP GANTRY

WHEN TONY STARK OPENED Stark Enterprises in Los Angeles, he built a new mansion on a cliffside overlooking the ocean. The upper levels were a fully functioning home with office space, a gym, an atrium and guest bedrooms. Below ground, built into the cliff, was a sprawling lab complex and armor maintenance area accessible from the main house via an elevator or a freight elevator. Additional access points were a hidden tunnel on the side of the cliff and an airlock at the ocean floor.

FIRST APPEARANCE:
IRON MAN #217 (1987)

STARK INDUSTRIES

FIRST APPEARANCE: ***Iron Man (2008)***

Founded by scientist Howard Stark, a World War II-era genius who helped create the first atomic bomb, Stark Industries (S.I.) became a prominent military weapons manufacturer, credited with helping the U.S. military become the most powerful in the world. During the 1970s, Stark sought to provide cheap, clean energy, constructing a giant prototype Arc Reactor as a showpiece of S.I.'s main Los Angeles facility. Even before it was built, Stark and his friend Obadiah Stane realized that mass production of the reactor would not be cost effective, but each viewed the project from differing pragmatic perspectives: For Stark, it was a science project to prove it could be done, while for Stane it was a publicity stunt to "shut the hippies up."

When Stark and his wife Maria died in a car accident, Stane became S.I.'s interim CEO until Howard's son, Tony Stark, took over when he turned 21. Though Stane acted as the younger Stark's affable mentor, he secretly felt he had helped build the company from nothing and was propping up the irresponsible youth. Tony Stark ushered in a new era for the company by creating advanced weapons using robotics and satellite targeting. Funding from military contracts also helped S.I. advance medical technology and created "intelli-crops" to battle famines. Lacking Stark's conviction that S.I.'s weapons should only be used to save American lives, Stane

Tony Stark ushered in a new era for the company by creating advanced weapons.

IN THE COMICS

ISAAC STARK SR. FOUNDED Stark Industries in the 19th century. During World War II, Howard Stark turned it into a major weapons manufacturer. Decades later, Howard and his wife, Maria, were murdered in a car accident arranged by a rival company, and Howard's adopted son, Tony, became S.I.'s new president. When rival businessman Obadiah Stane made a successful corporate takeover, Stark International became Stane International. Tony rallied, starting up Stark Enterprises, and eventually reclaimed Stane International years later, returning the company to its roots as Stark Industries.

FIRST APPEARANCE:
TALES OF SUSPENSE #39 (1963)

secretly and illegally sold them to terrorists. Eventually, when Stark visited Afghanistan for a military demonstration, Stane paid the Ten Rings terrorist organization to kill him. Stark survived but was captured, and learned they were armed with weapons built by his own company, forcing him to re-evaluate S.I.'s role in the world. After escaping by constructing a suit of powered armor, Tony announced to the press that S.I. was quitting weapons manufacturing. Caught off-guard by this unexpected proclamation, Stane convinced Stark to lie low while he "placated S.I.'s board of directors," then used Stark's absence to claim he was suffering from PTSD. As S.I. stock dropped precipitously, Stane successfully filed an injunction to lock Stark out of the company.

After seeing more examples of S.I. weapons being used by the Ten Rings to terrorize civilians in Gulmira, Afghanistan, and hearing news reports of his alleged mental problems, Stark confronted Stane at the Stark Industries' Annual Benefit for the Firefighters' Family Fund, and Stane admitted his involvement in the injunction and weapons sales. Wanting hard evidence of Stane's criminal dealings, Stark had his personal assistant Pepper Potts hack S.I.'s computers, but Stane learned of this breach. After bragging he would use Stark's miniature Arc Reactor to turn S.I. into a global power, Stane donned his own massive "Iron Monger" armor based on Stark's designs and built by S.I. scientists. Stane battled an armored Stark in and around S.I.'s Long Beach facility, a conflict that ended when Stark had Potts deliberately overload S.I.'s original Arc Reactor, killing Stane and destroying the reactor building.

FACT SHEET

- HOWARD AND MARIA'S CAR ACCIDENT OCCURRED ON LONG ISLAND IN MID-DECEMBER 1991. HOWARD HAS A STRETCH OF LONG BEACH HIGHWAY DEDICATED TO HIM, THE HOWARD STARK MEMORIAL PARKWAY.
- STARK INDUSTRIES MISSILES INCLUDE THE SIX45, ABLE TO INTERCEPT AIRCRAFT AT MACH 1.1. THE JERICHO MISSILE SYSTEM WAS PART OF THE STARK INDUSTRIES "FREEDOM LINE" OF WEAPONS.
- JERICHO WAS THE FIRST MISSILE TO INCORPORATE S.I.'S PROPRIETARY REPULSOR TECHNOLOGY, WHICH STARK LATER BUILT INTO HIS "IRON MAN" ARMOR.
- WHEN STARK ANNOUNCED S.I. WOULD CEASE PRODUCING WEAPONS, COMPANY STOCK DROPPED 56.5 POINTS, WELL BEYOND STARK'S INITIAL ESTIMATE OF 40.

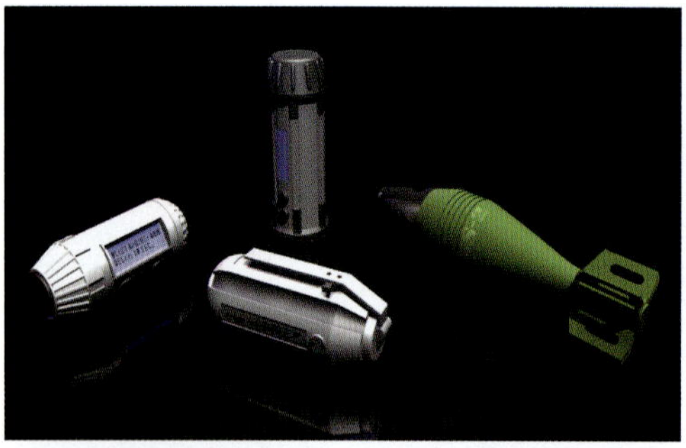

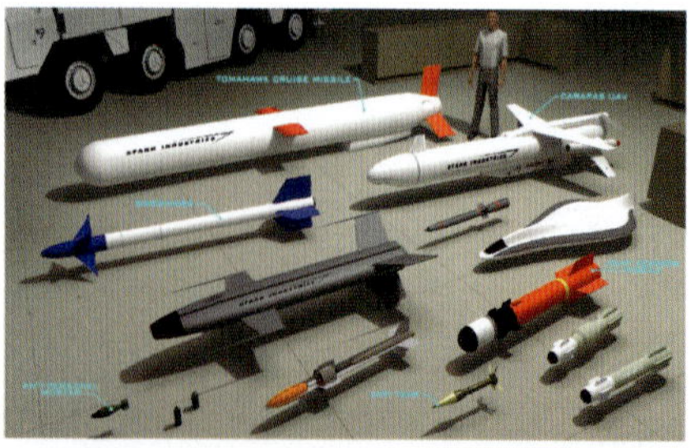

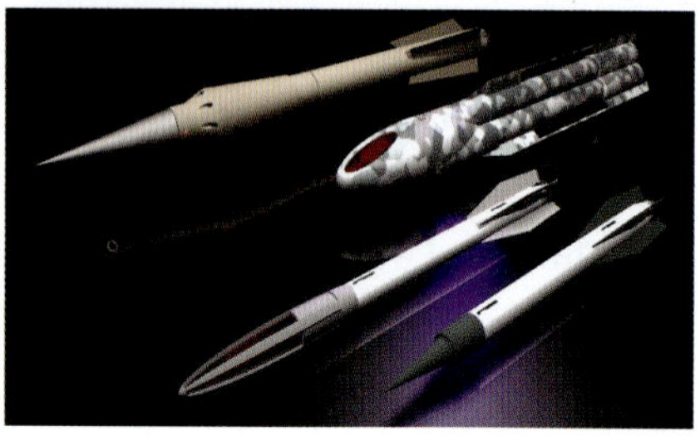

DUM-E (BACKGROUND) WITH FIRE EXTINGUISHER ATTACHMENT

STARK'S WORKSHOP ROBOTS

FIRST APPEARANCE: ***Iron Man [2008]***

While an undergraduate at MIT and exploring artificial intelligence (A.I.) technology, 16-year-old genius Tony Stark created two smart machines, which he eventually named Dum-E and U. Stark theorized that A.I. could be given personality through alternative programming and claimed his two prototype robots could understand voice commands and learn from his behaviors. Decades later, the abidingly loyal Dum-E and U still aid Stark in his workshop. Each robot can move independently on a wheeled chassis; both are equipped with a multi-jointed arm and three-pronged hand that can manipulate a variety of items, hand Stark tools and, if necessary, provide life-saving assistance such as fire extinguishing. Stark often addresses his workshop robots more as intelligent beings than mere automated attendants.

After Stark was severely injured and kidnapped by the terrorist organization the Ten Rings—a plot orchestrated by his corrupt business partner, Obadiah Stane—he eventually escaped and returned home with a miniaturized Arc Reactor implanted in his chest to prevent shrapnel from entering his heart. Dum-E was present when Stark attempted to replace the original device with an upgraded reactor, but was unable to help when a potentially life-threatening problem developed during the procedure. After Stark called his assistant Pepper Potts for assistance, Stark berated Dum-E, calling it "butterfingers" and telling it to clear the clutter on his desk. Potts was told to destroy the now-obsolete mini-reactor, but instead had it sealed in a display case as a gift for Stark. Later, when Stark began building his Mark II armor prototype, Dum-E assisted as best it could, holding a magnifying glass so Stark could see the tiny parts he soldered together on the armor's boot. When Stark tested the

Mark II's boot jets for the first time, Dum-E was equipped with a fire extinguisher while U recorded the event on video camera. Dum-E doused Stark with the extinguisher after the failed attempt even though Stark wasn't on fire. Dum-E and U kept their assigned jobs on Stark's next several flight attempts, though Dum-E was warned that it'd be donated to a city college if it unnecessarily doused Stark again. However, even after Stark finally achieved success in hovering in the lab, Dum-E continued aiming the extinguisher at him until Stark scolded Dum-E into standing down. After successfully field-testing the completed Mark II armor's flight capabilities, Stark returned to his Malibu estate and abruptly cut the armor's power while hovering over the roof—underestimating its weight—and crashed through three floors; Dum-E was waiting with the extinguisher and doused Stark.

Dum-E doused Stark with the extinguisher after the failed attempt even though Stark wasn't on fire.

Later, seeking a power source to empower his own armored suit, Stane temporarily paralyzed Stark with a sonic weapon and removed the miniature Arc Reactor from Stark's chest, leaving him to die. A weakened Stark struggled to get to his workshop and the original Reactor that Potts had preserved, but collapsed. Dum-E handed its longtime master the device, saving his life and enabling him to confront Stane; Stane subsequently died during an armored battle against Stark.

FACT SHEET

- STARK'S ORIGINAL WORK ON THE PAIR OF PROTOTYPE ROBOTS WAS FAR BEYOND ANY SEASONED MIT PROFESSOR'S COMPREHENSION.
- STARK'S WORK ON THE ROBOTS WON THE FOURTH ANNUAL MIT ROBOT DESIGN AWARD AND EARNED HIM THE LABEL "MIT'S ROBOTIC WUNDERKIND." U AND STARK WERE LATER PHOTOGRAPHED TOGETHER AT STARK INDUSTRIES FOR AN ARTICLE IN MIT TECHNOLOGY REVIEW.
- U FREQUENTLY SERVES AS VIDEOGRAPHER OF STARK'S EXPERIMENTS, AND APPARENTLY HAS SINCE ITS CREATION.
- THE ROBOTS' REACTIONS TO STARK'S COMMANDS, INCLUDING HUMANLIKE MOTIONS AND NOISES, MAY INDICATE THAT THEY WERE DESIGNED TO MIMIC EMOTIONAL RESPONSES.

U (BACKGROUND - L) WITH CAMERA ATTACHMENT; DUM-E (BACKGROUND - R) WITH FIRE EXTINGUISHER ATTACHMENT

IN THE COMICS

THE TEN RINGS WERE ARTIFICIALLY intelligent alien artifacts that could be worn as rings, each with its own unique power set, created by the dragon-like Kakaranatharan race. A Chinese nobleman called the Mandarin discovered the rings inside a crashed spaceship and began using them as weapons in his criminal endeavors. Mandarin formed a strong psychic link to the rings and sometimes loaned them to others. His son Temujin utilized them while his father was in a coma, but Mandarin reclaimed them upon awakening. After Mandarin's later death, the sentient rings attempted to take control of Iron Man's enemies in their quest to destroy Stark, but were defeated by Stark with help from his adoptive brother Arno and former ring-bearer Red Peril (Abigail Burns).

FIRST APPEARANCE:
TALES OF SUSPENSE #50 (1964)

TEN RINGS

FIRST APPEARANCE: ***Iron Man (2008)***

One of the cells of the Ten Rings terrorist organization was based in Afghanistan, where they focused their attention on the Middle East. The Rings secretly bought weapons from the U.S.A.'s Stark Industries through corrupt Obadiah Stane, who later hired the Rings to kill Stark Industries' CEO Tony Stark after a weapons test in Kunar Province. However, Stane left the Rings in the dark about their target's true identity. During the attack on Stark's convoy, the Rings mortally wounded Stark but reneged on their deal with Stane upon realizing who their target was. They kept him alive, ordering Ho Yinsen, a brilliant surgeon they had abducted from Gulmira, to save Stark's life and demanded more money from Stane to kill Stark; they then ordered Stark to build a Jericho missile for them. Stark, knowing the Rings would not free him as they had promised, instead built a prototype suit of armor with Yinsen's aid to use against his captors. The Rings eventually realized the two were not building the missile, and Yinsen sacrificed his life to buy Stark more time to activate the armor. During his escape, Stark destroyed most of the terrorists' weaponry.

TEN RINGS INSIGNIA

The Ten Rings' leader Raza combed the desert with his men, collecting the discarded parts of Stark's armor. After acquiring more weapons from Stane, including the coveted Jericho, the Ten Rings continued their terror campaign in Gulmira. When this news reached Stark, he returned to Afghanistan clad in upgraded armor and put an end to the terrorists' actions, leaving commander Abu Bakaar at the mercy of the locals. Raza later offered Stark's reassembled prototype armor to Stane in exchange for several more armors of the same kind for the Ten Rings to use in conquering Asia. But Stane, no longer interested in aiding the terror group, paralyzed Raza with a sonic device, stole the prototype armor and had his armed forces eliminate Raza's Ten Rings cell.

FACT SHEET

- THE TEN RINGS IS A MULTINATIONAL GROUP; ITS MEMBERS SPEAK ARABIC, DARI, ENGLISH, FARSI, HUNGARIAN, MONGOLIAN, PASHTO, RUSSIAN AND URDU.
- RAZA AND HIS TROOPS MAKE THEIR CAMP IN A REMOTE AND HEAVILY FORTIFIED CAVE IN THE AFGHANISTAN MOUNTAINS.

HO YINSEN

FIRST APPEARANCE: ***Iron Man [2008]***

A brilliant surgeon and engineer from the Afghan village of Gulmira, Ho Yinsen attracted the unwanted attention of the terrorist organization the Ten Rings, who killed Yinsen's family and kidnapped him to remote caves deep within Afghanistan's mountains. Later, during the Ten Rings' kidnapping of weapons designer Tony Stark, Stark was wounded by an explosion that left shrapnel moving slowly toward his heart. Ordered by the Ten Rings to save Stark's life, Yinsen surgically installed a makeshift electromagnet into Stark's chest which prevented the shrapnel from moving. After Stark's recovery, the Ten Rings ordered him to create a sophisticated missile for them, promising freedom after it was completed.

Yinsen and Stark both knew the Ten Rings would not keep their promise. Stark feigned compliance but secretly began work on a prototype armored suit he would use against the terrorists. Though initially leery of Yinsen, Stark used his help to create a miniaturized Arc Reactor, which they installed in Stark's chest to power the magnet. Yinsen soon earned Stark's trust and Stark revealed his true plans; the two became friends as they worked together for three months. However, when the Ten Rings' leader, Raza, did not see progress on the missile, he threatened to torture and maim Yinsen if he did not reveal what Stark was truly up to. Stark saved Yinsen's life by claiming he could not work without Yinsen's assistance. Raza gave the two an ultimatum: The missile had to be delivered the next day.

Stark and Yinsen rushed to complete the armor, then assembled it onto Stark. When the Ten Rings observed their activities through surveillance cameras, two terrorists rushed to confront the scientists but were killed by an explosive booby trap left by Stark. Yinsen, realizing the armor would not finish booting up before the other terrorists responded, ignored Stark's protests, grabbed one of the dead men's machine guns and rushed into the caves. Randomly firing the weapon as he ran, Yinsen successfully stalled the Ten Rings long enough for Stark to activate the armor. However, Raza and the Ten Rings rallied and fatally shot Yinsen.

During his escape, Stark was distraught to find his dying friend. Believing he would soon be reunited with his family, Yinsen was at peace with his death. After Stark thanked Yinsen for saving him, Yinsen had one dying wish: that Stark would not waste his life. With those words ringing in his ears, Stark escaped the Ten Rings, halted his company's weapons manufacturing and perfected the armor, using it to become the heroic Iron Man.

IN THE COMICS

HO YINSEN, FROM THE TINY country of Timbetpal, had multiple PhDs in physics, robotics and medicine. While working to cure mental illness through neural impulse manipulation, he was forced to design weapons to receive government funding. Eventually abducted by the Sin-Cong, Yinsen helped save fellow prisoner Tony Stark's life from shrapnel in his chest and assisted in building a suit of armor to use against their captors. However, Yinsen sacrificed his life to delay guards while the armor completed charging.

The sinister Doctor Midas harvested Yinsen's brain and used it to create armor for himself. Yinsen's former students—now called the Sons of Yinsen—rescued their mentor's brain and housed it in a sophisticated armor. This being later sacrificed itself to defeat the murderous robot Ultron; whether this armor was animated by Yinsen or another program remains unrevealed.

FIRST APPEARANCE:
TALES OF SUSPENSE #39 (1963)

FACT SHEET

- YINSEN SPOKE NUMEROUS LANGUAGES, INCLUDING ENGLISH AND ARABIC, AND SERVED AS TRANSLATOR BETWEEN STARK AND THE TEN RINGS.
- YINSEN WAS A GIFTED SURGEON, RENOWNED FOR HIS STEADY HANDS.
- YINSEN FAMILIARIZED HIMSELF WITH HIS PRISON BY MEMORIZING STEPS HE TOOK WHILE WALKING THE CORRIDORS; SHARING THIS INFORMATION WITH STARK ENABLED HIS ESCAPE.
- YINSEN AND STARK MET YEARS BEFORE AT A CONFERENCE IN BERN, SWITZERLAND, BUT STARK WAS TOO DRUNK DURING THIS FIRST ENCOUNTER TO LATER REMEMBER THEIR INTERACTION.
- DESPITE BEING HELD IN A CAVE, YINSEN MAINTAINED HIS RESPECTABLE APPEARANCE, DRESSING ONLY IN SUITS AND TIES.

ABU BAKAAR

FIRST APPEARANCE: ***Iron Man [2008]***

Zealous and brutal, Abu Bakaar became a secondary leader in Raza's Ten Rings terrorist group in Afghanistan. When U.S. weapons designer Tony Stark journeyed to Afghanistan to exhibit his new Jericho missile system for the American military, the Rings were secretly hired by Stark's corrupt business partner Obadiah Stane to kill Stark. However, once the Rings learned Stark was their target, they demanded more money from Stane. Under Raza's orders, Bakaar demanded Stark build a Jericho missile for the group, and tortured him until he seemingly complied. Instead, Stark—with the aid of fellow captured scientist Ho Yinsen—secretly built a crude suit of weaponized armor. Yinsen sacrificed his life so Stark could use the armor to escape. After upgrading his armor, Stark later returned to Afghanistan when he learned that the Rings were terrorizing Yinsen's home village Gulmira with Stark Industries weapons secretly provided by Stane. The armored Stark found Bakaar and his men pillaging the countryside. As Bakaar issued orders, including the kidnapping of the displaced villagers and the execution of one terrified captive, Stark arrived and easily eliminated the Rings' threat. Bakaar attempted to hide and contact Raza, but Stark found him, smashed him through a solid concrete wall and threw the dazed terrorist to the villagers to dispense whatever justice they deemed appropriate.

FACT SHEET

- VIA SECURITY CAMERAS, BAKAAR WAS RESPONSIBLE FOR MONITORING STARK'S WORK, BUT COULD NOT UNDERSTAND WHAT STARK WAS DOING.
- BAKAAR DOESN'T SPEAK A WORD OF ENGLISH, AND DIDN'T REALIZE THAT STARK AND YINSEN CONSPIRED TO ESCAPE DIRECTLY IN FRONT OF HIM.

IN THE COMICS

IN THE MARVEL UNIVERSE, SGT. NICK Fury led the Howling Commandos during World War II, battling Axis forces and occasionally fighting alongside Captain America (Steve Rogers) and Bucky (James Barnes). Given the age-slowing Infinity Formula, Fury remained in his physical prime for decades. After the war, Fury joined the CIA, becoming a spy. Decades later, Col. Fury, now wearing an eyepatch, was recruited into spy agency S.H.I.E.L.D. and became its director at Tony Stark's recommendation. Fury and S.H.I.E.L.D. often worked alongside the Avengers and other heroes.

FIRST APPEARANCE:
SGT. FURY AND HIS HOWLING COMMANDOS #1 (1963)

IN THE ULTIMATE UNIVERSE, THE court-martialed Pvt. Nick Fury became an unwilling participant in the government's attempt to create super-soldiers during WWII; the process granted Fury super-strength and slowed his aging, but he escaped and went AWOL. Decades later, Fury rejoined the Army; now wearing an eyepatch, he was eventually put in charge of creating new super-soldiers for the government. Later promoted to director of the spy agency S.H.I.E.L.D., Gen. Fury gathered the Ultimates for superhuman world-protection.

FIRST APPEARANCE:
ULTIMATE MARVEL TEAM-UP #5 (2001)

NICK FURY

FIRST APPEARANCE: ***Iron Man [2008]***

Director of the extra-governmental Strategic Homeland Intervention, Enforcement and Logistics Division, Nick Fury learned of Tony Stark's tech-aided escape from the Ten Rings terrorists and covertly kept his eye on the weapons mogul as he further refined his armor. After Stark publicly revealed that he was the armored Iron Man, Fury broke into Stark's estate by hacking its artificial-intelligence system, JARVIS, and told Stark he wasn't the only super hero in the world. He identified himself, then told Stark he was there to discuss S.H.I.E.L.D.'s Avenger Initiative. However, Stark turned Fury down without listening to what he had to say, so Fury prepared an alternate plan to monitor Stark: plant a S.H.I.E.L.D. agent within Stark Industries.

FACT SHEET

- S.H.I.E.L.D. IS AN INDEPENDENT GOVERNMENTAL ORGANIZATION WITH A MORE SPECIFIC FOCUS THAN THE FBI, CIA OR DOD; ITS MEMBERS APPEAR MAINLY CONCERNED WITH MONITORING BEINGS OF ENHANCED POWER.
- NICK FURY WEARS AN EYEPATCH THAT COVERS A HEAVILY SCARRED AND NON-FUNCTIONAL LEFT EYE.

MARVEL'S *INCREDIBLE HULK*

GUIDEBOOK TO THE MARVEL CINEMATIC UNIVERSE

MARVEL

THE INCREDIBLE HULK

UNIVERSAL PICTURES AND MARVEL ENTERTAINMENT PRESENT A MARVEL STUDIOS PRODUCTION A VALHALLA MOTION PICTURES PRODUCTION EDWARD NORTON "THE INCREDIBLE HULK" LIV TYLER TIM ROTH TIM BLAKE NELSON TY BURRELL AND WILLIAM HURT CASTING BY LARAY MAYFIELD MUSIC BY CRAIG ARMSTRONG MUSIC SUPERVISOR DAVE JORDAN VISUAL EFFECTS SUPERVISOR KURT WILLIAMS EDITORS JOHN WRIGHT ACE RICK SHAINE ACE PRODUCTION DESIGNER KIRK M. PETRUCCELLI DIRECTOR OF PHOTOGRAPHY PETER MENZIES, JR., ACS EXECUTIVE PRODUCERS STAN LEE DAVID MAISEL JIM VAN WYCK

SOUNDTRACK AVAILABLE AT amazon.com® THIS FILM CONTAINS DEPICTIONS OF TOBACCO CONSUMPTION PRODUCED BY AVI ARAD GALE ANNE HURD KEVIN FEIGE SCREEN STORY AND SCREENPLAY BY ZAK PENN DIRECTED BY LOUIS LETERRIER

MARVEL PG-13 PARENTS STRONGLY CAUTIONED Some Material May Be Inappropriate for Children Under 13 SEQUENCES OF INTENSE ACTION VIOLENCE, SOME FRIGHTENING SCI-FI IMAGES, AND BRIEF SUGGESTIVE CONTENT ®

A UNIVERSAL RELEASE UNIVERSAL

Covering Marvel's *The Incredible Hulk (2008)*.

HEAD WRITER/COORDINATOR: **MIKE O'SULLIVAN**

COORDINATORS: **DARON JENSEN** AND **JEPH YORK**

WRITERS: **TROY BENJAMIN**, **ANTHONY COTILLETTA**, **ROB LONDON**, **MARKUS RAYMOND**, **MARC RIEMER**, AND **STUART VANDAL**

ARTISTS: **MURPHY ANDERSON**, **VINCE COLLETTA**, **MICHAEL GOLDEN**, **JACK KIRBY**, **ARIEL OLIVETTI**, **JEROME OPEÑA**, **PAUL PELLETIER**, AND **LIAM SHARP**

COVER ARTIST: **MIKE DEL MUNDO**

SPECIAL THANKS TO DAVE ALTHOFF, CHRIS BUCHNER, SHAWN "KEEBLER" BYERS, MADISON CARTER, JEFF CHRISTIANSEN, MATT DELMANOWSKI, ERIKA DENTON, TIM DILLON, PERCIVAL LANUZA, JACQUE PORTE, AND RYAN POTTER

HULK CREATED BY STAN LEE AND JACK KIRBY

ABOMINATION
EMIL BLONSKY

FIRST APPEARANCE: ***The Incredible Hulk (2008)***

Russian-born but raised in England, Emil Blonsky was a born fighter who joined the Royal Marines. By age 39, the career military man was aware he was slowing down but felt that his operational experience more than compensated. Loaned to United States Special Operations Command, he joined Gen. Thaddeus "Thunderbolt" Ross' special-ops team sent to apprehend fugitive scientist Bruce Banner in Brazil. However, Gen. Ross declined to inform the team that Banner could transform into a hulking monster and they were decimated. When Blonsky made it clear he was determined to face the creature again, Gen. Ross gave Blonsky a bio-tech force enhancement serum developed to create super-soldiers. A small dose gave Blonsky superhuman strength, speed, and agility, but these still proved insufficient when the army confronted the Hulk at Culver University, an encounter that ended with the Hulk crushing most of the bones in Blonsky's body.

Blonsky was not expected to survive, yet he fully healed within hours. Hoping to even the playing field, Blonsky took a much higher serum dose, but this had unexpected side effects including enhancing his already well-known belligerence. Blonsky joined the special-ops team sent to Manhattan where Banner was testing Dr. Sam Sterns' possible cure for his affliction. Temporarily unable to transform, Banner's capture proved annoyingly easy for Blonsky. Learning Sterns had synthesized Banner's gamma-contaminated blood and wanting the Hulk's power, Blonsky went rogue, forcing Sterns to give him a transfusion—despite Sterns' warning that mixing the blood with the serum might create an abomination. Transforming into an 11-foot-tall behemoth, the "Abomination" rampaged through Harlem, forcing Banner to transform and confront him. Bigger, smarter, stronger, and a better fighter for much of the battle, the Abomination had the upper hand until he threatened Banner's beloved, Dr. Elizabeth "Betty" Ross. His strength increasing with his rage, the Hulk rallied and beat the Abomination into submission.

IN THE COMICS

YUGOSLAVIAN-BORN KGB SPY

Emil Blonsky was assigned to sabotage Bruce Banner's work at New Mexico's Los Diablos Missile Base nuclear research facility and deliberately exposed himself to gamma radiation, hoping to gain Hulk-like powers. He became a powerful and monstrous creature like the Hulk, and when Betty Ross called him an abomination, he proudly adopted the description as his codename. After battling the Hulk repeatedly over the years, the Abomination poisoned Betty to hurt his foe. In retaliation, Betty's father, Gen. "Thunderbolt" Ross, killed the Abomination after Gen. Ross was empowered as the Red Hulk.

FIRST APPEARANCE:
TALES TO ASTONISH #90 (1967)

FACT SHEET

- BLONSKY'S STERLING RECORD MEANT HE COULD HAVE BECOME A COLONEL, BUT HE REJECTED PROMOTIONS, PREFERRING FRONTLINE COMBAT.
- GEN. JOE GRELLER PICKED THE BRAZILIAN ASSAULT TEAM ON ROSS' BEHALF, DESCRIBING THEM AS ALL GOOD MEN, WITH ONE "ACE"—BLONSKY.
- BLONSKY WAS GIVEN A SERUM DEVELOPED BY DR. REINSTEIN FOR PROGRAM WEAPONS PLUS, SPECIFICALLY SERUM 7922-8209, BATCH 006*V2, VARIANT NUMBER RB*227.6.

HULK
BRUCE BANNER

FIRST APPEARANCE:
The Incredible Hulk [2008]

Dr. Bruce Banner was a bioscience professor at Culver University in Virginia working on a gamma radiation resistance project. However, Banner was unaware he was actually participating in a sub-project of Gen. Thaddeus "Thunderbolt" Ross' U.S. Army infantry weapons development program focused on biotech force enhancement, a venture similar to the WWII-era Super-Soldier project. Banner worked with Gen. Ross' daughter, fellow Harvard graduate and scientist Dr. Elizabeth "Betty" Ross, with whom Banner was also romantically involved. Banner was so confident in his research that he tested it on himself, unwittingly transforming himself into a super-strong green creature that destroyed the Culver University laboratory and left both Dr. Ross and Gen. Ross injured. As Dr. Ross recovered, Banner went into hiding, becoming a fugitive as Gen. Ross hunted him in hopes of weaponizing the creature.

Banner evaded capture for five years, continuing his research and exploring botany as a possible source of a cure for his condition. Eventually settling in Rio de Janeiro's Rocinha Favela, Brazil and working at the Pingo Doce soda bottling factory, Banner began studying Brazilian martial arts, learning various breath-control techniques, and using a metronome to stifle his anger and resulting transformations. Through an encrypted satellite link, Banner communicated with Dr. Samuel Sterns, a cell biologist at Grayburn College in New York City, under the aliases Mr. Green (Banner) and Mr. Blue (Sterns). Sterns recommended serums derived from various plants as possible methods of counteracting the radiation, but every attempt failed. Needing more data, Sterns convinced Banner to send him a blood sample, which Sterns secretly mass-produced, believing Banner's blood could be a cure for countless afflictions.

Banner was so confident in his research that he tested it on himself.

While working at the factory, Banner cut himself performing routine repairs. He was unaware a drop of blood fell into a soda bottle that was later shipped to the U.S., where a Milwaukee man drank it and became ill with gamma radiation poisoning. Gen. Ross and the military tracked the soda to Brazil where career military operative Emil Blonsky and a black-ops team located Banner. Banner fled to the factory, which was closed for the night, but was also pursued by co-workers who disliked him; when they caught Banner and assaulted him, Banner transformed and retaliated. The black-ops team surrounded the factory and attacked, but their weaponry proved ineffective against the green monster, who easily decimated their ranks and hurled a forklift at Blonsky before escaping. Gen. Ross subsequently seized Banner's equipment and learned of his interactions with Mr. Blue.

Banner secretly traveled to the U.S. and arrived at Culver University 17 days later, where he observed Dr. Ross from afar and learned she was now dating a psychotherapist named Leonard. Banner received help from friend and restaurateur Stanley, who gave him pizzas to use in bribing university security and a student to allow him computer access to search for his original gamma pulse research data, which Mr. Blue believed he could use to cure Banner. However, Banner discovered his data had been removed from the university records. He returned to Stanley's restaurant only for Dr. Ross to see him when she stopped in for a late dinner. Banner tried to flee, but Dr. Ross found him and insisted he let her help. At her home, Ross gave Banner a thumb drive containing his data, which she had been secretly hiding for five years.

Banner and Dr. Ross were unaware that Leonard, fearing for Dr. Ross' safety, had called Gen. Ross and notified him Banner was at the university. While leaving town, Banner saw Gen. Ross' forces approaching and fled, swallowing the thumb drive to keep it out of the general's hands. When Banner saw Dr. Ross being roughly restrained by Gen. Ross' soldiers, he became angry and transformed. The soldiers attacked the creature, but they were soundly defeated. Now enhanced by Gen. Ross' biotech force serum, Blonsky directly attacked the creature and led him into the blast range of two powerful Stark Industries sonic cannons. Though stunned by the attack, the creature heard Dr. Ross' screams for her father to stop the assault and rallied, destroying both cannons. Against Gen. Ross' orders, Blonsky challenged the creature again and was nearly killed when the creature kicked him. Amidst the confusion, Dr. Ross approached the creature and calmed him. When a gunship opened fire, the creature shielded Dr. Ross with his body and hurled a piece of metal at it, causing it to crash; the creature protected Dr. Ross from the conflagration and fled with her unconscious form. When an eyewitness, student Jim Wilson, was interviewed by the local news about the battle, he dubbed the creature the "Hulk."

The Hulk and Dr. Ross took refuge in the Smoky Mountain National Forest until Banner regained human form. Short on money, Dr. Ross sold her deceased mother's necklace for cash. Using an unsecure computer connection at a gas station, Banner sent Sterns his original data, inadvertently alerting defense agency S.H.I.E.L.D. and the military, who were monitoring

IN THE COMICS

DR. ROBERT BRUCE BANNER SUFFERS from Multiple Personality Disorder due to the traumatic murder of his mother at the hands of Banner's alcoholic father when Banner was a child. Graduating with a doctorate in nuclear physics from the California Institute of Technology, Banner worked at the U.S. Defense Department nuclear research facility's Los Diablos Missile Base in New Mexico under Gen. Thaddeus "Thunderbolt" Ross and fell in love with Ross' daughter, Betty. Banner designed the highly radioactive gamma bomb and during its first test, teenager Rick Jones infiltrated the restricted site on a dare. Banner saved Jones but not before the bomb detonated, irradiating Banner with gamma particles, which caused him to transform into the monstrous, simple-minded grey Hulk at night, eventually becoming a green version whenever angry. His periodic rampages often resulted in a negative portrayal to the world, and Hulk was frequently pursued by Gen. Ross and authorities despite being a founding member of the heroic Avengers, repelling alien invasions and subterranean conquerors, and defeating numerous super-criminal endeavors. In modern times, while working for S.H.I.E.L.D., Banner was shot twice in the head; Tony Stark's Extremis biogenetic human genome improvement technology was implanted in his brain to repair the damage. The infusion of Extremis brought out a hyper-intelligent "Doc Green" persona. Both individually and alongside the Avengers, Banner strives to control his Hulk personas and use his power to benefit and protect the world.

FIRST APPEARANCE:
THE INCREDIBLE HULK #1 (1962)

the internet for uses of "Mr. Blue" and "Mr. Green." On the way to meet Sterns in New York City, Dr. Ross asked Banner to describe his transformation. Banner replied it was similar to induced hallucination experiments they had volunteered for years prior at Harvard—amplified 1,000 times. He only remembered jumbled fragments of the Hulk's actions.

Once in NYC, Banner was willing to proceed with Sterns' potential cure despite warnings that a slight miscalculation could kill him. Sterns' antidote reversed a provoked transformation, but he was uncertain if the serum had simply suppressed this single event or if Banner was permanently cured. Afterward, Banner was horrified to learn Sterns had concentrated and reproduced Banner's blood sample and conducted experiments with it. Banner demanded Sterns incinerate the supply, fearing the ramifications. As they argued, Banner was tranquilized by a U.S. Army sniper and taken into Gen. Ross' custody. Soon after, Blonsky forced Sterns to inject Banner's blood into him, turning Blonsky into the Hulk-like Abomination.

While leaving NYC via helicopter, Gen. Ross, Banner and Dr. Ross saw live video feed from a soldier on the ground that showed the Abomination attacking soldiers and civilians; as Gen. Ross turned the helicopter around, Banner accused Gen. Ross of participating in the creature's inception. Banner convinced Gen. Ross to let him direct the Hulk in engaging the Abomination. Banner leapt from the helicopter, triggering his transformation; once on the ground, the Hulk roared, gaining Blonsky's attention. The two battled, their ferocious rampage destroying much of Harlem. Gen. Ross ordered the helicopter's gunner to fire on the Abomination, which drew his attention. The Hulk moved to stop the Abomination from attacking the helicopter, but Blonsky still grabbed it, their additional weight forcing a crash landing. Seeing Dr. Ross' life in danger from a potential gas leak explosion, the Hulk extinguished the fire and resumed battling his foe until the Abomination threatened Dr. Ross again; the Hulk used a chain to strangle him until Dr. Ross stopped the Hulk from killing Blonsky. Triumphant, the Hulk fled the scene. Banner secretly relocated to remote Bella Coola, British Columbia, to live a solitary life and work toward controlling the Hulk.

THE HULK VS. THE ABOMINATION IN HARLEM

FACT SHEET

- AFTER SIGHTINGS IN AMERICA, THE PRESS DUBBED THE HULK THE "GREEN MONSTER" AND "GREEN SASQUATCH."
- WHILE BANNER WAS A FUGITIVE, AUTHORITIES MONITORED HIS KNOWN ASSOCIATES, INCLUDING BETTY ROSS, PSYCHIATRIST DR. L. SAMSON, AND FORMER STUDENT RICHARD "RICK" JONES.
- BANNER TAUGHT HIMSELF BASIC PORTUGUESE DURING HIS TIME IN BRAZIL, USING A BATTERED DICTIONARY AND TRANSLATED BROADCASTS OF A POPULAR U.S. CHILDREN'S TELEVISION SHOW FEATURING PUPPETS.
- GEN. ROSS' MEN USED WEAPONS AND EQUIPMENT PURCHASED FROM TONY STARK'S STARK INDUSTRIES IN THEIR PURSUIT OF BANNER AND IN BATTLES WITH THE HULK.
- BANNER PARTIALLY BUILT HIS LAB EQUIPMENT IN BRAZIL WITH SCAVENGED TRASH, SUCH AS AN OLD RECORD PLAYER AND A SMALL TIRE.
- BANNER MUST KEEP HIS HEART RATE UNDER 200 BPM OR RISK TRANSFORMING INTO THE HULK. WHEN BANNER AND DR. ROSS TRIED TO CONSUMMATE THEIR RENEWED FEELINGS, BANNER MADE THEM STOP BECAUSE HIS HEART BEGAN RACING.
- BANNER LEARNED OF A FLOWER THAT COULD POTENTIALLY CURE HIM BY READING *INVENTORY OF RARE AND ENDANGERED TRACHEOPHYTA OF AMAZONIA* BY AMANDA KIRCHOFF.
- BANNER WEARS READING GLASSES OCCASIONALLY AND, TO PREVENT EXPOSING HIS BLOOD TO OTHERS, CARRIES SUPERGLUE TO INSTANTLY SEAL ANY CUTS IN HIS SKIN.
- GEN. ROSS BELIEVES THE HULK'S RAMPAGES ARE RESPONSIBLE FOR THE DEATHS OF AT LEAST SEVEN PEOPLE BETWEEN THE HULK'S CREATION AND LOCATING BANNER IN BRAZIL.
- THE HULK'S VOCABULARY APPEARS VERY LIMITED.
- BANNER HONORED HIS PROMISE TO RECOVER DR. ROSS' MOTHER'S NECKLACE FROM THE PAWN SHOP AND SECRETLY MAILED IT BACK TO HER.

BETTY ROSS

FIRST APPEARANCE: ***The Incredible Hulk (2008)***

A cellular biologist at Culver University, Dr. Elizabeth "Betty" Ross was in love with colleague Dr. Bruce Banner. Through their research in gamma radiation resistance, Drs. Ross and Banner unknowingly contributed to her father Gen. Thaddeus "Thunderbolt" Ross' military projects. Confident in his work, Banner used himself as a test subject, which somehow transformed him into a monstrous, super-strong green creature that destroyed the lab and gravely wounded Dr. Ross and Gen. Ross. Banner fled, inciting Gen. Ross' manhunt for the creature he wanted to weaponize. Recovering, Dr. Ross became estranged from her father because of his actions against Banner. Sometime in the next five years, she found companionship with Leonard, a psychotherapist at Culver.

During a date with Leonard at Stanley's Pizza Parlor, Dr. Ross was reunited with the fugitive Banner, who had secretly returned to the university seeking his former research data hoping it would cure him. Having held on to the data for safekeeping, Dr. Ross took Banner home and gave him the files. However, Leonard notified Gen. Ross that Banner had returned, and the following morning the U.S. Army ambushed Banner at Culver. When pleading with her father to stop the assault failed, Dr. Ross was shocked to see Banner transform into the creature. Despite the danger, Dr. Ross entered the battlefield to reason with Banner; the creature saved her life when an attacking gunship crashed on top of them. After carrying Dr. Ross away from the conflict, the creature, now dubbed the "Hulk" by a bystander, calmed and transformed back into Banner.

The two traveled to New York City to meet Dr. Samuel Sterns who had developed a possible antidote for Banner's condition. There, Dr. Ross and Banner were ambushed and taken into military custody, but one of their pursuers, soldier Emil Blonsky, transformed himself into the super-strong Abomination through a combination of Banner's blood and a serum provided by Gen. Ross and rampaged through Harlem. Dismayed to learn Blonsky's transformation was her father's doing, Dr. Ross watched Banner convince her father to allow him to battle the Abomination. When the Hulk won the fight, Dr. Ross stopped him from delivering a killing blow. After a tender goodbye, the Hulk fled.

IN THE COMICS

ELIZABETH "BETTY" ROSS, daughter of Gen. Thaddeus "Thunderbolt" Ross, met Dr. Bruce Banner while he helped design weapons for the military and fell in love with him, much to her father's dismay. Their relationship suffered years of tribulation after Banner's own gamma bomb transformed him into the monstrous Hulk. Betty later became the Red She-Hulk for a time before being depowered by a now-intelligent Hulk.

FIRST APPEARANCE:
THE INCREDIBLE HULK #1 (1962)

FACT SHEET

- DURING THEIR FLIGHT FROM VIRGINIA, DR. ROSS SOLD HER DECEASED MOTHER'S NECKLACE TO BUY A USED PICK-UP TRUCK; BANNER LATER SECRETLY PURCHASED THE NECKLACE AND RETURNED IT TO HER.
- BANNER ATTEMPTED TO CONTACT DR. ROSS ON FEBRUARY 7, 2006, BUT THE MESSAGE WAS INTERCEPTED BY S.H.I.E.L.D.

THE ROSS FAMILY

THADDEUS ROSS

FIRST APPEARANCE: ***The Incredible Hulk [2008]***

U.S. Army Gen. Thaddeus "Thunderbolt" Ross revived Weapons Plus, a dormant World War II-era Super-Soldier program. In hopes of discovering a breakthrough, he secretly kept tabs on a gamma radiation resistance project led by his daughter, Dr. Elizabeth "Betty" Ross, and Dr. Bruce Banner, whom Betty loved. When Banner used himself as a test subject, the experiment transformed him into a super-strong green creature that destroyed the lab and injured both Dr. Ross and the general. After recovering, Gen. Ross dedicated himself to finding the fugitive Banner and unlocking the secret of Banner's power for military use; the obsession led to estrangement with his daughter. He led a special military unit dedicated to tracking Banner, but the scientist's trail went cold. Following Tony Stark's invention of the Iron Man armor and Stark's subsequent withdrawal from munitions manufacturing, a reluctant Gen. Ross was ordered by Senator Stern to shift his focus from genetic enhancement to technology and was assigned to develop a one-man combat vehicle with industrialist Justin Hammer, but when the prototype crashed in hostile territory, Iron Man had to be sent in to rescue the pilot. After Stark declined to kill any of the enemy soldiers he faced during the mission, Gen. Ross admonished Stark for turning his back on the military.

Eventually locating Banner in Rio de Janeiro's Rocinha Favela, Brazil, Gen. Ross assembled a cadre of elite soldiers to apprehend Banner—but opted not to inform them of Banner's condition, deeming it need-to-know information. Banner escaped the ambush because the squad was unprepared for the monstrous creature. One of the soldiers, the aging-yet-determined Royal Marine Emil Blonsky, particularly impressed the general. When Blonsky confronted Gen. Ross over the monster, the general saw an opportunity to both gain his own enhanced soldier and apprehend the creature. Taking an experimental Weapons

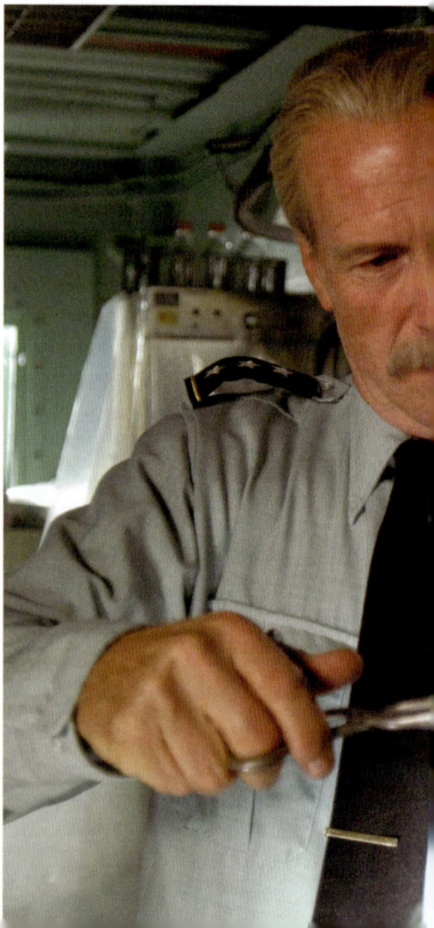

Plus Super-Soldier serum out of cold storage, Gen. Ross had it administered to Blonsky. Tipped off to Banner's current location by his daughter's new companion Leonard, Gen. Ross launched an assault on Banner at Culver University, but the mission ended in disaster: The monster pulverized Blonsky, Dr. Ross was injured in the crossfire, and the creature escaped with her; a bystander named the creature the "Hulk."

S.H.I.E.L.D. soon intercepted communications between Banner and biologist Dr. Samuel Sterns of New York City's Grayburn College. Gen. Ross set out for New York City—accompanied by Blonsky, whose enhancement had rapidly healed his injuries. Banner was apprehended, but Blonsky, driven by a lust for power, forced Dr. Sterns to inject him with Banner's blood, transforming him into the similarly super-strong Abomination. Rampaging through Harlem, Blonsky demanded a rematch with the Hulk. Confronted by Dr. Ross and Banner for creating a monster, Gen. Ross reluctantly turned Banner loose to transform and battle Blonsky, even assisting the Hulk by firing on the Abomination from his gunship. The Hulk saved the general and Dr. Ross when the gunship crashed and caught fire, then defeated the Abomination, throwing him at Ross' feet. Powerless to stop him, the general stood by as the Hulk escaped. As Gen. Ross later drowned his sorrows in a bar, he was approached by Tony Stark, who told the disgruntled general that a team was being formed.

WITH ENHANCEMENT SERUM

IN THE COMICS

GEN. THADDEUS "THUNDERBOLT" ROSS supervised the gamma bomb test that accidentally transformed scientist Bruce Banner into the Hulk. He single-mindedly led the hunt for the rampaging beast, often over the objections of his daughter, Betty, who loved Banner. Ross' mania drove him to the brink of madness and death on multiple occasions. In recent years, his obsession reached its natural conclusion: To defeat the Hulk, he became a Hulk. After being transformed into the Red Hulk by the Intelligencia cabal, and feeling disillusioned after the apparent assassination of Captain America (Steve Rogers), Ross nearly overthrew the U.S. government until the Hulk defeated him. Later, he was assigned to the Avengers and formed his own black-ops Thunderbolts team before the now-intelligent Hulk stripped him of his powers.

FIRST APPEARANCE:
THE INCREDIBLE HULK #1 (1962)

FACT SHEET

- GEN. ROSS TRACKED BANNER TO BRAZIL AFTER A DROP OF BANNER'S BLOOD CONTAMINATED A SODA BOTTLE IN THE FACTORY WHERE BANNER WORKED AND A MILWAUKEE MAN CAME DOWN WITH GAMMA POISONING BY DRINKING IT.
- GEN. ROSS' CHIEF AIDE WAS THE CAPABLE MAJOR KATHLEEN SPARR, WHO WAS ASSAULTED BY EMIL BLONSKY WHEN HE WENT ROGUE.
- GEN. ROSS DEPLOYED VARIOUS WEAPONS AGAINST THE HULK, INCLUDING TRANQUILIZER RIFLES, KNOCKOUT GAS GRENADES, AND STARK-CREATED MOBILE SONIC CANNONS.

IRON MAN UPDATE

FIRST APPEARANCE:
Iron Man [2008]

Billionaire industrialist Tony Stark led the advanced technology developer Stark Industries. Almost killed by terrorists using his company's munitions, he ended his company's weapons development, but used his Iron Man armor to stop criminals and help those in need. His heroic actions caught the attention of S.H.I.E.L.D. Director Nick Fury. With Stark Industries out of the weapons business, the U.S. military contracted Hammer Industries to design a single-pilot attack vehicle under Gen. Thaddeus "Thunderbolt" Ross' supervision; when it was shot down during a field test in the Congo, Iron Man was sent to rescue the pilot, but, aware the U.S. military hoped to manipulate him into killing the Congolese Army in the region, deliberately avoided slaying any of the pilot's captors. Gen. Ross scolded Stark for turning his back on the military. S.H.I.E.L.D. deemed Stark too reckless for Fury's Avengers Initiative and relegated him to consultant status. After Gen. Ross failed to capture the Hulk (Bruce Banner) and one of his soldiers, Emil Blonsky, was transformed into the Abomination thanks to Ross' actions, Stark approached a drunken and forlorn Gen. Ross in a bar. Stark initially chided Gen. Ross for reviving the Super-Soldier program because it had proved largely unstable, as evidenced by the now captive Blonsky. Stark then gained the general's attention by informing him a team was being put together.

> **S.H.I.E.L.D. deemed Stark too reckless for Fury's Avengers Initiative.**

FACT SHEET

- STARK INDUSTRIES SUPPLIED THE NON-LETHAL SONIC CANNONS USED BY GEN. ROSS AGAINST THE HULK.
- THE SUPER-SOLDIER SERUM THAT AUGMENTED EMIL BLONSKY WAS STORED IN A STARK INDUSTRIES "CRYOSYNC" CONTAINER.

SAMUEL STERNS

FIRST APPEARANCE:
The Incredible Hulk [2008]

Cell biologist Dr. Samuel Sterns was communicating with Bruce Banner via encrypted satellite connection as Mr. Blue (Sterns) and Mr. Green (Banner), aiding Banner in seeking a cure for his gamma irradiation. After many failures, Sterns convinced Banner to send him a blood sample, which Sterns secretly mass-produced and tested on animals, hoping to make humans impervious to disease and win a Nobel Prize. When Banner sent Sterns data of the original experiment that irradiated Banner, their unsecured contact alerted S.H.I.E.L.D. and the military. Finally meeting in person in Manhattan, Sterns managed to temporarily suppress Banner's transformation with his test antidote. However, when Sterns revealed his own research, a shocked Banner deemed it too dangerous and demanded the blood be destroyed. Before Sterns could take action, the military captured Banner. Unsatisfied with the anticlimactic arrest and desperate to match the power of Banner's creature, artificially enhanced soldier Emil Blonsky forced Sterns to inject Banner's blood into Blonsky's body. Turned into the Abomination, Blonsky struck Sterns, injuring his head. As Banner's blood dripped into the open wound, Sterns began visibly mutating; considering the Hulk to be godlike, he apparently welcomed his transformation.

IN THE COMICS

GAMMA RADIATION TRANSFORMED high school dropout Samuel Sterns into the hyperintelligent Leader; he repeatedly aimed for world domination, but was often thwarted by the Hulk (Bruce Banner). The Leader's goals have included starting a global war to rule the remains and enhancing humans with gamma radiation.

FIRST APPEARANCE:
TALES TO ASTONISH #62 (1964)

FACT SHEET

- STERNS WORKS AT GRAYBURN COLLEGE IN NEW YORK CITY.
- STERNS BELIEVES IT SERVES HIM WELL TO BE MORE CURIOUS THAN CAUTIOUS IN HIS WORK.

MARVEL'S *IRON MAN 2*

GUIDEBOOK TO THE MARVEL CINEMATIC UNIVERSE

MARVEL

IRON MAN 2

PARAMOUNT PICTURES AND MARVEL ENTERTAINMENT PRESENT A MARVEL STUDIOS PRODUCTION IN ASSOCIATION WITH FAIRVIEW ENTERTAINMENT A JON FAVREAU FILM ROBERT DOWNEY JR. "IRON MAN 2" GWYNETH PALTROW DON CHEADLE SCARLETT JOHANSSON SAM ROCKWELL MICKEY ROURKE AND SAMUEL L. JACKSON AS NICK FURY MUSIC BY JOHN DEBNEY MUSIC SUPERVISOR DAVE JORDAN VISUAL EFFECTS AND ANIMATION BY INDUSTRIAL LIGHT & MAGIC COSTUME DESIGNER MARY ZOPHRES CO-PRODUCERS JEREMY LATCHAM VICTORIA ALONSO EDITORS RICHARD PEARSON, A.C.E. DAN LEBENTAL, A.C.E. PRODUCTION DESIGN BY J. MICHAEL RIVA DIRECTOR OF PHOTOGRAPHY MATTHEW LIBATIQUE, ASC EXECUTIVE PRODUCERS DENIS L. STEWART LOUIS D'ESPOSITO JON FAVREAU SUSAN DOWNEY EXECUTIVE PRODUCERS ALAN FINE STAN LEE DAVID MAISEL PRODUCED BY KEVIN FEIGE SCREENPLAY BY JUSTIN THEROUX DIRECTED BY JON FAVREAU

AC/DC: IRON MAN 2 AVAILABLE ON COLUMBIA RECORDS

Covering Marvel's *Iron Man 2 (2010)*, *Iron Man 2 (2010) #1-2*,
Iron Man 2: Agents of S.H.I.E.L.D. (2010) #1, and *Iron Man 2: Public Identity (2010) #1-3*.

HEAD WRITER/COORDINATOR: **MIKE O'SULLIVAN**

COORDINATORS: **DARON JENSEN** AND **JEPH YORK**

WRITERS: **TROY BENJAMIN**, **MADISON CARTER**, **PATRICK DUKE**, **MIKE FICHERA**, **DARON JENSEN**, **ROB LONDON**, **CHRIS MCCARVER**, **MARKUS RAYMOND**, **MARC RIEMER**, **JACOB ROUGEMONT**, **STUART VANDAL**, AND **JEPH YORK**

ARTISTS: **CARLOS ANGUIANO**, **JONATHAN BACH**, **TONY BOHORQUEZ**, **STEVE BRAGGS**, **TIM BRAKENSIEK**, **ELIOT R. BROWN**, **GENE COLAN**, **NATASHA DEVAUD**, **MARKO DJURDJEVIC**, **DOUBLE NEGATIVE**, **KALENE DUNSMOOR**, **MONICA FEDRICK**, **RENE GARCIA**, **JOHN GOODSON**, **ADI GRANOV**, **DON HECK**, **BRUCE HOLCOMB**, **KEVIN HOPGOOD**, **ILM**, **JACK KIRBY**, **ROBERT KOSAI**, **BOB LAYTON**, **RON LIM**, **M3**, **ALITHA MARTINEZ**, **SCOTT MAY**, **AARON MCBRIDE**, **LUKE MCDONNELL**, **RYAN MEINERDING**, **RON MENDELL**, **KAORI OGINO**, **BRANDON PETERSON**, **PROLOGUE**, **JOHN ROMITA, SR.**, **PAUL THURIOT, JR.**, **JOHN WALKER**, **RON WOODALL**, AND **MARY ZOPHRES**

COVER ARTIST: **PASCAL CAMPION**

SPECIAL THANKS TO DAVE ALTHOFF, SHAWN "KEEBLER" BYERS, JEFF CHRISTIANSEN, MATT DELMANOWSKI, ERIKA DENTON, TIM DILLON, PERCIVAL LANUZA, JACQUE PORTE, AND RYAN POTTER

IRON MAN CREATED BY STAN LEE, LARRY LIEBER, DON HECK, AND JACK KIRBY

WRIST-MOUNTED WEAPONS

BLACK WIDOW
NATASHA ROMANOFF

FIRST APPEARANCE: ***Iron Man 2 [2010]***

S.H.I.E.L.D. Agent Black Widow (Natasha Romanoff) was tasked with infiltrating Stark Industries to assess Tony Stark's viability for the Avengers Initiative. Given the cover identity "Natalie Rushman," Black Widow was hired as a notary by Bambi Arbogast for Stark Industries' Legal Department. When S.H.I.E.L.D. learned the Arc Reactor in Stark's chest was killing him, Black Widow drugged a co-worker, Samantha Carlisle, and took her place to get closer to Tony Stark. Delivering documents to Stark's home to finalize Pepper Potts' promotion to Stark Industries CEO, "Natalie" made an impression on Stark when she easily pinned Stark's chauffeur Happy Hogan during a sparring session; Stark promoted "Rushman" to his personal assistant. Accompanying Stark to the Monaco Historic Grand Prix, "Rushman" facilitated Stark's schedule and witnessed Iron Man's battle with the terrorist Ivan Vanko, subsequently dealing with the press for Potts. When Stark asked "Rushman" how she'd spend her last birthday, to gather more information for his personality profile, she provocatively replied she'd do "whatever she wanted." Stark subsequently started a drunken, armored brawl with his friend Lt. Col. James Rhodes at Stark's birthday party. When S.H.I.E.L.D. Director Nick Fury later confronted Stark over his recent impulsive actions, Stark was shocked to learn that "Rushman"

FACT SHEET

- BLACK WIDOW SPEAKS SEVERAL LANGUAGES, INCLUDING ENGLISH, FRENCH, ITALIAN, RUSSIAN, AND LATIN.
- BLACK WIDOW'S S.H.I.E.L.D. DUTIES INCLUDE WORK AS A FIELD AGENT AGAINST ENEMY COMBATANTS AND AS A SHADOW AGENT FOR INFILTRATION MISSIONS.
- BLACK WIDOW'S S.H.I.E.L.D. WEAPONS INCLUDE SHOCK DISCS, SMOKE DISCS, A GARROTE, PEPPER SPRAY, A WALTHER PPK/S .380 ACP PISTOL, AND SPECIALIZED BRACELETS.
- WHEN BLACK WIDOW AND "HAPPY" HOGAN STORM HAMMER INDUSTRIES, BLACK WIDOW SUBDUED TWELVE GUARDS IN THE SAME TIME IT TOOK HOGAN TO DEFEAT ONE.

was actually a S.H.I.E.L.D. agent. On Fury's order, Black Widow administered lithium dioxide to Stark, which briefly abated the symptoms of palladium poisoning caused by the Arc Reactor.

Returning to Stark Industries with her cover intact, Romanoff attended Hammer Industries' weapons presentation at the Stark Expo with her new CEO Potts, where Hammer Industries' war drones and an armored Rhodes, both remote-controlled by Vanko, attacked Iron Man. After forcing Hammer Industries CEO Justin Hammer to reveal Vanko's involvement, Romanoff and Hogan broke into Hammer Industries to stop Vanko, but he escaped. Romanoff hacked Vanko's computers, restored Rhodes' armor controls, and remotely provided tactical support to Iron Man in his battle with Vanko. Later, Black Widow's assessment of Stark reported his compulsive behavior, self-destructive tendencies, and textbook narcissism; she recommended Iron Man — but not Stark — for the Avengers Initiative. Elsewhere, Fury and Black Widow discussed recruiting Rhodes into the Avengers Initiative.

IN THE COMICS

NATALIA ROMANOVA ("NATASHA ROMANOFF"), BORN IN THE U.S.S.R. in the late 1920s, was raised by Ivan Petrovitch. During WWII, Natalia was placed in a Soviet assassin training facility; when she escaped, Ivan went AWOL, and the two became mercenaries. In 1956, the Winter Soldier — a brainwashed Bucky Barnes — offered the pair a modified Soviet Super-Soldier serum that would extend their lifespans if they returned to the U.S.S.R.; since Ivan was injured, Natalia agreed. Enrolled in the Red Room Academy, Natalia was extensively trained and educated; her memories were altered to strengthen her loyalty to the U.S.S.R. and enhance her cover stories while on missions. Years later Natalia was retired, her memories of espionage erased and she was married to Soviet test pilot Alexi Shostakov, but when Alexi seemingly died, Natalia demanded to become a spy. With Ivan as her handler, Natalia became known as "Black Widow" because she seduced and killed her targets.

Taking an espionage job against Stark Industries, Black Widow romanced Tony Stark but was ultimately discovered. Seeking revenge against Iron Man, Black Widow recruited Hawkeye, skilled archer Clint Barton, to assist her in sabotaging Stark Industries. After several failed attempts, Black Widow was eventually recruited into S.H.I.E.L.D. by Nick Fury, who put her skills to good use and she once went undercover as teacher "Nancy Rushman." In the ensuing years, Black Widow regained her memories, partnered with crime fighter Daredevil (Matt Murdock), helped formed the Champions of Los Angeles super-team, and joined the Avengers, even leading them for a time. Black Widow continues to work with S.H.I.E.L.D. and the Avengers to protect the world.

FIRST APPEARANCE: *TALES OF SUSPENSE #52 (1964)*

NICK FURY UPDATE

FIRST APPEARANCE: ***Iron Man [2008]***

After failing to recruit Tony Stark for the Avengers Initiative himself, S.H.I.E.L.D. Director Nick Fury ordered one of his operatives, Black Widow (Natasha Romanoff), to go undercover within Stark Industries. Providing Black Widow with the cover identity "Natalie Rushman," Fury tasked her with getting close to Stark to assess his viability for the Avenger Initiative. Meanwhile, Fury monitored Iron Man's attacks on various Ten Rings terror cells across the globe. When Stark refused to cooperate with Gen. Thaddeus "Thunderbolt" Ross and the U.S. military, Fury realized he might be able to work with Stark's rebellious personality.

Learning the mini-Arc Reactor in Stark's chest was killing him, Fury surprised Stark by revealing that "Rushman" was actually Black Widow, putting Stark off his guard. Fury confronted Stark about his recent destructive behavior, demonstrating that Stark couldn't handle everything on his own, and scolded Stark for becoming a problem that he had to address personally — pointing out that Stark was not the center of Fury's universe, and he had bigger issues to deal with in the southwest region of the country. In a gesture partially meant to show Stark that he could accept help from others, Fury supplied Stark with lithium dioxide, a compound that temporarily inhibited the palladium poisoning from Stark's mini-Arc Reactor. Fury explained that he knew Stark's father Howard, one of S.H.I.E.L.D.'s founders, and that the Arc Reactor was unfinished technology meant to be fueled by a new element that would dwarf nuclear power; Howard had never finished the project, but if Tony could, it would mean a cure for his condition. Fury gave Howard's notes and research to Stark and challenged him to finish the job, indicating to Stark that being a team player has its benefits. Fury left Black Widow at Stark Industries with her cover intact and assigned S.H.I.E.L.D. Agent Phil Coulson to keep Stark on task, but soon reassigned Coulson to the southwest.

Later, Fury revealed to Stark Black Widow's negative assessment of him. Trying a new approach to entice Stark, Fury told him that S.H.I.E.L.D. was no longer interested in him for the Avengers Initiative; instead, Fury offered to bring Stark on as a consultant. To show Stark he could play ball, Fury did him a favor by arranging for Senator Stern, a rival of Stark's, to publicly award Stark for his heroic actions. Elsewhere, Fury and Black Widow discussed recruiting Stark's friend James Rhodes into the Avengers Initiative.

FACT SHEET

- FURY LIKES TO JOKE ABOUT HIS DAMAGED LEFT EYE TO EASE THE PRESSURE IN TENSE SITUATIONS.
- FURY IS A MASTER TACTICIAN, UTILIZING EVERY RESOURCE AVAILABLE TO HIM, AND IS ABLE TO ALTER HIS PLANS WHEN THE SITUATION DEMANDS IT.
- FURY HOLDS THE RANK OF COLONEL.
- WHEN FURY OFFERED STARK A CONSULTANT POSITION WITH THE AVENGERS INITIATIVE, THEY WERE MONITORING NEWS FOOTAGE OF THE HULK'S RAMPAGE AT CULVER UNIVERSITY.

IN THE COMICS

JUSTIN HAMMER

FIRST APPEARANCE: ***Iron Man 2* (2010)**

Arms-maker Justin Hammer, CEO of Hammer Industries, profited from his rival Tony Stark's departure from the weapons business when he gained a valuable government contract. Under Gen. Thaddeus Ross' supervision, Hammer designed a single-pilot attack vehicle. Despite Hammer's claim it wasn't vulnerable to surface-to-air assaults, it was shot down in the Congo during its first field test; the U.S. military sent in Iron Man (Tony Stark) to save the pilot. Despite this setback, the Department of Defense allowed Hammer to design a suit of armor for them. Called in as an expert by the Senate Armed Services Committee for a public hearing concerning the government's attempt to commandeer the technology behind the Iron Man suit, Hammer lost his government contract after Stark showed humiliating footage of Hammer's suit gravely injuring a test pilot during simple movement tests.

Later, Hammer attended the Monaco Historic Grand Prix and witnessed Ivan Vanko's use of Stark's Arc Reactor technology in an attempt to kill Tony Stark for slights he believed his father suffered at the hands of Stark's father. Sensing an opportunity to get back at Stark, Hammer arranged Vanko's escape from prison and took him to Hammer Industries in Queens, New York. Hammer admitted his attack suits' production was rushed and miscalculations were made, but he still hoped they would put him in the Pentagon's good graces for the next 25 years. Trusting Vanko to improve the suits for the Stark Expo, Hammer was disappointed when Vanko turned the suits into unmanned drones. Meanwhile, the military provided Hammer with the opportunity to apply Hammer technology in weaponizing an Iron Man suit acquired by Stark's close friend Lt. Col. James Rhodes. Despite Vanko's claims that the drones were not ready for demonstration, Hammer introduced them at the Stark Expo alongside the Variable Threat Response Battle Suit, a.k.a. "War Machine," worn by Rhodes. When Vanko remote-controlled the drones and War Machine suit to attack Iron Man, S.H.I.E.L.D. Agent Romanoff forced Hammer to reveal Vanko's location. Stark Enterprises CEO Pepper Potts subsequently had Hammer arrested.

INDUSTRIALIST JUSTIN HAMMER, owner of Hammer Industries and various subsidiaries, controlled his business from a heavily armed and protected floating villa usually located in the Mediterranean. He took over many of Stark's clients when Stark abandoned the weapons business and financed super-criminals, providing them with advanced weaponry, sometimes stolen from Stark, in exchange for 50 percent of his clients' revenue. For years, Iron Man not only ran afoul of Hammer's operatives, but also fought off Hammer's attempts to destroy or take over his business. After a confrontation aboard Hammer's space station, Stark left Hammer adrift in space, trapped inside frozen water which apparently killed him. Hammer's daughter Justine continued her father's legacy until her daughter Sasha apparently killed her.

FIRST APPEARANCE:
IRON MAN #120 (1979)

FACT SHEET

- HAVING LONG LIVED IN STARK'S SHADOW, HAMMER STRIVES TO SURPASS STARK BY ANY MEANS NECESSARY.
- WIRED MAGAZINE CALLED HAMMER THEIR MOST ELIGIBLE TECH-BACHELOR, BUT A PROFILE OF HAMMER FOR VANITY FAIR WAS PRE-EMPTED WHEN STARK DISTRACTED CHRISTINE EVERHART, THE VANITY FAIR INTERVIEWER.
- HAMMER HAS A FLAMBOYANT PERSONALITY, AND DANCED HIS WAY ONSTAGE WHILE PRESENTING AT THE STARK EXPO.

HAMMER INDUSTRIES

FIRST APPEARANCE: *Iron Man 2 (2010)*

Led by CEO Justin Hammer, Hammer Industries (H.I.) is a corporation known primarily for weapons manufacturing, and as a fierce competitor to Stark Industries. When Stark Industries dropped out of weapons manufacturing, H.I. gained crucial U.S. military contracts.

After Stark's technological breakthrough with the Iron Man armor, H.I. provided design specifications for a military attack craft, but it was shot down by the Congolese army during its field test. The pilot was rescued with no bloodshed — thanks to Iron Man's intervention. Hammer's Advanced Weapons Systems then began attempts to recreate a "weaponized suit" of their own, but met with failure when the suit violently twisted at the waist, gravely injuring its test pilot. When Stark displayed footage of this failure at a Senate hearing, H.I. was publicly embarrassed and its Department of Defense contract was revoked. To prove his company's worth, Hammer arranged an H.I. presentation at the Stark Expo and facilitated terrorist Ivan Vanko's escape from prison, intending to use Vanko's engineering skills to discredit Tony Stark. After setting Vanko to work on his armored prototype battle suits from a Hammer facility in Queens, New York, Hammer reluctantly allowed Vanko to convert the prototypes into remote-controlled drones. Meanwhile, Hammer also weaponized a functional Iron Man suit for the U.S. military, planning to publicly reveal it at the Stark Expo as the Variable Threat Response Battle Suit.

During the Stark Expo presentation,

IN THE COMICS

HAMMER INDUSTRIES (H.I.) IS A corrupt corporation that publicly operated as a weapons manufacturer. However, H.I. ran a number of front companies such as Electronica Fabrizzi and Crecy Enterprises while surreptitiously manufacturing high-tech weapons, armor, and gadgetry for criminal clientele including the winged Beetle (Abe Jenkins), three ice-themed villains named Blizzard (Gregor Shapanka, Donald Gill, and Mickey Quaid), weapons expert Boomerang (Fred Meyers), the massive gamma-powered Rhino (Aleksei Sytsevich), the crazed tail-lashing Scorpion (Mac Gargan), the ultimate copycat fighter Taskmaster (Tony Masters), and Whiplash (Mark Scarlotti). Hammer ran his company from a villa on a floating island which moved about the Mediterranean Sea.

H.I. once created a device which could override Stark's Iron Man armor, leaving the hero to believe he was malfunctioning. After the device caused Iron Man to accidentally kill an ambassador, causing a scandal for Stark Industries (S.I.) while profiting H.I., Iron Man discovered Hammer's involvement and captured him. H.I. later secretly acquired control of S.I. rival Stane International and teamed with other S.I. competitors in an attempt to destroy their common foe; Iron Man eventually forced Hammer to relinquish his holdings of Stane back to Stark. After Hammer's apparent death, his daughter Justine, the criminal Crimson Cowl, inherited her father's fortunes and continued the family business.

FIRST APPEARANCE:
IRON MAN #120 (1979)

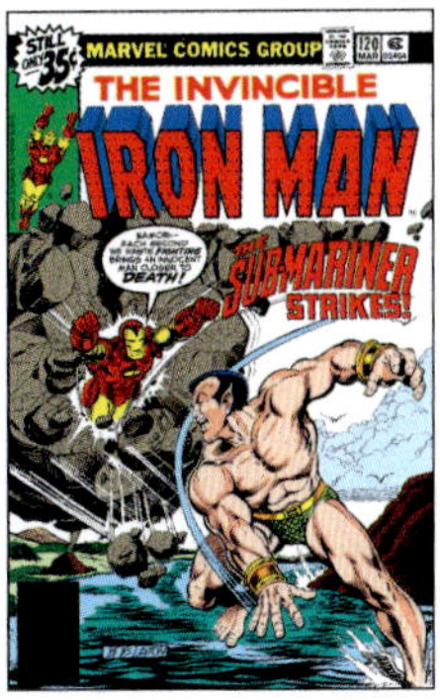

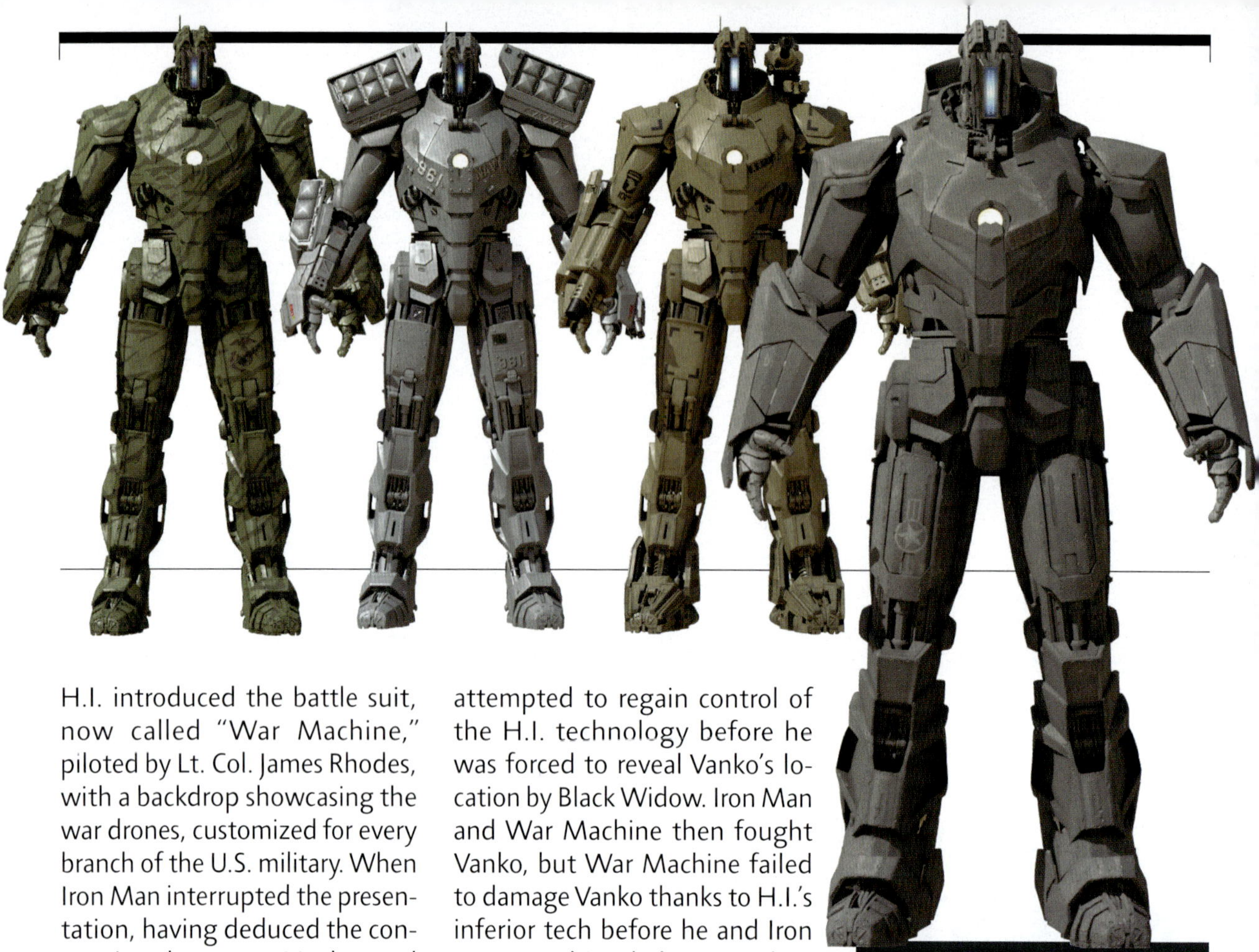

H.I. introduced the battle suit, now called "War Machine," piloted by Lt. Col. James Rhodes, with a backdrop showcasing the war drones, customized for every branch of the U.S. military. When Iron Man interrupted the presentation, having deduced the connection between Vanko and Hammer, Vanko activated the war drones and remotely took control of Rhodes' battle suit and attacked Iron Man. Hammer attempted to regain control of the H.I. technology before he was forced to reveal Vanko's location by Black Widow. Iron Man and War Machine then fought Vanko, but War Machine failed to damage Vanko thanks to H.I.'s inferior tech before he and Iron Man combined their repulsor beams to defeat Vanko. Stark Industries' CEO Pepper Potts called the police and had Hammer arrested.

THE HAMMERDRONES: (TOP ROW-L TO R) MARINE, NAVY, ARMY, AIR FORCE (FAR RIGHT)

HAMMER INDUSTRIES LAB

FACT SHEET

- INITIALLY COSTING $125.7 MILLION EACH, THE HAMMER DRONES WERE SPECIALIZED FOR EACH BRANCH OF THE U.S. MILITARY: ARMY DRONES HAVE M32 M6L MULTI-GRENADE LAUNCHERS, NAVY DRONES HAVE FIXED-POINT COIL LASERS AND FIM-92 STINGER MISSILES, AIR FORCE DRONES ARE EQUIPPED FOR FLIGHT AND HAVE THERMAL VISION VORTEX RING GUNS, AND MARINE DRONES HAVE HIGH-DEFINITION CAMERAS.
- HAMMER INDUSTRIES' KINETIC-KILL SIDEWINDER MISSILE WAS NICKNAMED "THE EX-WIFE" BY JUSTIN HAMMER HIMSELF. THOUGH TOUTED BY HAMMER FOR ITS DESTRUCTIVE POTENTIAL, THE EX-WIFE FAILED TO DETONATE WHEN FIRED BY WAR MACHINE IN BATTLE WITH WHIPLASH.

IRON MAN UPDATE

FIRST APPEARANCE: *Iron Man [2008]*

Young Tony Stark often argued with his demanding father, Howard. Jarvis, the family butler, frequently comforted Tony when Howard lost his temper and claimed that Tony was not living up to his full potential; Tony later named his artificial intelligence (A.I.) system after Jarvis. When Tony graduated summa cum laude from Cambridge University at a young age, Howard accused him of deliberately racing through school out of boredom, but Tony angrily ended the discussion. It was the last time they talked before his parents died.

After Stark refused to join S.H.I.E.L.D.'s Avengers Initiative, Director Nick Fury ordered S.H.I.E.L.D. Agent Natasha Romanoff, a.k.a. Black Widow, to get close to Stark. Stark hunted down Ten Rings terrorist cells and became the world's first celebrity super hero. Though he aided the U.S. military when asked, he also sometimes got in their way as he rushed in to save lives, so U.S. Senator Stern contracted arms-manufacturer Justin Hammer to develop a one-man vehicle to match Iron Man. When it was shot down in the Congo, Stark rescued the pilot, but deliberately failed to recover the vehicle.

Stark soon discovered he was slowly being poisoned by toxic palladium from the miniature Repulsor Technology (R.T.) Arc Reactor embedded in his chest. Unable to find a suitable replacement substance, Stark kept the realization he was dying to himself. Increasingly thinking of his legacy, he arranged a Stark Expo inspired by the ones his father held previously. Six months after his public debut, Stark testified before Senator Stern's Senate Armed Services Committee. To pressure Stark into handing over his Iron Man technology to the U.S. government, Stern cited intelligence that hostile governments had developed their own weaponized suits, but Stark showed footage of their failed attempts as evidence that rival armors were years away from being operational.

Not revealing his imminent mortality, Stark made his assistant Pepper Potts his successor as chairman and CEO. Stark's friend Lt. Col. James Rhodes informed Stark that the Pentagon still wanted their own Iron Man; he was trying to convince them to hire Stark as an autonomous contractor instead of simply seizing the suits. Seemingly ignoring Rhodes' concerns, Stark instead goaded Rhodes into trying out a suit and taught his friend to pilot it. Having infiltrated Stark Enterprises as Natalie Rushman, Romanoff became Stark's new personal assistant. While attending Monaco's Historical Grand Prix, Stark impulsively decided to drive in the race, but was attacked by Ivan Vanko, armed with his own R.T.-powered weapons; Vanko blamed the Stark family for his own family's misfortunes. Potts and Stark's chauffeur Happy Hogan delivered Stark's portable armor to him, and Stark subdued Vanko, but the attack was seen as evidence that others were closer to duplicating Stark's technology than Stark had

FACT SHEET

- STARK DRANK 80 OUNCES OF CHLOROPHYLL DAILY TO REDUCE THE PALLADIUM'S POISONING EFFECTS. DESPITE THIS, HIS BLOOD'S TOXICITY LEVELS ROSE TO 53 PERCENT BEFORE HE WAS CURED.
- CERTAIN HE WAS DYING, STARK DONATED HIS ENTIRE MODERN ART COLLECTION TO THE BOY SCOUTS OF AMERICA, WHICH ANGERED POTTS, AND AWARDED CONTRACTS TO WIND FARMS AND PLASTIC PLANTATION TREE GROWERS.
- WHEN TONY DROVE IN THE MONACO HISTORICAL GRAND PRIX, HE REPLACED STARK RACING TEAM DRIVER DEFILIPPO, WHO WAS NOT PLEASED WITH LOSING HIS POSITION.

claimed. Back in California, at what he believed would be his final birthday party, Stark drunkenly showed off his suit's firepower, rudely rebuffing Potts' admonishments. Disgusted, Rhodes donned the armor he had been taught to pilot and tried to stop Stark. After the resultant brawl ended, an angry Rhodes took the armor he had claimed to the military, hoping to placate his superiors.

The next morning, Fury revealed Rushman's true identity as a S.H.I.E.L.D. operative to Stark and encouraged him to continue searching for the palladium replacement. Fury gave Howard's personal lockbox to Tony, revealing that Howard was a founding member of S.H.I.E.L.D. The box contained reels of film, one of which depicted Howard admitting his love for his son, and hinting that he had hidden an important discovery for Tony to find and complete.

After this, having realized that he loved Potts, Stark tried to apologize and tell her, but her continued anger stymied him. Seeing a model of the 1974 Stark Expo in Potts' office and realizing that Howard modeled the Expo layout after the atomic structure of a new element he had discovered but could not produce due to the limitations of technology at the time, Stark manufactured the element and created a new miniature R.T. reactor chestpiece, which reversed the damage to his body. A taunting phone call from Vanko warned Stark he was planning to strike at the Expo, where Hammer was unveiling new Hammer drones and Rhodes' Hammer-upgraded "War Machine" armor. Iron Man raced there, but Vanko remotely controlled both Rhodes' armor and the drones to attack Stark and the Expo. While the Expo was evacuated, Black Widow rebooted War Machine, restoring Rhodes' control, and Rhodes helped Iron Man destroy the drones and defeat the armored Vanko. Triggering the drones' self-destruct explosives, Vanko demolished the Expo, but Stark and Rhodes escaped, the former rescuing Potts en route. Stark and Potts finally revealed their love for each other.

Later, Fury informed Stark that S.H.I.E.L.D. now only wanted him as a consultant. With Rhodes and Stark due to be publicly awarded medals for stopping Vanko, Stark agreed to Fury's request with the proviso that Fury pressure Senator Stern into presenting the award personally.

TONY'S R.T.

HOWARD STARK AND SOVIET PHYSICIST ANTON VANKO DESIGNED THE ARC REACTOR TOGETHER UNTIL ANTON WAS CAUGHT TRYING TO SELL THE TECHNOLOGY, RETURNED TO RUSSIA AND IMPRISONED. YEARS LATER, HIS SON IVAN USED THE BLUEPRINTS TO BUILD HIS OWN MINIATURE ARC REACTOR, CREATING WEAPONS TO USE AGAINST STARK AS WHIPLASH, BUT STARK WON THEIR FIRST BATTLE. SIMULTANEOUSLY, NEUTRON DAMAGE FROM THE REACTOR WALL CAUSED THE PALLADIUM CORES OF TONY'S CHEST-INSTALLED MINI-ARC REACTOR TO CORRODE, LEAKING TOXINS INTO HIS BLOOD. SYNTHESIZING THE NEW ELEMENT HIS FATHER HAD DISCOVERED BUT NEVER ACTUALIZED, STARK REPLACED THE PALLADIUM WITH A NEW MINIATURE REPULSOR TECHNOLOGY (R.T.) ARC REACTOR WITH A TRIANGULAR CORE. MEANWHILE, TAKING STARK'S OFFHAND RECOMMENDATION TO DOUBLE HIS FIRST REACTOR'S ROTATIONS, VANKO ALSO BUILT A NEW R.T. REACTOR TO POWER THE SECOND ITERATION OF HIS OWN ARMOR.

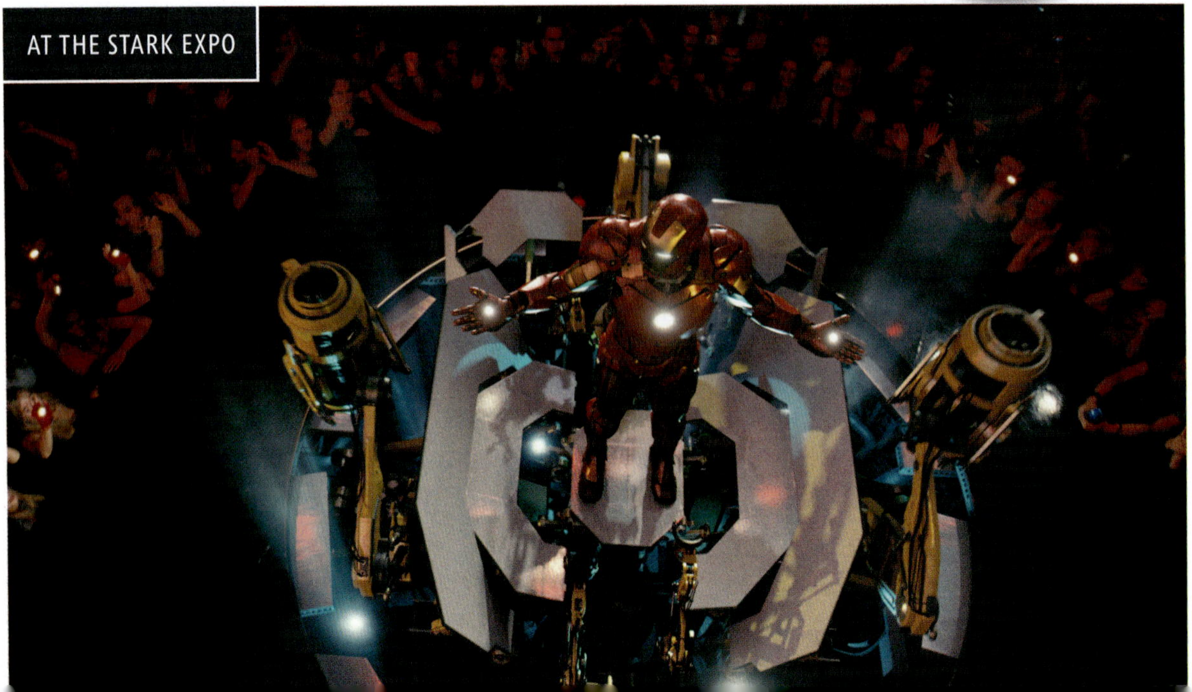

AT THE STARK EXPO

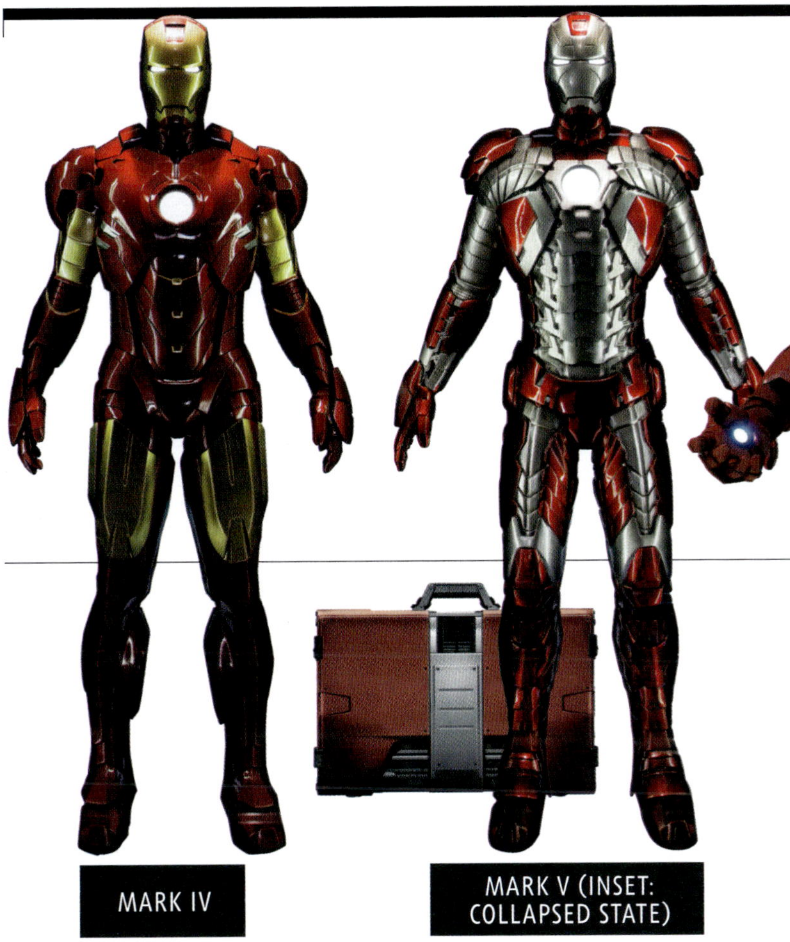

IRON MAN'S ARMORS UPDATE

FIRST APPEARANCE: ***[Mark IV-VI] Iron Man 2 [2010]***

Tony Stark continued developing the Iron Man armor technology, increasing his arsenal of suits by three: the Mark IV, a replacement for the battle-damaged Mark III; the Mark V, a collapsible suit of portable travel armor; and the Mark VI, a technological evolution of the Mark IV designed to handle the increased power output of Stark's redesigned miniature Repulsor Technology (R.T.) Arc Reactor.

The Mark IV became Stark's primary armor during Stark's personal peacekeeping missions and self-promotion junkets. Stark piloted the Mark IV during his dramatic entrance at the Stark Expo opening ceremonies and during his drunken stupor at his Stark Estate birthday party that led to a protracted battle with James Rhodes, who donned the Mark II armor in order to stop Stark's increasingly self-destructive behavior. The fight ended when the two fired repulsor bursts at one another that met in midair and caused a massive explosion, heavily damaging the estate. With Stark subdued by the blast, Rhodes departed with the Mark II, which he later enhanced with many weapons systems and dubbed "War Machine."

FACT SHEET

- THE MARK IV WAS FUNCTIONALLY IDENTICAL TO THE MARK III AND BOASTED MINIMAL DIFFERENCES IN TERMS OF EXTERIOR DESIGN OR ONBOARD FEATURES AND WEAPONRY.
- THE MARK V COULD BE CARRIED AS A BRIEFCASE-LIKE BLOCK UNTIL NEEDED; A FOOT PEDAL ACTIVATED THE SUIT, WHICH COULD FORM ONTO STARK'S BODY IN SECONDS.
- THE MARK VI FEATURED NEW WEAPONS IN THE SUIT'S FOREARM BRACES, INCLUDING MICRO-MISSILE LAUNCHERS AND SINGLE-USE, HIGH-POWERED LASERS.
- STARK MODIFIED PART OF HIS GARAGE TO ACT AS A "GALLERY" FOR HIS PREVIOUS SUITS, INCLUDING A RECONSTRUCTION OF THE MARK I ARMOR HE BUILT ALONGSIDE HO YINSEN IN AFGHANISTAN.
- WHEN SENATOR STERN SAID THAT THE IRON MAN ARMOR WAS A WEAPON DURING A U.S. SENATE HEARING, STARK DENIED THIS, INSISTING IT WAS A HIGH-TECH PROSTHESIS.

THE HALL OF ARMOR

The Mark V armor was designed for situations when Stark had to suit up and traveling to the Stark Estate to do so was unfeasible. Stark entrusted the Mark V to Happy Hogan during his vacation to Monaco and found himself in dire need of the armor when Ivan Vanko attacked him at the Monaco Historic Grand Prix. Hogan and Pepper Potts delivered the Mark V, which allowed Stark to defeat Vanko, but the Mark V was heavily damaged by Vanko's energized whips.

After developing a new element based on his father's research that would replace the poisonous palladium core in his mini-Arc Reactor, Stark designed and built the Mark VI, a replacement for the Mark IV that could utilize his miniature R.T. Arc Reactor's increased power output. Alongside Rhodes in his modified Mark II War Machine armor, Stark fought and destroyed Justin Hammer's rogue military drones; the pair defeated an armored Ivan Vanko with a tandem repulsor attack that triggered the same sort of explosion that had ended their fight at the Stark Estate.

IN THE COMICS

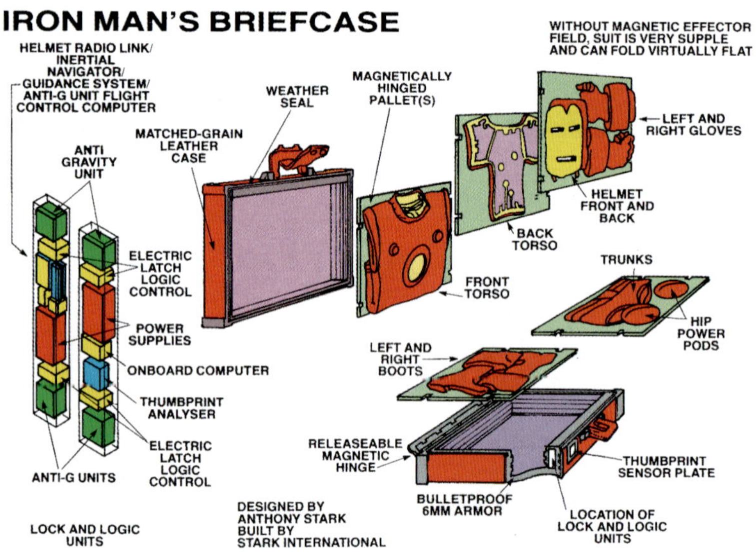

AFTER RETURNING TO AMERICA from his ordeal in Southeast Asia, Tony Stark decided to use his prototype Iron Man armor to operate as a masked hero, which required a means to conveniently transport the armor to make quick changes into his armored alter ego. Stark streamlined the prototype into a collapsible, less bulky design and created a modified attache case that could store the armor when not in use. The case carried the armor's pieces on stacked trays, and was fitted with bulletproof armor and fingerprint sensors that kept the armor out of unfriendly hands.

The briefcase became Stark's go-to method for transporting later versions of the armor as he transitioned from a collapsible armor-plate design to suits that employed forcefield-reinforced micro-chainmail; even James Rhodes used the case to carry the Model 04 armor during his stint as Iron Man. In later years, Stark learned that the systems that made the suit portable were adversely affecting his health, requiring him to develop a new suit without the hazardous equipment. The lack of collapsibility in the new armor made the briefcase obsolete.

FIRST APPEARANCE:
TALES OF SUSPENSE #40 (1963)

PEPPER POTTS UPDATE

FIRST APPEARANCE: *Iron Man (2008)*

After Tony Stark's grandstanding at a Senatorial hearing, exorbitant spending of resources for a year-long expo, and other neglectful and indulgent incidents, executive assistant Virginia "Pepper" Potts became increasingly frustrated with Stark's lackadaisical attitude toward his business. As she confronted Stark about her concerns, he responded by making her the CEO of Stark Industries, a decision he'd been considering for a while. The transfer paperwork was notarized by company paralegal "Natalie Rushman" (secretly S.H.I.E.L.D. Agent Natasha Romanoff), whom Stark hired as his new assistant. On a business trip in Monaco, Stark spontaneously abandoned Potts at a restaurant to participate in a televised Grand Prix race. Seeing Stark on the restaurant's big screen, Potts sent "Rushman" to collect Stark's driver, Happy Hogan. As Potts waited, Russian scientist Ivan Vanko, a.k.a. Whiplash, entered the racetrack and, using weapons powered by technology similar to Stark's, attacked the oncoming racers to get to Stark. Hogan arrived with a "briefcase" (actually a compact suit of Iron Man armor) and rushed Potts to the raceway, driving the limousine onto the track in the opposite direction of the race. When they reached Stark, Whiplash completely destroyed the limo; Potts got the armor to Stark, and he defeated Vanko.

Potts quickly called police and took over Justin Hammer's control center.

Potts suspected Stark was hiding something from her, and on the flight back to the U.S., she confronted him, but he evaded answering her, trying to convince her to go on vacation with him. In light of the Monaco incident, Potts refused — she needed to handle damage control for the company's public image. When Stark endangered guests at his birthday party by drunkenly showing off his armor's repulsor rays, Potts tried to close the revels down, but Stark rudely belittled her instead. The next day, Stark tried to apologize to Potts while she was instructing Stark Industries' lawyers to retrieve Stark's Mark II armor confiscated by Lt. Col. James Rhodes during the party; still angry, Potts refused to accept the apology. Later, at the Stark Expo, Stark Industries' competitor Hammer Industries displayed high-tech military drones and the modified Mark II armor worn by Rhodes, but they were remotely hijacked by Whiplash and used to attack Stark and the Expo. Potts quickly called police and took over Justin Hammer's control center, trying to regain control of the situation. She chose to stay until the park was completely evacuated, unaware that the drones were set to explode when Stark defeated Whiplash. Although Stark rescued her from the subsequent explosions, the stress of recent experiences overcame her, and she and Stark shared a kiss, after which they began a romantic relationship.

FACT SHEET

- POTTS IS ALLERGIC TO STRAWBERRIES.
- POTTS SPENT TEN YEARS ACCUMULATING AND CURATING STARK'S LARGE COLLECTION OF MODERN ART; STARK THEN DONATED IT TO THE BOY SCOUTS OF AMERICA, ANGERING POTTS.
- POTTS WAS ALSO ANGERED TO LEARN ABOUT STARK DYING DUE TO A FLAW IN THE MINI-ARC REACTOR IN HIS CHEST BY OVERHEARING RADIO CHATTER BETWEEN STARK AND ROMANOFF.

STARK EXPO

FIRST APPEARANCE: ***Iron Man 2 [2010]***

Believing technological advances could improve the public's quality of life, Stark Industries founder Howard Stark sponsored multinational technology expositions intended to bring together scientists and great thinkers from across the globe in hopes that they would pool their resources and create inventions that would better the world. Stark World Expositions were held in 1954 and 1964 in New York's Flushing Meadows-Corona Park, the site of the 1939-1940 New York World's Fair. Following the 1964 Stark World Expo, Flushing Meadows also hosted the 1964-1965 New York World's Fair, which resulted in the construction of the park's now-iconic Unisphere globe.

In the 1960s, Stark and Anton Vanko invented the Arc Reactor, an energy-generating device powered by palladium. Stark conceived of a synthetic element that would power the reactor more efficiently, but lacked the technology to physically synthesize it. Unwilling to leave clear notes about this proposed element, Stark instead encoded its atomic structure in a scale model of the upcoming 1974 Stark Exposition, using the Unisphere statue as its nucleus and the Expo's pavilions as the protons and neutrons. Stark recorded a message for his young son Tony, alluding to the model's importance and hoping Tony would one day solve the riddle and use superior future technology to synthesize the element. For unrevealed reasons, the 1974 show — its name shortened to simply "Stark Expo" — was Howard Stark's last; Howard died in 1991.

In modern times, Tony Stark, now Stark Industries' CEO and the super hero Iron Man, learned that the palladium in his chest-mounted mini-Arc Reactor was poisoning him. Facing his own mortality, Stark revived the Expo, hoping to leave a legacy of beneficial technology for future generations. Launching a year-long show in the Expo's traditional Flushing Meadows location, Stark made a grand entrance in typical flamboyant fashion — flying in as Iron Man through fireworks and landing amidst several Iron Man-themed dancers ("Ironettes") — and delivered the Expo's keynote speech. Weeks later, Stark went through his father's belongings and discovered Howard's cryptic message. Noticing the structure of the 1974 Expo model, Stark soon discovered and synthesized the hidden element, completing his father's Arc Reactor research and saving his own life.

Stark's rival Justin Hammer scheduled a weapons demonstration at

1974 EXPO SCALE MODEL

POSTERS OF PAST EXPOS

the Expo, hoping to show up Stark at his own event. He debuted his military Hammer drones and Lt. Col. James Rhodes' "War Machine" armor — but Anton Vanko's son Ivan betrayed his uneasy ally Hammer, overriding War Machine and the drones and forcing them to attack Iron Man, whom he blamed for his family's misfortunes. The battle raged across the Expo, causing widespread damage. Hoping to lure the drones away from civilians, Iron Man led them through the parking lots, but several turned back to attack the Expo itself, and Iron Man was forced to return. As Pepper Potts oversaw the Expo's evacuation, Iron Man disabled several drones by flying through the Unisphere, his pursuers crashing on its interior walls, but the Vanko-controlled War Machine tackled him into a pavilion themed as a Japanese garden. Black Widow rebooted War Machine's armor remotely, freeing Rhodes; he and Iron Man battled and disabled the remaining drones. Vanko arrived as the armored Whiplash but was defeated by Iron Man and War Machine. In defeat, Whiplash activated the drones' self-destruct sequence. Iron Man flew Potts to safety as the drones exploded, severely damaging the Expo grounds. Whether Stark repaired and reopened the Expo after Whiplash's attack is unrevealed.

FACT SHEET

- HOWARD STARK LABELED THE 1974 EXPO MODEL "THE KEY TO THE FUTURE IS HERE," A HINT FOR TONY.
- THE STARK EXPO THEME SONG IS TITLED "MAKE WAY FOR TOMORROW TODAY."
- POTTS CONSIDERED THE STARK EXPO A WASTE OF THE COMPANY'S TIME, CALLING IT STARK'S EGO GONE WILD.
- STARK INSTALLED A MOBILE SUIT-UP GANTRY IN THE MAIN PAVILION'S FLOOR, ALLOWING HIM TO REMOVE THE IRON MAN ARMOR DURING HIS GRAND ENTRANCE.
- SEVERAL PEOPLE IN THE STARK EXPO CROWD WORE TOY IRON MAN MASKS AND GLOWING GAUNTLETS PRESUMABLY SOLD AT THE EXPO.

CREATING DIGITAL PROJECTION OF EXPO MODEL

WAR MACHINE ARMOR

WAR MACHINE
JIM RHODES

FIRST APPEARANCE: ***Iron Man [2008]***

An Air Force weapons procurement officer and military liaison to Stark Industries (S.I.), Lt. Col. James "Rhodey" Rhodes is a longtime friend to Tony Stark, although his attempts to corral the immature and narcissistic playboy occasionally strained that friendship. Though initially resistant to Stark's shutdown of S.I.'s weapons manufacturing efforts, Rhodes reconsidered once he learned of Obadiah Stane's illicit dealings and of Stark's efforts to stop Stane and his Ten Rings allies as Iron Man.

Rhodes was called by Senator Stern to appear before the Senate Armed Services Committee in Washington, D.C., to use excerpts of his report on the Iron Man armor in an unsuccessful attempt to coerce Stark into turning the suit over to the U.S. government. Rhodes later learned that Stark was being slowly poisoned by the palladium core within his Arc Reactor implant and unsuccessfully pled with him to accept help.

Rhodes later learned that Stark was being slowly poisoned by the palladium core.

The following evening, Rhodes arrived at Stark's birthday party to find a drunken armored Stark endangering the guests. Rhodes donned the Mark II armor, evacuated the guests and demanded Stark shut down his armor, but the two friends brawled throughout the Stark Estate before an explosion caused by their repulsor bursts meeting in midair

FACT SHEET

- AT STARK'S INSISTENCE, RHODES HAD TAKEN THE MARK II ON A PRACTICE FLIGHT DAYS BEFORE HIS CONFRONTATION WITH STARK.
- THOUGH HAMMER TOUTED "THE EX-WIFE" AS A POWERFUL PIECE OF ORDNANCE, THE SMALL MISSILE SIMPLY BOUNCED OFF VANKO'S ARMOR AND FAILED TO DETONATE.
- NICK FURY VETOED RHODES' RECRUITMENT INTO THE AVENGERS INITIATIVE, THINKING HIM BETTER SUITED FOR SOLO STRATEGIC OPERATIONS MISSIONS.

subdued Stark and allowed Rhodes to fly the Mark II to Edwards Air Force Base. Stark's rival Justin Hammer upgraded and armed the Mark II, transforming it into the Variable Threat Response Battle Suit or, as Stark called it during the fight at the estate, the "War Machine." The minimally armed Mark II was fitted with additional armor plating, a minigun on a shoulder swivel mount, forearm-mounted sub-machine guns, and a shoulder-mounted launcher carrying a missile dubbed "The Ex-Wife" by Hammer.

Rhodes appeared in the War Machine armor as part of Hammer's public unveiling of his military drones at the Stark Expo, but upon Stark's arrival to confront Hammer about his alliance with terrorist Ivan Vanko, Vanko remotely commandeered the drones and Rhodes' armor and set them all against Stark and the Expo spectators. Once S.H.I.E.L.D. Agent Natasha Romanoff remotely rebooted Rhodes' armor, Rhodes joined Stark in defeating the drones and an armored Vanko. After confirming that Stark and Pepper Potts survived self-destruction detonations of Vanko's armor and drones, Rhodes flew off, claiming his car was destroyed in the explosions, so he had to use the suit to transport himself. Days later, Rhodes and Stark were presented medals in Washington, D.C., begrudgingly bestowed by Senator Stern.

IN THE COMICS

MARINE CORPS HELICOPTER PILOT

James "Rhodey" Rhodes encountered Tony Stark in his Iron Man guise after his helicopter was shot down near the Sin-Cong terrorist camp from which Stark had escaped. A friendship was struck between the pair after they helped one another escape to friendly territory, and Stark rewarded Rhodes' courage by hiring him as his personal pilot. When Stark briefly descended into drunken poverty, Stark entrusted his Model 04 armor to Rhodes, who operated as Iron Man until Stark regained his sobriety and fortune.

When Stark thought himself terminally ill, he developed the heavily armed Model 11 "War Machine" Iron Man armor to launch an offensive on Justin Hammer, who had framed Stark for criminal negligence. Upon his supposed death, Stark willed Stark Enterprises and the War Machine armor to Rhodes, but Rhodes was infuriated to learn Stark was simply placed in stasis until his damaged nervous system could be repaired. Rhodes eventually reconciled with Stark and has operated as a super hero in various powered suits, including the alien Eidolon Warwear and various redesigns of the Iron Man, War Machine and Iron Patriot armors.

FIRST APPEARANCE: *IRON MAN #118 (1978)*

WHIPLASH
IVAN VANKO

FIRST APPEARANCE: ***Iron Man 2 [2010]***

Raised by his father Anton to believe that Howard Stark was the source of all his family's misfortune, Ivan Vanko became a physicist, but when he tried to sell plutonium to Pakistan, he was arrested and imprisoned for 15 years. Emerging a bitter man, Vanko lived with his dying father in Moscow. Howard's son Tony's revelation to the world that he was the armored hero Iron Man, combined with Anton's death, spurred Ivan to destroy the Stark legacy. He built his own miniature Arc Reactor, using it to power a weapons harness that focused repulsor energy through plasma channels, and created two powerful energized whips mounted on his arms. Using fake credentials, he infiltrated the Monaco Historic Grand Prix as a crew member. Vanko attacked the participating Stark as Whiplash, but Stark donned Iron Man armor and defeated Vanko.

MINIATURE ARC REACTOR

Industrialist Justin Hammer broke Vanko out of prison, faked the Russian's death, and brought Vanko to America to put him to work on his armor prototypes, hoping to use them to show up Stark. Vanko disappointed Hammer: He made Hammer's armors into drones and told him they wouldn't be functional in time for the Hammer presentation at the Stark Expo. Unbeknownst to Hammer, the

FACT SHEET

- VANKO'S SOLE CONFIDANT WAS A WHITE COCKATOO; HE ASKED HAMMER TO HAVE IT BROUGHT TO HIM FROM RUSSIA, BUT HAMMER TRIED TO FOOL VANKO WITH A REPLACEMENT BIRD INSTEAD.
- VANKO USED THE ALIAS BORIS TURGENOV TO ENTER MONACO.
- WHILE HE SPEAKS AND UNDERSTANDS ENGLISH, VANKO OFTEN PRETENDS OTHERWISE TO MAKE OTHERS UNDERESTIMATE HIM.
- VANKO IS A SKILLED BRAWLER AND CAN BREAK A MAN'S NECK WITH HIS BARE HANDS.

WHIPLASH'S FULL ARMOR

drones were fully operational and under Vanko's control — as was Hammer's newly acquired "War Machine" armor, piloted by Stark ally Lt. Col. James "Rhodey" Rhodes. Vanko also used Hammer's resources to upgrade his weapons harness and integrate it into an armored suit. Vanko called Tony Stark, revealing that he was still alive, to lure him to the Hammer demonstration. There, Iron Man was ambushed by the drones and War Machine, much to Rhodes' displeasure. After War Machine was remotely freed from Vanko's control by the Black Widow, he helped Stark destroy the drones — only for Whiplash to arrive himself, clad in his new armor. Whiplash had the upper hand until Stark and Rhodes joined their repulsor beams together, creating a massive blast of energy that ruined Vanko's armor. Vanko then revealed his trump card: self-destruct mechanisms in his suit and all the wrecked drones. Stark and Rhodes escaped moments before the bombs detonated, apparently killing Vanko.

ANTON VANKO

FIRST APPEARANCE:
Iron Man 2 [2010]

Soviet physicist Anton Vanko defected from the U.S.S.R. and cocreated the Arc Reactor with Howard Stark, but when he was accused of espionage, he was deported. Unable to reproduce his designs for the Soviet government, he was exiled to Siberia. Raising his son, Ivan, in Moscow, he finally passed away, inspiring Ivan to seek vengeance against Howard's son Tony.

IN THE COMICS

MARC SCARLOTTI WAS A member of the criminal Maggia organization who used an electrified whip as the superhuman enforcer Whiplash; he repeatedly clashed with Iron Man, and was eventually killed by Iron Man's Ultron-possessed armor.

FIRST APPEARANCE:
TALES OF SUSPENSE #97 (1968)

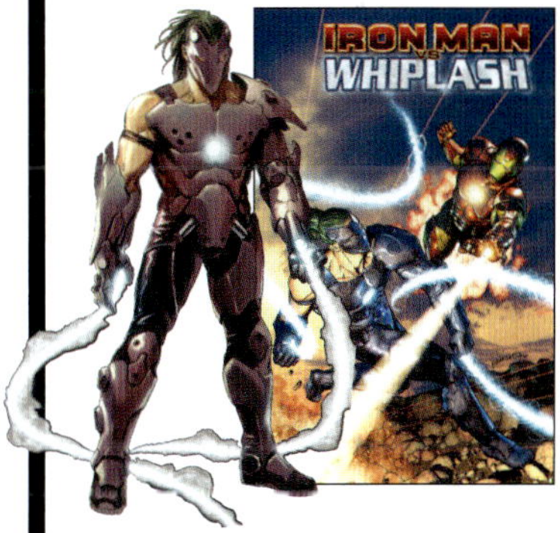

RECENTLY, A NEW WHIPLASH has taken up Scarlotti's mantle; when Anton Vanko's village was massacred, he swore vengeance on Tony Stark, who he believed had perpetrated the attack. Vanko created his Whiplash armor to attack Stark, only to learn that Stark had been framed. Since then, he's joined the Masters of Evil and participated in an attempted heist to steal Iron Man's armors.

FIRST APPEARANCE:
IRON MAN VS. WHIPLASH #1 (2010)

ANTON VANKO WAS AN AGENT of the Russian government, sent to destroy Iron Man with his electric Crimson Dynamo armor, but was killed in battle with the next wearer of the Dynamo armor, Boris Turgenov.

FIRST APPEARANCE:
TALES OF SUSPENSE #46 (1963)

PHIL COULSON UPDATE

FIRST APPEARANCE: ***Iron Man [2008]***

After having served as Tony Stark's liaison to S.H.I.E.L.D. at the time of the Iron Man suit's invention, Coulson was assigned to monitor Hendricks, a new S.H.I.E.L.D. recruit, whom he put through a realistic but manufactured scenario involving the Ten Rings terrorist organization to test Hendricks' field readiness.

S.H.I.E.L.D. Director Nick Fury again assigned Coulson to Stark while the dying billionaire attempted to create a suitable replacement element for the poisonous palladium that powered the mini-Arc Reactor in his chest. In order to help maintain Stark's focus, Coulson and the Black Widow disabled all of the incoming and outgoing communications to the Stark Estate. In response to Stark's more erratic behavior of late, Coulson was also authorized by Nick Fury to keep Stark on the premises using any means necessary; however, Stark snuck away to meet with Pepper Potts.

Later, during Stark's remodel of his workshop while creating the replacement element, Coulson chastised him for breaking his house arrest. However, Coulson ended up assisting Stark in the task of leveling out synthesizer coils with an unlikely tool: an incomplete replica of Captain America's shield. Coulson told Stark he was reassigned to New Mexico, where he later located an item that had impacted the Earth and carved a large crater out of the New Mexico desert: a mysterious, unmovable hammer.

FACT SHEET

- WHEN STARK REQUESTED S.H.I.E.L.D. MAKE A COFFEE RUN FOR HIM DURING HIS HOUSE ARREST, COULSON THREATENED TO TASE STARK AND WATCH EPISODES OF *SUPERNANNY* WHILE STARK DROOLED INTO THE CARPET.
- WHEN LEAVING FOR NEW MEXICO, COULSON BADE TONY STARK FAREWELL BY REITERATING HOW MUCH S.H.I.E.L.D. NEEDED HIM.

CHRISTINE EVERHART UPDATE

FIRST APPEARANCE: ***Iron Man [2008]***

Following Tony Stark's public admission that he was the armored adventurer Iron Man, Christine Everhart continued in her role as journalist for Vanity Fair magazine, and attended the Monaco Historic Grand Prix race to interview high-profile celebrities gathered there. Eager for self-promotion, Stark rival and weapons industrialist Justin Hammer tried to impress her during his afternoon interview for the magazine's forthcoming feature on him, but she was distracted by Stark's sudden appearance. Although somewhat ideologically at odds with Stark, Everhart was keen for a comment from the famous industrialist and remained focused on Stark despite Hammer's attempts to keep himself the subject of conversation. Everhart gracefully ignored Stark's continued jabs about their previous romantic encounter, and was amused when Stark took the opportunity to point out that Hammer Industries recently had their military contract revoked and still had no slot for the upcoming Stark Expo, which was set to showcase international cutting-edge technology. Hammer told Everhart he did not consider Stark a competitor, but the damage had been done: Immediately after Stark left to personally join the race, Everhart lost interest in Hammer and left to call her editor.

FACT SHEET

- EVERHART'S JOURNALIST JOB SECURES HER ACCESS TO HIGH-PROFILE CELEBRITY EVENTS WORLDWIDE.
- EVERHART SOUGHT A QUOTE FROM NEW STARK INDUSTRIES CEO PEPPER POTTS FOR THE MAGAZINE'S POWERFUL WOMEN ISSUE.
- EVERHART KEEPS A HANDHELD RECORDER ON HER AT ALL TIMES IN CASE AN INTERESTING STORY POPS UP.

HAPPY HOGAN UPDATE

FIRST APPEARANCE:
***Iron Man* (2008)**

After Tony Stark's speech at the Stark Expo, his chauffeur Harold "Happy" Hogan escorted him out through an enthusiastic crowd. As Hogan showed Stark a newly purchased car, the two bantered with an attractive U.S. Marshal — who served Stark with a subpoena. Hogan took the paperwork, explaining that his eccentric employer disliked being handed things.

Later, the two sparred in Stark's home gymnasium. Stark elbowed Hogan in the face; Hogan warned him against dirty boxing. When Natalie Rushman arrived to finalize Pepper Potts' promotion to Stark Industries' CEO, Stark offhandedly suggested that Hogan and Rushman spar. However, when Hogan taunted "Rushman" — secretly the undercover Black Widow — she quickly flipped and disabled him.

With Potts now CEO, Hogan became her chauffeur, though he still maintained great loyalty to Stark. When Whiplash attacked Stark's racecar at the Monaco Historic Grand Prix, Hogan drove his limousine onto the racetrack, smashing the villain against a wall and delivering Stark's collapsible Mark V armor.

When Hammer drones attacked the Expo, Black Widow had Hogan drive her to Hammer Industries, though he was very distracted as she changed into her S.H.I.E.L.D. uniform in the back seat. Despite Widow's instructions to watch the building's perimeter, Hogan entered with her and attacked a security guard. He eventually won by biting his opponent's ear, resorting to "dirty boxing" of his own, but was shocked to see Black Widow had defeated all the other guards by herself.

FACT SHEET

- HOGAN IS AN AMATEUR BOXING ENTHUSIAST.
- HOGAN HAS EXCELLENT DRIVING REFLEXES; HE AVOIDED ONCOMING RACECARS WHILE DRIVING THE WRONG WAY AROUND THE GRAND PRIX TRACK.

JARVIS UPDATE

FIRST APPEARANCE:
***Iron Man* (2008)**

Tony Stark's artificial intelligence program JARVIS helped him locate and defeat Ten Rings terrorist cells throughout the Middle East, though Stark began controlling many of his Iron Man armor's functions himself, rather than using JARVIS as an interface. When the palladium core in Stark's mini-Arc Reactor chestpiece began poisoning him, JARVIS monitored Stark's health and ran simulations on every known element, unsuccessfully searching for alternate materials to power the reactor. JARVIS recommended Stark tell assistant Pepper Potts that he was dying, but Stark refused.

After Ivan Vanko attacked Stark as Whiplash, JARVIS scanned newspaper archives and revealed Ivan and Anton Vanko's ties to Stark's father, Howard. S.H.I.E.L.D. tasked Stark with completing Howard's Arc Reactor research; when Stark noticed that Howard's 1974 Stark Expo model resembled an atom, he had JARVIS scan it, then manipulated JARVIS' 3-D wireframe representation to uncover the theoretical element Howard had encoded. JARVIS determined the new element could serve as a non-toxic power source for Stark's chestpiece; Stark soon synthesized it and upgraded his miniature Repulsor Technology (R.T.) Arc Reactor.

When Whiplash called and taunted Stark, JARVIS attempted to trace the call, and Stark deduced Whiplash's plans. As Iron Man, Stark headed to the Stark Expo, where Whiplash remotely controlled Lt. Col. Rhodes' "War Machine" armor to attack him. JARVIS tried unsuccessfully to hack into War Machine's armor; eventually Black Widow remotely rebooted the suit.

FACT SHEET

- JARVIS ROUTES AND ANNOUNCES ALL TELEPHONE CALLS TO THE STARK ESTATE.
- STARK CAN "MUTE" JARVIS, TURNING ALL ITS SPEAKERS AND MONITORS OFF SIMULTANEOUSLY.
- STARK HAS INSTALLED JARVIS INTERFACE PANELS IN HIS PRIVATE JET AND HIS FATHER'S FORMER HOME.

SENATOR STERN

FIRST APPEARANCE: *Iron Man 2 [2010]*

Convinced that Tony Stark's Iron Man technology was a threat to national security, Senator Stern consulted with Stark's ally, Lt. Col. James Rhodes, and Army Gen. Thaddeus Ross about Stark. Afterward, Stern led a Senate Armed Services Committee hearing to persuade Stark to hand over his Iron Man armor to the U.S. military, relying on testimony from industrialist Justin Hammer and a reluctant Rhodes. Stern held the stance that the armor was a deadly weapon and that other nations were creating similar weapons. Hacking into computer systems worldwide, Stark demonstrated that enemy nations' attempts at duplicating the armor were unsuccessful. Stark then made a speech about his own success at privatizing world peace, inspiring applause from observers and effectively humiliating Stern. After Stark's televised battle against the armored villain Whiplash (Ivan Vanko), Stern publicly pointed out that Stark's claims that no one could duplicate his armor were now proven false. When Stark defeated Whiplash a second time, as a favor to Stark, Stern was coerced by S.H.I.E.L.D. Director Nick Fury into serving as presenter at a medal ceremony honoring Stark and Rhodes; Stern took joy in sticking Stark with a needle while pinning the medal on him.

IN THE COMICS

SENATOR STERN HAS NO DIRECT comic counterpart, but his role is similar to Senator Harrington Byrd, who demanded Stark identify the man in the Iron Man armor, citing national security. Although long critical of Stark and Iron Man, Byrd eventually became convinced of Stark's patriotism.

FIRST APPEARANCE:
TALES OF SUSPENSE #46 (1963)

FACT SHEET

- STERN REPRESENTS THE STATE OF PENNSYLVANIA IN THE U.S. SENATE AND IS THE CHAIRMAN OF THE SENATE ARMED FORCES COMMITTEE.
- STERN ENJOYS GOLF AND HAS DISCUSSED BUSINESS WITH JUSTIN HAMMER ON THE GREENS.
- STERN PRESENTS RHODES WITH MERITORIOUS SERVICE MEDAL AND STARK WITH THE ARMY'S DISTINGUISHED SERVICE MEDAL.

HOWARD STARK

FIRST APPEARANCE: *Iron Man [2008]* [PHOTO]; *Iron Man 2 [2010]* [FULL APPEARANCE]

A WWII-era genius who helped create the first atomic bomb, Howard Stark founded both Stark Industries, a prominent munitions company, and S.H.I.E.L.D., an extra-governmental spy organization. In the 1960s, Stark recruited Soviet defector Anton Vanko to help invent the Arc Reactor, an energy-generating device powered by palladium, which Stark believed could help end humanity's reliance on nuclear power. After Vanko attempted to sell the technology, Stark reported him, and Vanko was deported. In the 1970s, Stark and his business partner Obadiah Stane realized that mass production of the Reactor would not be cost effective. Stark conceived of a new element that would power the Reactor more efficiently, but lacked the technology to create it. Unwilling to let his notes fall into rivals' possession, Stark coded his research and hoped that his son Tony could one day solve the riddle with advanced technology. When Howard and his wife Maria died in a car accident in 1991, Stane became the company's interim CEO until Tony took over at age 21.

INDUSTRIALIST AND INVENTOR
Howard Stark, adoptive father of Tony Stark, was a member of the Brotherhood of the Shield, a predecessor to spy agency S.H.I.E.L.D., and encountered such historical figures as Isaac Newton, Nikola Tesla, and Leonardo da Vinci. He and his wife, Maria, were murdered in a car accident arranged by a rival company.

FIRST APPEARANCE:
IRON MAN #28 (1970)

FACT SHEET

- STARK, OFTEN INFURIATED BY HIS YOUNG SON TONY'S IMMATURE BEHAVIOR, CARED DEEPLY FOR HIS SON TONY BUT NEVER TOLD HIM. A VIDEO RECORDING OF STARK MADE BEFORE HIS DEATH REVEALED STARK FELT TONY WAS HIS GREATEST CREATION.
- AMONG STARK'S STORED ITEMS IS A COPY OF *CAPTAIN AMERICA COMICS #1.*

MARVEL'S *THOR*

GUIDEBOOK TO THE MARVEL CINEMATIC UNIVERSE

MARVEL

THOR

PARAMOUNT PICTURES AND MARVEL ENTERTAINMENT PRESENT A MARVEL STUDIOS PRODUCTION A FILM BY KENNETH BRANAGH "THOR" CHRIS HEMSWORTH NATALIE PORTMAN TOM HIDDLESTON STELLAN SKARSGÅRD COLM FEORE RAY STEVENSON IDRIS ELBA KAT DENNINGS WITH RENE RUSSO AND ANTHONY HOPKINS AS ODIN MUSIC BY PATRICK DOYLE MUSIC SUPERVISOR DAVE JORDAN CO-PRODUCERS CRAIG KYLE VICTORIA ALONSO COSTUME DESIGNER ALEXANDRA BYRNE EDITOR PAUL RUBELL, A.C.E. PRODUCTION DESIGNER BO WELCH DIRECTOR OF PHOTOGRAPHY HARIS ZAMBARLOUKOS, BSC EXECUTIVE PRODUCERS ALAN FINE STAN LEE DAVID MAISEL EXECUTIVE PRODUCERS PATRICIA WHITCHER LOUIS D'ESPOSITO PRODUCED BY KEVIN FEIGE STORY BY J. MICHAEL STRACZYNSKI AND MARK PROTOSEVICH SCREENPLAY BY ASHLEY EDWARD MILLER & ZACK STENTZ AND DON PAYNE DIRECTED BY KENNETH BRANAGH

MARVEL

Collecting information from Marvel's *Thor (2011)* and *Marvel's Thor Adaptation (2013)*.

HEAD WRITER/COORDINATOR: **MIKE O'SULLIVAN**

COORDINATION: **DARON JENSEN**

WRITERS: **TROY BENJAMIN**, **ANTHONY COTILLETTA**, **PATRICK DUKE**, **DARON JENSEN**, **ROB LONDON**, **CHRIS MCCARVER**, **SEAN MCQUAID**, **MARKUS RAYMOND**, **JACOB ROUGEMONT**, AND **STUART VANDAL**

ARTISTS: **STEFANO CASELLI**, **FRANK CHO**, **OLIVIER COIPEL**, **PASQUAL FERRY**, **DON HECK**, **JACK KIRBY**, **VANCE KOVACS**, **E.J. KRISOR**, **BEN LAI**, **LUMA PICTURES**, **JAMIE MCKELVIE**, **JORGE MOLINA**, **CHRIS NICHOLS**, **SARA PICHELLI**, **ESAD RIBIC**, **RAJ RIHAL**, **WERNER ROTH**, **CRAIG SHOJI**, **RYAN STEGMAN**, **DALIBOR TALAJIC**, **GREG TOCCHINI**, **GUS VASQUEZ**, AND **WHISKEYTREE**

COVER ARTISTS: **WILL SLINEY** AND **ANDY TROY**

SPECIAL THANKS TO DAVE ALTHOFF, STEVEN BOYD, SHAWN "KEEBLER" BYERS, JEFF CHRISTIANSEN, MATT DELMANOWSKI, ERIKA DENTON, TIM DILLON, MIKE FICHERA, PERCIVAL LANUZA, AMANDA NALLEY, JACQUE PORTE, RYAN POTTER, AND JEPH YORK

IN LOVING MEMORY OF MAHOGANY WILLIAMS JENSEN, 2000-2015

THOR CREATED BY STAN LEE, LARRY LIEBER, AND JACK KIRBY

ASGARD

FIRST APPEARANCE: ***Thor (2011)***

Home to the long-lived Asgardians, and one of the Nine Realms of their cosmology, Asgard, the Realm Eternal, is a flat, floating planetary body with a gravitational pull and day-and-night intervals. Asgard hosts a vast city of unsurpassed beauty, mixing immense golden architecture, ornate statues and decor, and verdant paradises. The realm ends where waters encircling the city come to a precipitous drop into the void of eternal space. The Bifrost, a glittering, rainbow-colored bridge extends across Asgard's water, connecting the massive, central castle to an ornate, circular observatory on the precipice edge which, when activated, can project the bridge to any location in the Nine Realms for rapid transport.

The ruling Asgardian royal family includes the All-Father, Odin, his queen, Frigga, and their sons Thor and Loki. Asgard is largely populated by warriors who have honed their craft to an art form; their victory celebrations are approached with equal passion. Odin refers to Asgard as a beacon of hope, shining out across the stars for all to see.

By 965 A.D., Earth's humans believed Asgard to be the realm of their gods, and the denizens of other realms their feared evils. When Jotunheim's Frost Giants

THRONE ROOM

IN THE COMICS

HOME TO THE ASGARDIANS and numerous other races, Asgard is a small planetary body, roughly the size of the United States, that was connected to Earth (Midgard) by the roots of Yggdrasil, a cosmic Asgardian tree. Asgard is one of Ten Realms of the Asgardian cosmology, which include Earth, Jotunheim, Hel, Heven, and five others; direct access to Earth (Asgardian thunder god Thor Odinson's adopted home) was accomplished via the Rainbow Bridge, Bifrost. In modern times, following a rebirth in the cyclical destruction of the Asgardians, Thor moved the city of Asgard to Earth, where it hovered over Oklahoma until it was destroyed in battle against corrupt Earth forces. Rebuilt (with help from Tony Stark) and rechristened Asgardia, the city currently resides between Earth and the Moon.

FIRST APPEARANCE:
JOURNEY INTO MYSTERY #85 (1962)

WEAPONS VAULT

kingdoms. The subsequent confrontation exhausted Odin to the point of falling into his regenerative Odinsleep, leaving Loki to claim the throne.

Loki approached Laufey, offering him entrance into Asgard to slay Odin and regain the Casket. Laufey agreed, unaware Loki intended to kill Laufey so Asgard would find Loki worthy of the throne. After sending the Destroyer to Earth to slay Thor, Loki killed Laufey in Odin's bedchamber. However, moments later, Thor returned to Asgard, his humbling experiences on Earth and personal sacrifice to defeat the Destroyer making him worthy to rule. The two brothers battled until Thor was forced to destroy the Bifrost to prevent Loki from slaughtering the Jotuns in an effort to further prove himself to Odin. An awakened Odin saved his sons from falling into the void of space, but when Odin disapproved of Loki's machinations, Loki allowed himself to fall into a space warp. Odin reclaimed the throne of Asgard, but the Realm Eternal was cut off from the other realms by the Bifrost's destruction.

invaded Earth, intending to regress it to an ice age, the Asgardian armies came to humankind's aid, repelling the Jotuns. Following the Jotuns' defeat, Asgard established universal peace and withdrew from the other realms, becoming the stuff of humanity's myths, legends, and fairy tales.

In modern times, Loki secretly enabled three Jotuns to covertly enter Asgard via a secret path and breach the Asgardian weapons vault, seeking to reclaim the Casket of Ancient Winters, their greatest weapon. As Loki hoped, this disrupted Thor's coronation and angered him into taking reckless retaliation. Disobeying Odin's commands, Thor and his closest allies journeyed to Jotunheim to confront Jotun king Laufey, who considered Thor's aggression an act of war. After saving Thor from Jotunheim, Odin ruled that Thor's dismissal of peace made him unfit to rule and banished him to Earth. Shortly after, Loki learned from Odin he was a Frost Giant, long ago adopted by Odin in hopes of one day uniting the

FACT SHEET

- ASGARD IS ONE OF NINE REALMS OF THE COSMOS LINKED BY THE BRANCHES OF YGGDRASIL, THE COSMIC "WORLDS TREE." OTHER REALMS INCLUDE EARTH (MIDGARD), JOTUNHEIM, ALFHEIM, NORNHEIM, VALHALLA, AND VANAHEIM.
- WHEN EXPLAINING ASGARD TO JANE FOSTER, THOR DESCRIBED IT AS A PLACE WHERE SCIENCE AND MAGIC EXIST AS ONE.
- ASGARD'S WEAPONS VAULT WAS STAUNCHLY PROTECTED BY THE DESTROYER AUTOMATON.
- LOKI CLAIMED TO KNOW WAYS IN AND OUT OF ASGARD THAT BYPASSED THE BIFROST.

BIFROST AND OBSERVATORY

FACEPLATE RETRACTED

DESTROYER

FIRST APPEARANCE: ***Thor (2011)***

The Destroyer construct was one of Asgard's most powerful weapons, stored behind a mystical wall of energy, stone, and spikes inside the royal weapons vault. When Jotunheim Frost Giants secretly breached the vault in an attempt to recover their confiscated Casket of Ancient Winters, Odin sensed their intrusion and activated the Destroyer to stop them. The Destroyer exterminated the Giants with powerful energy beams projected from its face. When Odin's son Thor disobeyed Odin's command and traveled to Jotunheim to confront the Frost Giants, their king, Laufey, considered Thor's actions to be an act of war, ending a long-standing truce between the kings. An enraged Odin stripped Thor of his powers and exiled him to Earth to learn humility. Soon after, Odin succumbed to his rejuvenating Odinsleep, leaving Loki to rule Asgard in his place. Thor's friends, Sif and the Warriors Three, privately felt Loki was not worthy of the throne and tried persuading him to reverse Thor's banishment, but Loki refused; the group left for Earth to find Thor. Incensed, Loki activated the Destroyer and sent it to Earth to destroy Thor and anything in its path. Upon its arrival, the Destroyer was met by a S.H.I.E.L.D. contingency led by Agent Phil Coulson; when asked to identify itself, the Destroyer responded by using its energy beam to destroy their vehicles. The Destroyer entered the town of Puente Antiguo, New Mexico, and demolished everything in its path without discrimination, and easily fended off an attack by the Warriors Three. Sif assaulted the Destroyer from above, driving her spear through its neck, temporarily halting its rampage. The Destroyer quickly recovered and continued to lay waste to the Asgardians and the town. Thor unsuccessfully attempted to reason with Loki through the Destroyer, instead receiving a fatal blow. Thor's selfless and humble sacrifice proved him worthy of his power: Thor's hammer, Mjolnir, instead flew to him and rejuvenated him. Creating a vortex powerful enough to lift the Destroyer into the air, Thor used Mjolnir to force the Destroyer's blasts back into itself, causing it to explosively malfunction and crash back to Earth.

IN THE COMICS

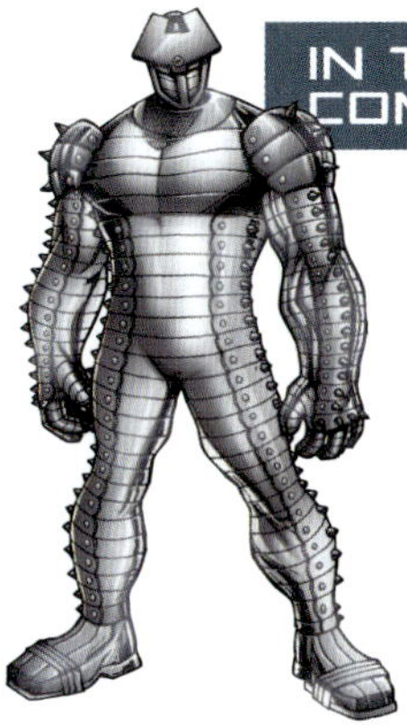

SEEKING DEFENSE AGAINST WORLD-destroying level threats, Asgardian All-Father Odin Borson enlisted the Dwarves of Nidavellir to construct the Destroyer, a vastly powerful, inert armor that is animated by absorbing the consciousness of any who touched it. Once activated, the armor destroys everything in its path, usually through the disintegrator ray contained behind its faceplate. Over its history, the Destroyer has been used for malicious and benevolent deeds; it remains one of Asgard's greatest weapons.

FIRST APPEARANCE:
JOURNEY INTO MYSTERY #118 (1965)

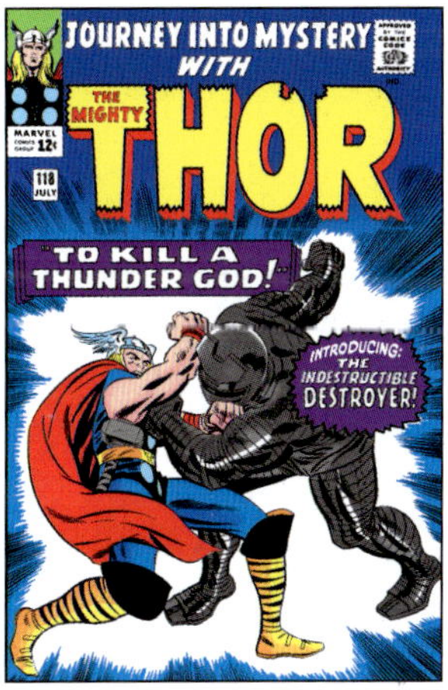

FACT SHEET

- THE DESTROYER CAN APPARENTLY BE SUMMONED ONLY BY ASGARD'S KING TO SWIFTLY ANNIHILATE ASGARD'S ENEMIES.
- THE ARMOR'S BODY CAN BE QUICKLY RECONFIGURED TO FACE THE OPPOSITE DIRECTION WITHOUT HAVING TO TURN AROUND.
- ASGARD'S KING CAN HEAR AND SEE WHAT THE DESTROYER DOES, EVEN ACROSS THE VOID SEPARATING THE NINE REALMS.

JANE FOSTER

FIRST APPEARANCE: ***Thor [2011]***

A brilliant astrophysicist, Jane Foster enlisted her late father's colleague Dr. Erik Selvig and her intern Darcy Lewis to document a recurring meteorological event near Puente Antiguo, New Mexico, believing the event tied into her research into spatial wormholes. Upon sighting the anomaly, Lewis inadvertently drove Foster's truck into the Asgardian warrior prince Thor, who had been exiled to Earth by his father Odin for inciting a war between Asgard and the Frost Giants of Jotunheim. Lewis subdued the ranting Thor with a stun gun, and the trio dropped him off at the local hospital before returning to their lab.

While reviewing their findings, Lewis showed Foster and Selvig a photograph of the anomaly with a human silhouette inside. Sensing a link between Thor and the anomaly, the trio drove to the hospital, but Foster accidentally backed her truck into the escaping Thor. Though stymied by Thor's arrogance, Foster and her colleagues supplied him with clothes and a meal at the local diner, where they heard locals speak of a crashed satellite 50 miles away that could not be pried from the ground; Thor correctly deduced this was his enchanted hammer Mjolnir, but, heeding Selvig's concerns that Thor appeared delusional and dangerous, Foster declined to drive him there. After Thor left to retrieve the hammer by himself, Foster discovered S.H.I.E.L.D. agents led by Agent Phil Coulson stripping her lab of data and equipment, citing a "security threat" as justification.

With years of her research confiscated and determined to learn Thor's connection to the anomaly, Foster, undaunted by Selvig's warnings about S.H.I.E.L.D., located Thor and drove him to the crash site; during the drive the two realized they were becoming attracted to one another. Finding the

FACT SHEET

- FOSTER'S PUENTE ANTIGUO LAB WAS THE UNUSED SMITH MOTORS AUTO DEALERSHIP. SHE FREQUENTLY SPENT SPARE TIME ON ITS ROOF TO THINK.
- FOSTER CONSIDERED HER EX-BOYFRIEND, DR. DONALD BLAKE, TO BE "GOOD WITH PATIENTS, BUT BAD AT RELATIONSHIPS."
- FOSTER'S FATHER AND ERIK SELVIG WERE PROFESSORS AT THE SAME UNIVERSITY.
- FOSTER'S TRUCK, A MODIFIED 1971 STEYR-DAIMLER-PUCH PINZGAUER, DOUBLED AS A MOBILE LABORATORY.

FOSTER'S LAB

site contained within a makeshift S.H.I.E.L.D. outpost, Foster left a voicemail with Selvig while watching from afar as Thor fought through several agents; Thor was disheartened when he couldn't lift Mjolnir from the ground and was taken into custody. Returning to the lab, Foster argued with Selvig that Thor seemed neither a liar nor a lunatic, despite Selvig showing her a Norse mythology book mirroring Thor's seemingly outlandish claims.

Selvig later convinced Coulson to release Thor, who presented Foster with her notebook, the one piece of her research he had managed to steal back, and explained how accurately her research lined up with the Nine Realms' cosmology. The arrival of Thor's Asgardian allies, Sif and the Warriors Three, and the Asgardian behemoth, the Destroyer, finally dispelled any remaining doubts in Thor's claims. Foster watched as the Destroyer struck Thor with a seemingly fatal blow, only for Mjolnir to return to Thor's hand, restoring his powers. After Thor dispatched the Destroyer and insisted that Coulson return Foster's equipment, Thor promised Foster he would return for her after he dealt with his treacherous adopted brother Loki back in Asgard. Foster accepted his oath with a passionate kiss, but Thor was soon forced to destroy the Bifrost to prevent Loki from destroying Jotunheim, trapping him in Asgard. Foster continued her research, now with S.H.I.E.L.D. participation, hoping to one day be reunited with Thor.

FOSTER'S MOBILE LAB

IN THE COMICS

JANE FOSTER WAS A REGISTERED nurse in the employ of physician Donald Blake, the secret alter ego of Asgardian thunder god Thor. Thor and Foster shared a mutual attraction, but Thor's father Odin considered the mortal Foster unworthy of a romance with his son. Foster eventually married another doctor, Keith Kincaid; had a son, Jimmy; and became a doctor herself—but her marriage ended in divorce, due in part to Jane's simmering feelings for Thor.

After Foster contracted breast cancer, she forbade Thor to seek non-Earthly treatments for her condition. When Thor became unworthy to wield his enchanted hammer, Mjolnir, Foster was deemed worthy and took possession of Mjolnir, despite knowing that wielding it would worsen her frail health. Mjolnir empowered Foster, transforming her into Thor, the Goddess of Thunder.

FIRST APPEARANCE:
JOURNEY INTO MYSTERY #84 (1962)

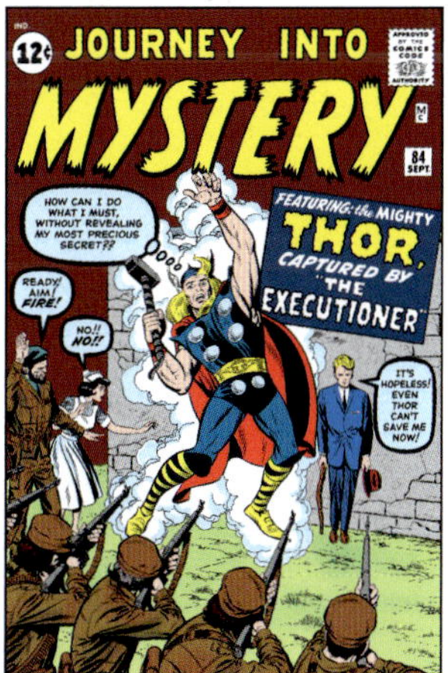

FRIGGA

FIRST APPEARANCE:
***Thor* [2011]**

Frigga is the Asgardian queen, wife of Odin and mother to Thor and Loki, the latter secretly an Asgardian-sized Frost Giant adopted in infancy by the couple. Despite Frigga's loving attention, Thor grew rash and developed a quick temper, and Loki became devious and jealous of Thor. When Odin decided to step down, Frigga attended Thor's coronation, but the ceremony was interrupted when Frost Giants from Jotunheim broke into Odin's vault, their entry into Asgard secretly facilitated by Loki. Though stopped, their intrusion led Thor to recklessly invade Jotunheim; Odin rescued him, but angrily exiled him from Asgard. An argument with Loki, who had realized his true parentage, combined with the other recent stress and exhaustion, plunged Odin unexpectedly into power-restoring Odinsleep. Fearing he wouldn't awaken, Frigga remained by his bedside, leaving Loki to rule Asgard in Odin's stead. When two Jotuns invaded Odin's chamber seeking to slay him while he slept, Frigga quickly dispatched one with her sword before the other, Frost Giant king Laufey, swatted her aside. She recovered to witness Loki slaying Laufey, but Thor arrived moments later, revealing to Frigga's shock that Loki had arranged the attack just to prove himself by stopping it, and had tried to kill Thor too; her sons battled, and Loki was seemingly slain. The warrior goddess Sif later offered Frigga condolences, but the queen was more concerned how Thor was coping with his losses.

FACT SHEET

- ALTHOUGH AMUSED BY THOR'S BOASTFULNESS, FRIGGA SILENTLY CAUTIONED HIM TO BE RESPECTFUL IN ODIN'S PRESENCE.
- FRIGGA BELIEVES THERE IS ALWAYS A PURPOSE TO ODIN'S ACTIONS EVEN WHEN OTHERS CANNOT COMPREHEND HIS REASONING.
- FRIGGA EXPLAINED THAT ODIN KEPT LOKI'S FROST GIANT ANCESTRY SECRET TO PREVENT LOKI FROM EVER FEELING AS IF HE WASN'T THEIR SON OR THEY HIS FAMILY.

IN THE COMICS

FRIGGA (A.K.A. FREYJA) MARRIED ODIN to end a war between their respective kingdoms, and is the adoptive mother of Thor Odinson and Loki Laufeyson and birth mother to Balder—whose eventual death would precipitate Ragnarok, the Twilight of the Gods. To prevent Ragnarok, Frigga convinced nearly every living entity in Asgard not to harm Balder, making him nearly invulnerable. Frigga also belonged to a pantheon of Earthly goddesses that watched over specially selected humans that represented humankind's full potential to satisfy the cosmic Celestials, who would judge humanity's worthiness to survive. When Ragnarok occurred, Frigga was slain but later resurrected, and Asgard was restored in the space over Broxton, Oklahoma, until it was destroyed by corrupt Earth forces. After Odin went into self-exile to serve as warden for his brother Cul, Frigga sought to unite nine of the Ten Realms into the republic of Asgardia, becoming All-Mother alongside Gaea and Idunn to rule in Odin's absence. When Odin returned, disagreement over who held the throne caused great tension between Frigga and Odin. Frigga later joined a battle against the Destroyer, which was sent by Odin to attack a new Thor (secretly Jane Foster). Frigga died while battling the Midgard Serpent, but was later reborn.

FIRST APPEARANCE:
JOURNEY INTO MYSTERY #92 (1963)

HAWKEYE
CLINT BARTON

FIRST APPEARANCE: ***Thor (2011)***

An expert marksman specializing in archery, Clint "Hawkeye" Barton is an agent for elite intelligence agency S.H.I.E.L.D. When Asgardian ruler Odin stripped his wayward son Thor of his powers and exiled him to Earth, he also sent Thor's mystic hammer Mjolnir there, enchanted such that only someone worthy of its power could lift it. Mjolnir landed in a New Mexico desert, where many curious locals tried and failed to remove it from its impact crater, unaware of its true nature. S.H.I.E.L.D. quickly built a make-shift facility around the hammer to protect and analyze this strange alien artifact. Barton was among the agents assigned to guard the facility under the command of Agent Phil Coulson.

Trying to retrieve Mjolnir, Thor invaded the S.H.I.E.L.D. facility and fought his way through many of its guards. Wanting a sharpshooter overhead to help contain the situation, Coulson had Barton lifted above the scene in a crane bucket, armed with a bow and arrows. Barton soon had Thor in his sights, ready to bring him down, but Coulson ordered Barton to hold his fire, wanting to see how the situation played out. When Thor finally reached Mjolnir, he was unable to lift it because of Odin's enchantment, still too arrogant and selfish to be worthy of wielding it. As Thor sank to his knees in despair and frustration, Coulson called off Barton and had his guards take Thor into custody.

FACT SHEET

- COULSON ASKED FOR "A GUN" OVERHEAD DURING THOR'S INVASION OF THE S.H.I.E.L.D. FACILITY. BARTON ALMOST TOOK A SNIPER RIFLE, BEFORE CHOOSING A BOW INSTEAD.
- BARTON WIELDED A COMPOUND BOW, WHICH INCORPORATES MORE MECHANICAL PARTS THAN A TRADITIONAL RECURVE BOW. SLOWER TO OPERATE AND LESS VERSATILE THAN TRADITIONAL BOWS, COMPOUND BOWS REQUIRE LESS PULL AND CAN FIRE ARROWS WITH GREATER VELOCITY, FORCE AND ACCURACY, GOOD FOR DISTANCE SHOOTING.
- BARTON SEEMED AMUSED AND IMPRESSED BY THOR DURING THE DESERT INCIDENT, EVENTUALLY WARNING COULSON HE NEEDED TO MAKE THE CALL "BECAUSE I'M STARTING TO ROOT FOR THIS GUY."

IN THE COMICS

ABUSED BY AN ALCOHOLIC FATHER whose drunk driving ultimately orphaned them, brothers Clint and Barney Barton spent time in an orphanage and abusive foster care before they ran away and joined the Carson Carnival of Traveling Wonders. Trained by star performers Trick Shot (Buck Chisholm) and the Swordsman (Jacques Duquesne), Clint became an expert archer, but both of his mentors turned out to be criminals. Barney also turned to crime, estranging the brothers. Working as carnival sideshow marksman Hawkeye, Clint saw Iron Man (Tony Stark) in action and was inspired to become a super hero, crafting a colorful purple-and-blue costume armed with mechanically gimmicked trick arrows. Mistaken for a criminal by the police, the fugitive Hawkeye fell in love with Russian spy Black Widow (Natasha Romanoff), who manipulated him into battling Iron Man. Soon reforming, Hawkeye joined the elite Avengers super-hero group, becoming one of the longest-serving key members. A team player, Hawkeye has served with the Defenders, the Thunderbolts and various incarnations of the Avengers, including founding their West Coast branch. Partnered with the time-lost Old West hero Two-Gun Kid for a time, he has more recently begun mentoring young archer Kate Bishop, also called Hawkeye. His romantic partners have included fellow adventurers Black Widow, Moonstone (Karla Sofen), Echo, Wasp (Janet Van Dyne), Spider-Woman (Jessica Drew), and his ex-wife, Mockingbird (Bobbi Morse).

FIRST APPEARANCE:
JOURNEY INTO MYSTERY #118 (1965)

HEIMDALL

FIRST APPEARANCE:
Thor (2011)

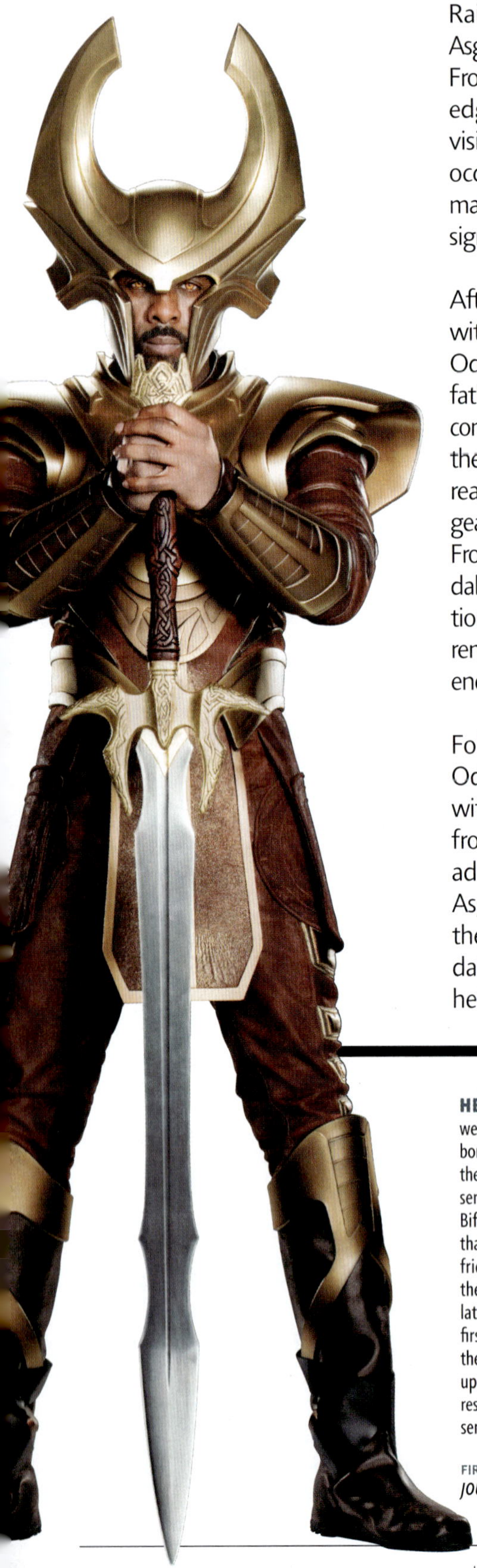

Gatekeeper of Asgard, Heimdall acts as the guardian of the Bifrost, the interdimensional Rainbow Bridge gateway linking Asgard to the rest of the Nine Realms. From his observatory at the Bifrost's edge, Heimdall's encompassing vision enables him to see all that occurs within the Nine Realms, making him ideally suited to his assigned station.

After Frost Giants invaded Asgard without Heimdall detecting them, Odin's son, Thor—in defiance of his father's orders—took a band of his comrades-in-arms to Heimdall so that they could travel to the Frost Giants' realm of Jotunheim to exact vengeance. Curious and frustrated that Frost Giants evaded his senses, Heimdall permitted the journey, but cautioned them that the Bifrost would remain closed should their actions endanger Asgard.

Following Thor's banishment by Odin for his disobedience, Heimdall witnessed Thor's struggles on Earth from his observatory. After Thor's adopted brother, Loki, ascended Asgard's throne when Odin fell into the regenerative Odinsleep, Heimdall observed his journey to Jotunheim. Unable to see Loki's actions there, Heimdall confronted him. Loki reminded Heimdall of his oath to obey Asgard's ruler and ordered him to keep the Bifrost closed.

Correctly suspecting Loki's culpability in the Frost Giants' incursion, Heimdall allowed Thor's remaining allies, Sif and the Warriors Three, to travel to Earth to rescue Thor. Loki charged Heimdall with treason and stripped him of his citizenship and position. No longer under oath to obey Asgard's ruler, Heimdall attacked Loki, who froze him with the Casket of Ancient Winters. Thor's later pleas to open the Bifrost spurred Heimdall into breaking free to bring Thor and his allies home. Though Thor destroyed the observatory and shattered the Bifrost to prevent Loki from using them to destroy Jotunheim, Heimdall returned to his post at the Bifrost's jagged edge, assuring Thor that his mortal love, Jane Foster, was searching for a way to reunite them.

FACT SHEET

- HEIMDALL'S SWORD ACTED AS A KEY THAT DIRECTED THE BIFROST TO WHICHEVER OF THE NINE REALMS PROSPECTIVE TRAVELERS WISHED.
- LEAVING THE BIFROST OPEN FOR TOO LONG WOULD UNLEASH THE BRIDGE'S FULL POWER AND DESTROY THE WORLD TO WHICH IT WAS DIRECTED.

IN THE COMICS

HEIMDALL AND HIS SISTER, SIF, were fabled in Norse mythology to have been born from nine mothers thought to represent the sea. Appointed by Odin to act as Asgard's sentry and guardian of the Rainbow Bridge Bifrost, so adherent to his oath was Heimdall that he would not violate it for enemies or friends. After the fire demon Surtur shattered the Bifrost, Heimdall served as a warrior and later Asgard's temporary ruler; as king, his first act was the Bifrost's restoration. When the Asgardians were transformed into mortals upon Ragnarok, the fabled end of Asgard, Thor restored Heimdall first, knowing his omniscient senses could locate the others.

FIRST APPEARANCE:
JOURNEY INTO MYSTERY #85 (1962)

HOGUN

FIRST APPEARANCE:
Thor (2011)

One of Asgard's heroic Warriors Three, Hogun journeyed with Thor, Sif, Loki, and fellow Warriors Three Volstagg and Fandral to Jotunheim, seeking revenge for a Frost Giant invasion of Asgard's weapons vault. In Jotunheim, Jotun King Laufey insinuated that there were traitors in Asgard and offered Thor and his allies the opportunity to leave, but a Giant's pointed insult angered Thor into combat. The Asgardians were soon overwhelmed and had to be rescued by an angry Odin, with Laufey declaring war with Asgard.

After Thor was banished to Earth by Odin for his arrogance, Thor's friends learned that Loki had notified Odin of their plans; most were grateful his message reached Odin in time to save them. Hogun was suspicious, however, thinking Loki might be the traitor of whom Laufey had spoken. Unaware that Odin had fallen into his rejuvenating Odinsleep, the group approached the throne to ask mercy for Thor, only to find Loki had become king in his father's absence. Unhappy with the situation, Hogun and his companions conspired to journey to Earth to retrieve Thor. They were surprised when Heimdall, guardian of the Bifrost bridge that enabled travel throughout the Nine Realms, allowed them to pass unhindered.

Although they found Thor, their reunion with their estranged friend was cut short by the Destroyer, a phenomenally powerful weapon sent by Loki to kill them. The Warriors Three distracted the Destroyer while Sif attacked it from behind, and Thor and his mortal allies evacuated civilians from the area. Hogun watched as Thor sacrificed himself defeating the Destroyer, showing himself worthy of his power once more. Hogun, Thor, and the other Asgardian warriors returned to Asgard in time for Thor to vanquish Loki and stop his attempt to destroy Jotunheim.

FACT SHEET

- HOGUN WIELDS A LARGE METAL MACE WITH RETRACTABLE SPIKES.
- IN CONTRAST TO JOVIAL VOLSTAGG AND SWASHBUCKLING FANDRAL, HOGUN TENDS TO BE SOMBER AND STOIC, USING VERY FEW WORDS.

IN THE COMICS

KNOWN AS "THE GRIM," HOGUN is one of the Warriors Three, a band of Asgardian heroes. His homeland within the Asgard dimension was destroyed by Mogul of the Mystic Mountain, and he met the other Warriors Three when Fandral and Volstagg asked him to judge a dare to see which could pet the monstrous Fenris Wolf. Becoming fast friends, the trio have shared many adventures, and they seldom travel apart from each other for very long.

FIRST APPEARANCE:
JOURNEY INTO MYSTERY #119 (1965)

LAUFEY

FIRST APPEARANCE: ***Thor (2011)***

Standing up to 10 feet tall, the blue-skinned Frost Giants of wintery Jotunheim can generate ice weapons at will, or freeze with a touch. Circa 965 A.D., the Jotun king Laufey led an invasion of Earth, intending to use the Giants' power source, the Casket of Ancient Winters, to plunge the planet into another ice age. King Odin and Asgard's army stopped the Jotuns in Tonsberg, Norway, and drove them back to Jotunheim. The war ended when Odin defeated Laufey and took the Casket. Odin also adopted Laufey's abandoned diminutive infant son, found in a Jotun temple, hoping the child could one day unite the kingdoms in permanent peace; an agreement forbade both sides from entering the other realms. The baby, named Loki, grew up in Asgard, but Odin kept his true heritage secret. Without the Casket, Jotunheim slowly fell apart.

In modern times, three Jotuns, aided by an Asgardian traitor, entered Asgard's weapons vault to retrieve the Casket during the coronation of Odin's other son, Thor. Sensing their presence, Odin activated the Destroyer armor to slay the Jotuns. Thor wanted to go to war with Jotunheim for breaking the truce, but Odin forbade it. Acting against his father's will, Thor led Loki, who secretly told a guard to inform Odin of Thor's plan, and the warriors Sif, Hogun, Fandral,

CASKET OF ANCIENT WINTERS

and Volstagg to Jotunheim. Confronting Laufey, Thor did not believe the claim that there was a traitor in Asgard. Laufey gave the belligerent Thor a chance to leave before his actions caused another war, which Loki accepted on the Asgardians' behalf, but a parting insult pushed Thor too far, and he attacked. During the ensuing battle, a Jotun's touch turned Loki's skin blue, but left him unharmed, leading him to suspect his true heritage. Forced to flee, the Asgardians were cornered by a Jotun horde. They were saved by Odin's timely arrival. Trying to reason with Laufey, Odin asked him to forgive Thor's immature actions, but Laufey declared war. Odin drove Laufey and the Jotuns back before returning the Asgardians to Asgard. Following this incident, Odin stripped Thor of his powers and banished him to Earth for his disobedience.

Later, Loki confronted Odin, who confirmed Loki's true ancestry, kept secret from Loki because Odin truly loved him and considered him his son. As the deeply hurt Loki railed against his adoptive father, Odin collapsed,

LAUFEY CONFRONTS ODIN

falling into the Odin-sleep so he could recuperate from recent stresses. As new regent, Loki traveled to Jotunheim, revealing to Laufey that he was the one who showed the Jotuns the secret path to Asgard and concealed them from the all-seeing Asgardian Heimdall's view. Loki offered to lead Laufey and a few soldiers to Odin and return the Casket of Ancient Winters to Jotunheim if Laufey slew Odin for him. Laufey accepted the deal. Later arriving in Odin's chamber, Laufey was stopped from murdering Odin with an ice dagger by a double-crossing Loki, who used an energy blast from Odin's spear to kill Laufey. Following Laufey's death, Loki, in an attempt to prove he was worthier than Thor, released the full power of the realm-traversing Bifrost bridge upon Jotunheim. However, a returning Thor prevented the genocide of the Jotun race by shattering the Bifrost with his hammer, Mjolnir.

IN THE COMICS

THE FROST GIANTS ARE A RACE OF Jotunheim giants, directly descending from primordial Frost Giant Ymir. Frost Giant king Laufey was killed during a battle in a war with Asgard by the Asgardian regent, Odin. Following the battle, Odin took Laufey's infant son, Loki, back to Asgard to raise as his own. Frost Giants lost Laufey's skull on Earth during a resurrection attempt thwarted by Thor and Viking warriors. Centuries later, the Frost Giants, led by Skrymir, formed an alliance with Dark Elf Malekith and Roxxon CEO Dario Agger to reacquire Laufey's skull in another resurrection attempt.

FIRST APPEARANCE:
JOURNEY INTO MYSTERY #112 (1965)

FACT SHEET

- AS A JOTUN, LAUFEY HAS FULL CONTROL OVER ICE, AND HIS MERE TOUCH CAUSES FROSTBITE.
- LAUFEY WIELDED THE CASKET OF ANCIENT WINTERS AS A WEAPON TO FREEZE ANYTHING OR ANYONE IN HIS PATH.
- LAUFEY DID NOT RECOGNIZE LOKI AS HIS LONG-LOST SON WHEN LOKI RETURNED TO JOTUNHEIM.

WITH JANE FOSTER

DARCY LEWIS

FIRST APPEARANCE: ***Thor [2011]***

Political science major Darcy Lewis was the only applicant when Jane Foster was looking for an assistant for her astrophysics research. While Foster and Erik Selvig were chasing meteorological disturbances in the New Mexico desert, Lewis acted as the driver of their truck. Despite the phenomenon generating visibility-obscuring mist, Foster insisted Lewis drive into the heart of the disturbance. Hesitating at the last moment, Lewis jerked the wheel, striking a glancing blow to a man stumbling through the fog. The trio rushed to the man's side, but he became belligerent as he came to, calling himself Thor. A spooked Lewis knocked him out with a stun gun, and they dropped him off at a hospital. Upon returning to their lab, Foster, Selvig, and Lewis reviewed the data from the disturbance when Lewis made a startling discovery: Thor had been in the middle of what they believed was an Einstein-Rosen Bridge.

Returning to the hospital to question him, they learned Thor had fled. When Foster became determined to search for him, Lewis readied her trusty stun gun, but the hunt ended swiftly when Foster accidentally backed the truck into Thor. Returning to the lab, Lewis was openly appreciative of Thor's ripped musculature and subsequently impressed by his massive appetite when the famished Thor remained hungry after consuming much food.

Overhearing three locals talking about a "satellite" that had fallen from the sky into the desert, and which had proven to be immovable, Thor believed it to be his hammer, Mjolnir. He bid the trio farewell and set off to retrieve his lost weapon. The scientists returned to their lab to find a team of S.H.I.E.L.D. agents led by Phil Coulson confiscating their equipment and research, even taking Darcy's digital music player, much to her dismay.

After Thor was taken into S.H.I.E.L.D. custody, Lewis posited that perhaps a primitive culture like the Vikings might have worshipped space travelers from an Einstein-Rosen Bridge as deities; it seemed to be the nudge that Selvig needed to be convinced to save Thor from captivity. The next morning, Lewis was taken aback by the arrival of other Asgardians, proving Thor's tales to be true. When Loki unleashed the Destroyer weapon on Earth to kill Thor, Lewis assisted in the evacuation of the townspeople to get them to safety. After defeating the Destroyer, Thor returned to Asgard to confront his brother, leaving Lewis and her friends behind.

Later, with the help of S.H.I.E.L.D. satellite codes, Lewis worked with Foster and Selvig to try to find Thor and his home in the Nine Realms.

FACT SHEET

- LEWIS FIRST PLACED THE BLAME FOR HITTING THOR WITH THEIR TRUCK ON JANE, THEN OFFERED TO GIVE HIM CPR AFTER SEEING HOW HANDSOME HE WAS.
- LEWIS HAD DIFFICULTY PRONOUNCING THE NAME OF THOR'S HAMMER, MJOLNIR, CALLING IT "MYEU-MUH."
- LEWIS WAS DISTRAUGHT THAT S.H.I.E.L.D. CONFISCATED HER IPOD, ONTO WHICH SHE HAD JUST LOADED 30 NEW SONGS.

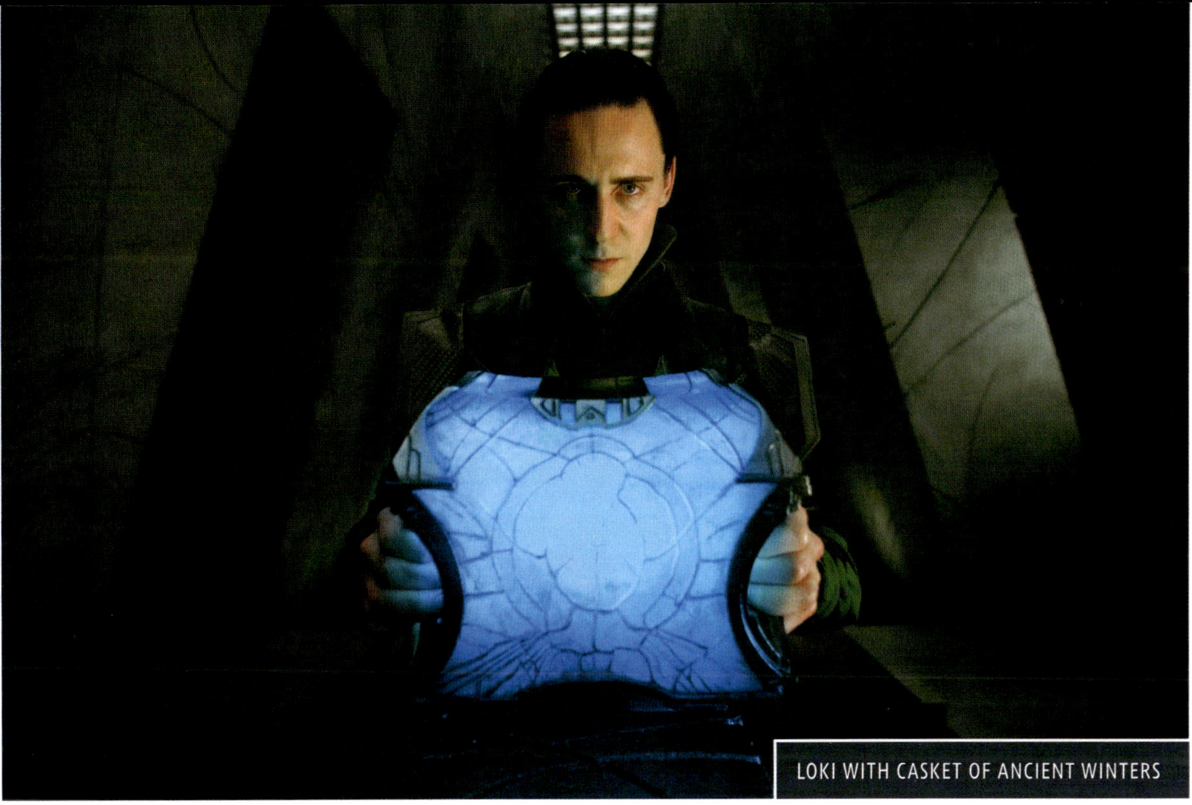

LOKI WITH CASKET OF ANCIENT WINTERS

LOKI

FIRST APPEARANCE: ***Thor [2011]***

When Odin, lord of Asgard, defeated the Frost Giants of Jotunheim in the final battle of a war between the two realms, he found an undersized Frost Giant infant—the forsaken son of the Jotun king, Laufey—abandoned in a temple. Hoping to one day use the boy, whom he named Loki, to unite the two warring kingdoms, Odin brought him back to Asgard and raised him alongside his own son, Thor. Odin and his wife, Frigga, kept the truth from both of them, never wanting Loki to feel different. The two brothers could not have been more different, however: While Thor grew to be a boisterous brawler and mighty warrior, Loki became adept at sorcery and deception. Ultimately, it was Thor who was groomed to inherit Odin's throne. While Loki maintained a façade of friendship in his adventures with Thor and their friends Sif and the Warriors Three, he secretly resented his brother and came to covet the throne himself.

Loki decided to ruin the ceremony by secretly helping a party of Frost Giants.

When the time came for Odin to pass the reins of power to Thor, Loki decided to ruin the ceremony by secretly helping a party of Frost Giants gain entry into Asgard. They breached Odin's weapons vault to steal the Casket of Ancient Winters, the source of Jotun power, which Odin had taken after their defeat, but were promptly dispatched by the Destroyer weapon. Loki subtly encouraged his brother to strike back at Jotunheim, defying Odin's orders, and he accompanied Thor and their friends—Fandral, Hogun, and Volstagg, known collectively as the Warriors Three, plus the warrior maiden Sif—to the Bifrost, the bridge connecting Asgard with the rest of the Nine Realms. Loki had planned to use his persuasive abilities to talk the Bifrost's gatekeeper, the all-seeing Heimdall, into letting them leave, but Heimdall was so perturbed by the Giants' undetected intrusion that he allowed them to travel to the icy world unbidden. Upon their arrival, Loki soon realized that they were woefully outnumbered, and he tried to talk his way into a truce with Laufey. But when one of the Giants insulted Thor, an all-out brawl erupted. During the battle, a Giant grabbed Loki—but instead of being burned by his icy touch, as Volstagg had been, his skin temporarily turned blue like a Frost Giant's. Soon, Fandral was badly wounded, and Loki and the others were cornered by a Frost Giant army. Loki had hedged his bets, however, by having Odin informed of their escapade after they left, and the All-Father arrived in time to rescue them. Furious that Thor had shattered the fragile peace between Asgard and Jotunheim, Odin stripped him of his enchanted hammer, Mjolnir, and exiled him to Earth until he proved worthy, despite Loki's facetious pleas for clemency.

When his friends asked Loki to petition Odin to end Thor's exile, he refused, as he believed Thor deserved his punishment. Later, Loki examined the Casket in the weapons vault and found that it responded to his touch. Loki confronted Odin, who admitted to Loki his true origins. Loki, incensed at having been deceived, verbally lashed out at Odin; this, combined with the stresses of Thor's banishment and the looming conflict with Jotunheim, prompted Odin to fall into the regenerative, coma-like Odinsleep. With Frigga staying at Odin's side, Loki became the new leader of Asgard. Soon, Thor's friends came to him and asked him to lift Thor's banishment, but Loki demurred, insisting that his first decree as king could not be to reverse Odin's last.

Loki subsequently came to Earth, where Thor had been imprisoned inside a S.H.I.E.L.D. base after a failed attempt to reclaim Mjolnir. Loki lied to Thor, saying Odin had died and a treaty had been signed with the Frost Giants that included Thor's continued banishment as a condition of the peace. Loki also told Thor that

LOKI AS KING OF ASGARD

Frigga had forbidden his return. After bidding his brother farewell, Loki tried to lift Mjolnir, which had been enchanted so that it could only be hefted by those worthy of its power; he was unable to budge it. He then journeyed to Jotunheim, where he offered Laufey a chance to sneak into Asgard to assassinate the helpless Odin. Upon Loki's return to Asgard, Heimdall expressed concern that he had not been able to see Loki during his visit to Jotunheim. Loki asserted his power as king, overruling Heimdall. This only further troubled Heimdall, who subsequently sent Thor's friends to Earth to retrieve him. When Loki learned of this, he turned on Heimdall, using the Casket to encase him in ice. Loki then sent the Destroyer to Earth to slay Thor. In the ensuing battle, Thor nobly sacrificed himself, proving himself worthy of Asgard and Mjolnir. Reclaiming his power, he defeated the Destroyer and returned to Asgard. Meanwhile, Loki brought Laufey to Asgard and took him to Odin, only to turn on the Frost Giant, slaying his birth father to save his adoptive one—making sure that Frigga was present to witness it. Before he could use his "heroic" act to his advantage, however, Thor returned to Asgard, now with full knowledge of Loki's deceptions.

Heimdall expressed concern that he had not been able to see Loki during his visit to Jotunheim.

Determined to prove his worth as a king and—thanks to Laufey's attempt on Odin's life—armed with an excuse to attack

IN THE COMICS

THE ADOPTED FROST GIANT SON of Asgardian All-Father Odin and brother of Thor, the god of thunder, the trickster god Loki resented Thor from childhood. As an adult, he became a renegade, conspiring with Asgard's enemies and learning forbidden black magic. He also sired a number of children, including Hela, ruler of the underworld; the ferocious Fenris Wolf; and the world-devouring Midgard Serpent. When Thor began adventuring on Earth, Loki continually bedeviled him, assaulting his brother and his newfound home with sinister spells and minions. One of his schemes inadvertently led to Earth's mightiest heroes assembling as the Avengers, much to his chagrin. Over the years, Loki's fortunes have waxed and waned; he has ruled Asgard, been imprisoned in Hel and even fought alongside Thor. His physical form is as malleable as his allegiance; in recent years, he has taken on many guises. He usurped the Lady Sif's body before returning to his original form, only to die and return to life as an innocent child. As a child, he sacrificed himself to stop the demon Mephisto, allowing his old devious self to truly return. The Young Avenger Wiccan later aged Loki's body to its teens to give him access to the power he needed to defeat the interdimensional parasite Mother. Loki has since served as an agent of Asgard (now called Asgardia), conducting secret missions for the All-Mother. No matter his form—man or woman, adult or child, hero or villain—Loki remains, at best, a mischievous trickster.

FIRST APPEARANCE:
JOURNEY INTO MYSTERY #85 (1962)

the Frost Giants, Loki blasted Thor aside and activated the Bifrost. He froze it in place so that its energies poured continuously into Jotunheim, threatening to destroy the realm and the entire Frost Giant race. Thor's warlike tendencies had been quelled by his time on Earth, and he demanded that Loki stop. Loki refused, proceeding to threaten the life of Jane Foster, Thor's newfound mortal love. The two brothers dueled atop the Bifrost. Ultimately, Loki's magic was no match for Thor's might, and Loki was powerless to stop his brother from destroying the Bifrost to save Jotunheim. The newly awakened Odin grabbed both Thor and Loki before they could fall off the shattered Bifrost. Rebuked by Odin after swearing that he had committed his evil deeds to please his adoptive father, Loki chose to let go, plunging into the space warp created by the Bifrost's destruction and leaving his family to mourn his loss. Loki survived, however, and came to exert his mental control over Thor's friend Dr. Erik Selvig, who S.H.I.E.L.D. had assigned to study a powerful cubical artifact.

FACT SHEET

- LOKI CAN MAKE ILLUSORY DUPLICATES OF HIMSELF, CONTROL OTHERS' MINDS AND RENDER HIMSELF INVISIBLE—EVEN TO THE ALL-SEEING HEIMDALL.
- LOKI KNOWS OF WAYS TO TRAVEL IN AND OUT OF ASGARD THAT BYPASS THE BIFROST.
- AS RULER OF ASGARD, LOKI WIELDED ODIN'S SPEAR, GUNGNIR, FIRING ENERGY BLASTS, CONTROLLING THE DESTROYER AND USING IT AS A MELEE WEAPON.
- WHEN LOKI VISITED THOR ON EARTH, HE REPLACED HIS USUAL ASGARDIAN GARB WITH A STYLISH BUSINESS SUIT.

ODIN

FIRST APPEARANCE: ***Thor [2011]***

In 965 A.D., Odin All-Father, king of Asgard, led his army to stop the Frost Giants of Jotunheim from invading Earth and using their Casket of Ancient Winters to throw the planet into a new ice age. Stopping the Jotun army in Tonsberg, Norway, the Asgardians drove them back to Jotunheim, where Odin defeated Laufey, the Frost Giant king—but lost an eye in the battle. In the aftermath, Odin found Laufey's abandoned infant son in a temple; hoping the child would one day unite the Asgardians and Jotuns, Odin adopted him and named him Loki, but kept his genealogy secret. Odin took the Jotuns' Casket and formed a treaty with Laufey based on the condition that neither's subjects could enter the other's realms.

Odin and his wife Frigga raised Loki as their own, alongside their firstborn son, Thor. Odin strived to teach the boys patience and wisdom as he prepared them to one day replace him as king. Yet Thor became boorish and prideful, while Loki grew devious and jealous.

Centuries later, Odin decided to abdicate the throne and held a coronation ceremony to crown Thor as Asgard's new king. Odin stressed guarding the Nine Realms while preserving the peace, calling for Thor to cast aside selfish ambition and to pledge himself to the good of the realm, but Odin sensed an attempt by the Frost Giants to secretly steal back the Casket of Ancient Winters and stopped the ceremony. Odin quickly commanded the deadly Destroyer weapon to dispatch the thieves, but two Asgardian guards were killed.

SLEIPNIR

FACT SHEET

- MJOLNIR WAS FORGED IN THE HEART OF A DYING STAR AS A WEAPON TO DESTROY OR AS A TOOL TO BUILD; WHEN ODIN TOOK IT FROM THOR, HE PLACED AN ENCHANTMENT ON IT: "WHOSOEVER HOLDS THIS HAMMER, IF HE BE WORTHY, SHALL POSSESS THE POWER OF THOR."
- WHEN THOR SACRIFICED HIMSELF TO STOP LOKI FROM KILLING HIS FRIENDS, ODIN, STILL IN THE ODINSLEEP, SHED A SINGLE TEAR.
- ODIN'S POWERFUL SPEAR, GUNGNIR, PROJECTS ENERGY BLASTS, CONTROLS THE DESTROYER, AND CAN OPERATE THE BIFROST.
- ODIN RIDES AN EIGHT-LEGGED HORSE, SLEIPNIR, AND IS OFTEN ACCOMPANIED BY TWO RAVENS NAMED HUGIN AND MUNIN.
- ODIN WEARS AN ARMORED EYEPATCH OVER HIS MISSING RIGHT EYE.

WITH HUGIN AND MUNIN

As Loki silently watched, Thor told Odin he wanted to make the Frost Giants pay for breaking the treaty, but Odin calmly reminded Thor the attackers had already paid with their lives. Angry at Odin's dismissal, Thor pointed out the Jotuns almost stole the Casket and implied the Frost Giants were taking advantage of Odin's age and weakness. He demanded that Odin allow him to march Asgard's army on Jotunheim and break the Frost Giants' spirits so they wouldn't attempt another uprising, but Odin pointed out Thor was thinking like a warrior and not a king: It would be foolish to punish an entire people for the actions of a few. Instead, Odin intended to find the breach in Asgard's defenses and to prevent further invasions. When Thor pressed the issue, Odin sternly told Thor it was not his decision and reminded him that Odin was still king.

When Thor disobeyed his father's orders and led a small group to confront the Frost Giants, Odin had to rescue them from the resultant battle. Odin tried to reason with Laufey and stave off further bloodshed, saying Thor's actions were those of a boy, but Laufey nonetheless declared war against Asgard. The Asgardians returned home, and Odin chastised Thor, who wanted the Jotuns to fear him as they once feared Odin. Declaring this motivation to not be of leadership but pride and vanity, Odin accused Thor of forgetting what he was taught. When Thor wouldn't back down, Odin angrily called Thor a vain, greedy, and cruel boy. Thor retaliated by labeling Odin an old man and a fool, and Odin agreed—he had been a fool to think Thor was ready to be king. At this, Loki tried to interrupt, but Odin only growled at him. Odin stated that Thor had disobeyed the express command of his king, and through arrogance and stupidity had exposed innocent lives to the horror and desolation of war. Declaring Thor unworthy of Asgard and his title, power, and family, Odin stripped

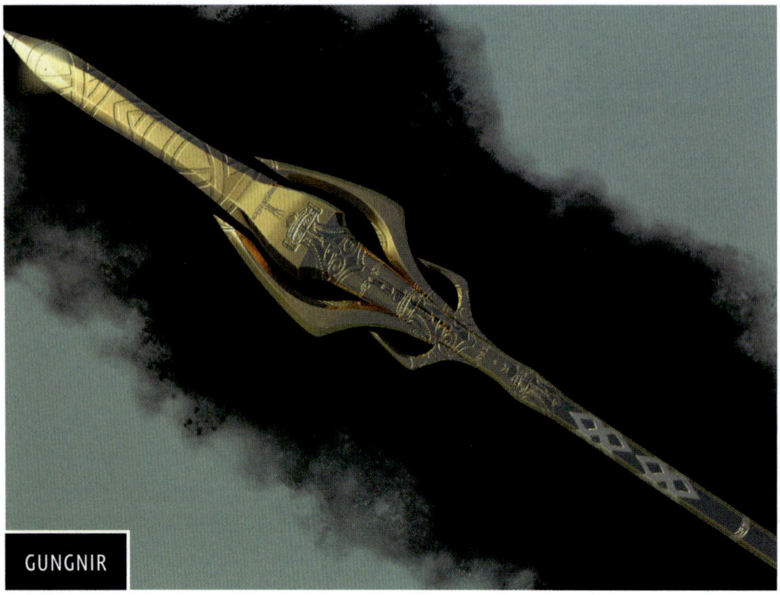

GUNGNIR

Thor of his armor and his hammer Mjolnir, and exiled Thor to Earth. Enchanting Mjolnir to be unmovable by any who were unworthy, Odin tossed the hammer after Thor so it would be available when Thor learned humility.

During Thor's exile, Loki confronted Odin over his suspicions of his true parentage. Odin revealed Loki's ancestry and explained he had hoped to use Loki to unite the two kingdoms, but with war declared, those plans were gone. Enraged, Loki demanded to know why Odin hadn't told him earlier; Odin replied that Loki was his son and he wanted to protect him from the pain of the truth. During Loki's resulting outburst, Odin was overwhelmed by the toll of recent events and collapsed into the rejuvenating, coma-like Odinsleep. Unprepared for it, Frigga remained unsure when, or if, Odin would awaken. With Odin indisposed, but still aware of everything transpiring around him, Loki was declared king; Frigga refused to leave her husband's side.

Seeking to manipulate events to prove himself worthy of the throne to those that doubted him, Loki secretly led Laufey to the helpless Odin. Frigga defended Odin but was quickly swatted aside. Loki killed Laufey, planning to use the assassination attempt as an excuse to wipe out the Jotuns. However, Thor, re-empowered since learning humility through difficult experiences on Earth, returned and revealed Loki's deception. Thor destroyed the Bifrost so Loki couldn't use it to commit genocide in Jotunheim; the bridge's destruction awakened Odin, who saved Thor and Loki from falling into the vast expanse of space off the Bifrost's shattered edge. Loki claimed he had acted in hopes that Odin would be proud of his accomplishments, but Odin rebuffed him; a dejected Loki subsequently allowed himself to fall into a looming space warp.

Later, Thor told Odin he realized he still had a lot to learn, and hoped he would one day make his father proud. Odin, pleased with his son's newfound maturity, told Thor he would be a wise king.

IN THE ODINSLEEP

IN THE COMICS

ODIN, KING OF ASGARD, FATHERED Thor with the Earth goddess Jord (Gaea); he has additional offspring by Frigga and others. He also adopted Loki, abandoned son of frost giant Laufey. When Thor grew arrogant, Odin banished Thor from Asgard and transformed him into the mortal Dr. Don Blake to teach him humility; Thor eventually returned to Asgard. When Odin temporarily died, Thor took his place on Asgard's throne. Later, Odin's brother Cul attacked Earth and was defeated. Afterward, Odin exiled himself as Cul's warden to keep Cul from harming innocents. Eventually freeing Cul out of necessity and in hopes of his brother's reformation, Odin returned to Asgard—and assumed the throne was still his. His arrogance caused great tension between himself and Frigga, who, alongside Gaea and Idunn as the All-Mother, ruled Asgard in his absence. Odin was greatly angered to learn a new Thor (secretly Jane Foster) had replaced his son and made it his mission to reclaim Mjolnir from her.

FIRST APPEARANCE:
JOURNEY INTO MYSTERY #85 (1962)

ERIK SELVIG

FIRST APPEARANCE: ***Thor [2011]***

Ex-university professor Dr. Erik Selvig traveled to Puente Antiguo, New Mexico to assist Jane Foster, the astrophysicist daughter of a former colleague, in studying atmospheric disturbances she believed to be gateways between Earth and other worlds. While witnessing one such event, Selvig, along with Foster and her intern Darcy Lewis, accidentally struck Thor, newly exiled from Asgard, with Foster's truck, then transported him to County Hospital.

The next day, locals spoke of an immovable "satellite" in the desert—actually Thor's enchanted hammer, Mjolnir. When Thor asked for assistance to retrieve it, Selvig advised Foster to refuse, as he perceived Thor to be a delusional and dangerous individual for claiming Norse mythological stories were real. Despite the warning, Foster accompanied Thor to the site where S.H.I.E.L.D. had constructed a base camp around Mjolnir. Thor breached S.H.I.E.L.D.'s defenses but was discovered, and Foster left Selvig a voicemail asking for help before she was detected. After much convincing by Foster, Selvig went to S.H.I.E.L.D. and fabricated a story that persuaded Agent Phil Coulson to release Thor into Selvig's custody.

Taking Thor to a local bar, Selvig told the Asgardian that Foster cared for him, and then suggested Thor leave town before he could emotionally hurt her. But against his own advice, Selvig engaged Thor in a drinking contest that night and developed a fondness for him. Selvig's doubts of Thor's authenticity were soon cast aside when he witnessed four Asgardian warriors battle the lethal Destroyer weapon, as well as Thor's reunion with Mjolnir and reclamation of his power.

Sometime later, S.H.I.E.L.D. Director Nick Fury solicited Selvig to aid in studying an ancient cubed energy source; Thor's mischievous brother, Loki, influenced Selvig's decision to consent.

IN THE COMICS

AT THE TIME OF THE FILM, ERIK Selvig had not appeared in the comics. Dr. Eric Solvang—a quantum cosmologist working to prove his theory of an interconnected, infinite array of universes consisting of infinite possibilities—is his closest counterpart. Solvang warned the Asgardians that while Asgard occupied the space above Broxton, Oklahoma, the terrifying World Eaters would attempt to fill the void where Asgard once existed. Solvang also briefly dated Jane Foster.

FIRST APPEARANCE:
THOR #615 (2010)

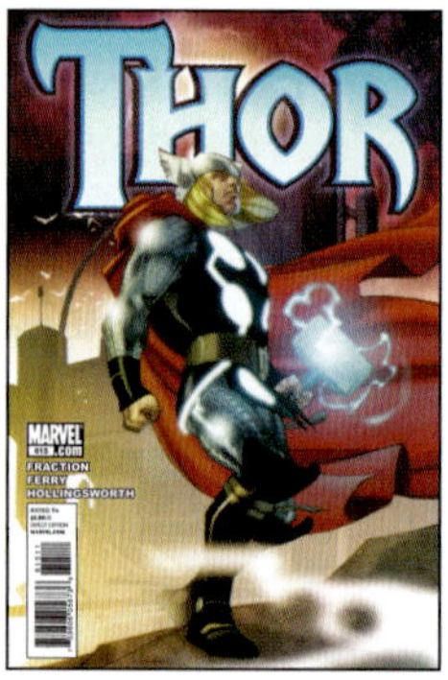

FACT SHEET

- SELVIG BELIEVED IT WAS DANGEROUS FOR FOSTER TO CHALLENGE S.H.I.E.L.D. BECAUSE A GAMMA SCIENTIST HE KNEW HAD DISAPPEARED IN EVENTS INVOLVING THE ORGANIZATION. WHEN LATER MEETING NICK FURY AT AN UNDISCLOSED S.H.I.E.L.D. FACILITY, SELVIG INITIALLY THOUGHT HE WAS BROUGHT THERE TO BE EXECUTED.
- ATTEMPTING TO PROVE TO FOSTER THAT THOR WAS DELUSIONAL, SELVIG BORROWED THE CHILDREN'S BOOK *MYTHS AND LEGENDS FROM AROUND THE WORLD* BY ANNEKA SUNDEN FROM THE LIBRARY.
- SELVIG TOLD AGENT COULSON THAT S.H.I.E.L.D. IS A "FACELESS ORGANIZATION OF JACK-BOOTED THUGS," BUT CLAIMED THE SENTIMENTS WERE NOT HIS WHEN COULSON APPEARED TO BE OFFENDED.

SIF

FIRST APPEARANCE: ***Thor [2011]***

In the male-dominated Asgard realm, female warriors are rare; many doubted that the maiden Sif could become one of the most feared fighters in the Nine Worlds, but she proved them all wrong. She frequently adventured with her closest friends: Fandral, Hogun, and Volstagg, collectively known as the Warriors Three; Thor, son of Asgard's king, Odin; and Thor's duplicitous brother, Loki.

After a party of Frost Giants breached Asgard's defenses with Loki's secret assistance, an infuriated Thor demanded to go to Jotunheim to retaliate, but Odin objected. Sif tried to dissuade Thor from defying Odin's command, but when he went anyway, the faithful Sif and the others accompanied him. She held her own against hordes of Frost Giants, but before long, Fandral was badly injured, and the Asgardians were enormously outnumbered. Odin saved the sextet of warriors and brought them back to Asgard; while Sif and the Warriors Three took Fandral to be healed, Odin stripped Thor of his magic hammer Mjolnir and banished him to Midgard. Sif and the Warriors tried to persuade Loki to intervene on Thor's behalf, but Loki agreed with Odin's judgment. Odin subsequently lapsed into the regenerative Odinsleep, leaving Loki as Asgard's ruler. When Sif and the others discovered this, they swore fealty to Loki, and once more asked him to rescind Thor's punishment; Loki again refused.

The despairing Warriors Three began feuding amongst themselves, requiring the level-headed Sif to calm them. Torn between their friendship with Thor and their loyalty to the Asgardian throne, Sif and the Warriors finally decided that the former outweighed the latter. With the aid of Bifrost guardian Heimdall, they travelled to Earth in search of their friend. Finding Thor in the small town of Puente Antiguo, New Mexico, they celebrated a joyful reunion. Soon, however, Loki dispatched the Destroyer weapon to Earth to kill Thor. Sif and the Warriors Three battled

FACT SHEET

- SIF'S WEAPONS OF CHOICE ARE TWO SWORDS THAT SHE CAN LINK AT THE POMMEL TO FORM A STAFF. SHE ALSO CARRIES A SHIELD.
- SIF IS HIGHLY ATTUNED TO THOR'S THOUGHTS AND FEELINGS; AFTER THOR RETURNED FROM HIS BANISHMENT, HIS MOTHER, FRIGGA, ASKED SIF FOR HER INSIGHTS ON HIS STATE OF MIND, HAVING LOST BOTH HIS BROTHER AND HIS LINK TO EARTH.

the enchanted construct while Thor and his human allies evacuated the town. Fearless despite the Destroyer's seeming invulnerability, Sif prepared to battle to the death, but Thor sacrificed himself to save his friends. In his sacrifice, he made himself worthy of his power; Mjolnir flew to Thor and rejuvenated him, and Thor quickly dispatched the Destroyer. Returning to Asgard to find Heimdall injured after a struggle with Loki, Sif and the Warriors helped him while Thor battled his brother, resulting in the destruction of the Bifrost and Loki's seeming death. Sif joined in the celebration of Thor's return and Odin's awakening, but still worried about Thor's newfound somber tone—and his preoccupation with Jane Foster.

IN THE COMICS

THE SISTER OF HEIMDALL, SIF befriended Thor in their youth; their friendship soon blossomed into romance. They eventually lost touch with each other, however; Sif left Asgard to further her warrior training, and Thor was banished to Earth (Midgard) by Odin to learn humility. Years later, they reunited and shared many adventures across the realms. They also continued their romance, and were even once betrothed, but Thor was often torn between his devotion to Sif and his drive to protect Earth. Sif adventured for a time alongside the spacefaring alien Beta Ray Bill. After the latest Ragnarok event, Loki usurped Sif's body and trapped her spirit in a dying elderly woman; Thor eventually rescued her and restored her to her true form. Sif remains one of Asgard's most stalwart defenders.

FIRST APPEARANCE:
JOURNEY INTO MYSTERY #102 (1964)

SITWELL (CENTER)

JASPER SITWELL

FIRST APPEARANCE: ***Thor [2011]***

While investigating a mysterious fallen object in a New Mexico desert, S.H.I.E.L.D. Agent Jasper Sitwell monitored the near-constant electromagnetic interference emanating from it and rerouted any aircraft that happened to pass over the temporary laboratory surrounding the object. When the Asgardian Thor invaded the laboratory to reclaim the object, which was actually his hammer weapon, Mjolnir, Sitwell sent agents Delaney and Jackson to investigate. Following Thor's capture, Sitwell fact-checked Dr. Erik Selvig's claim that Thor was his colleague Dr. Donald Blake, ultimately learning the identification was falsified.

Agent Sitwell later accompanied Agent Phil Coulson to the arrival site of Thor's allies, Sif and the Warriors Three, and was ordered to enlist S.H.I.E.L.D.'s Linguistics Department to identify the runes left on the ground following their transport. When the Destroyer weapon arrived to kill Thor at the command of his conniving adopted brother, Loki, Sitwell took cover during the attack. Following its defeat, Sitwell was present when Thor pronounced himself S.H.I.E.L.D.'s ally on the condition that Jane Foster's confiscated scientific equipment was returned.

FACT SHEET

- WHEN SEEING IT FOR THE FIRST TIME, SITWELL THOUGHT THE DESTROYER MIGHT HAVE BEEN TONY STARK'S CREATION.
- AT THE S.H.I.E.L.D. LAB, SITWELL REPORTED DIRECTLY TO AGENT PHIL COULSON.

IN THE COMICS

AS ZOMBIE

JASPER SITWELL WAS AN EARLY agent of S.H.I.E.L.D., graduating top in his training class. Despite his often irritating demeanor, Sitwell proved his loyalties to S.H.I.E.L.D. Director Nick Fury, becoming part of Fury's trusted inner circle. Over the years, Sitwell served as S.H.I.E.L.D.'s liaison to Stark Industries and to the heroic Avengers team, monitoring them on S.H.I.E.L.D.'s behalf. Eventually reassigned, Sitwell oversaw the demolition of S.H.I.E.L.D.'s former New York branch office and served as commander of their Chesapeake Bay base.

Shortly after being promoted, Sitwell was replaced by a rogue Life Model Decoy called the Deltite and placed in suspended animation, where he was later revived and brainwashed into serving the terrorist Hydra group before being deprogrammed by Nick Fury. Returning to S.H.I.E.L.D., Sitwell later supervised Agent G.W. Bridge's unofficial pursuit of the vigilante Punisher (Frank Castle). When corrupt tycoon Norman Osborn disbanded S.H.I.E.L.D., Sitwell remained loyal to Fury, joining his mercenary Howling Commandos unit and aiding with Winter Soldier (Bucky Barnes)'s missions; during one such operation, he was apparently killed by a brainwashed Black Widow (Natasha Romanoff), but was somehow later resurrected as a zombie and assigned to S.H.I.E.L.D.'s Howling Commandos extranormalities unit.

FIRST APPEARANCE:
STRANGE TALES #144 (1966)

THOR

FIRST APPEARANCE: ***Thor [2011]***

Circa 965 A.D., the Asgardians, an advanced race worshipped as gods on Earth, fought a war against Jotunheim's Frost Giants. The Asgardian king, Odin All-Father, defeated the Frost Giant ruler Laufey, claiming both the Giants' most powerful weapon, The Casket of Ancient Winters, and Laufey's infant son, Loki, who had been abandoned to die because he was considered weak. Odin and his wife, Frigga, raised Loki alongside their son, Thor Odinson, also born around this time, though neither boy was aware of Loki's true heritage. Odin told the siblings war tales, warning that one day it would be their turn to defend the fragile

Odin told the siblings war tales, warning that one day it would be their turn to defend the fragile peace between the realms.

peace between the realms and advising that while only one could ascend to Asgard's throne, both were born to be kings. Unfortunately, this well intended guidance inspired in Loki a growing jealousy towards Thor, as Loki—not entirely unjustly—concluded that Thor was too rash to make a good king. Over the next millennium, Thor forged strong friendships both on and off the battlefield with the "Warriors Three"—Fandral, Hogun, and Volstagg—and the war maiden Sif. Armed with the

MJOLNIR

mystic hammer Mjolnir, which could summon and control storms and lightning, Thor led his friends in defending Asgard against threats from other realms. His public popularity grew, and Thor became increasingly overconfident. Though quietly concerned his son was not yet ready to rule, Odin recognized that age was finally taking its toll on him, forcing him to periodically enter coma-like Odinsleep to rebuild his strength, and decided to pass his crown to Thor. Dismayed, Loki plotted to prove Thor's incompetence.

On the day of the succession, Loki's magic secretly allowed three Jotuns to enter Asgard unseen and breach the Vault that held Asgard's greatest weapons. Sensing the intrusion, Odin had the animated Destroyer weapon slay the Jotuns. The incursion disrupted Odin's proclamation, and the Jotuns' affront at entering Asgard enraged Thor, all as Loki had intended. While Odin felt that the intruder's deaths had ended the matter and did not want to risk the fragile truce, Thor announced his intent to invade Jotunheim, eventually forcing Odin to angrily remind him that he was not yet king. With ill grace, Thor submitted to his father's order, but Loki slyly encouraged his brother to disobey Odin, and Thor led Loki, Sif, and the Warriors Three to Jotunheim via the Bifrost, a Rainbow Bridge that connected Asgard to the other eight realms. They confronted Laufey, who taunted Thor by telling him that the House of Odin was full of traitors. Noticing that their group was severely outnumbered, Loki accepted on his group's behalf when Laufey offered them a last chance to withdraw, but a Giant's final insult pushed Thor over the edge, and battle ensued. Finally fleeing as the enemies' numbers swelled, the group was saved by Odin's arrival. Thor joyfully suggested they finish off the Jotuns together, only for Odin to chastise him. When it became clear Laufey now wanted war, Odin withdrew all the Asgardians. Both enraged at the other's actions, father and son angrily argued until Odin declared Thor unready to rule. Odin

ORNAMENTAL HELMET

AS MORTAL MAN

stripped him of his Asgardian powers, pronouncing him unworthy of Mjolnir, and banished him to Midgard (Earth). Hoping the depowered Thor would eventually learn humility, Odin enchanted Mjolnir so that only the worthy might wield it and in so doing gain Thor's power. After a magical inscription of interlocking lines appeared and vanished on Mjolnir, Odin sent it to Earth after his exiled son.

Landing near Puente Antiguo, New Mexico, Thor soon discovered he was now mortal and, after some initial misunderstandings caused by his aggressive attitude, was taken in by astrophysicist Jane Foster, who was investigating the "phenomenon" that had brought Thor to Earth. Taken to a diner to eat, Thor overheard locals discussing the object that had crashed in the desert fifty miles away, which the government had now claimed. Realizing it was Mjolnir, Thor asked Foster to drive him there, but her colleague Erik Selvig convinced her not to, believing Thor was delusional. However, Foster changed her mind when S.H.I.E.L.D. government agents, also investigating recent events, confiscated her equipment and research. During the drive, Thor found himself increasingly attracted to the mortal scientist, and promised to return what S.H.I.E.L.D. had taken as soon as he had Mjolnir. Easily penetrating S.H.I.E.L.D.'s security surrounding the immobile hammer, Thor discovered to his surprise that he could not lift it. Humbled, Thor let himself be taken into custody.

When Thor was left unattended, Loki visited him. Since Thor's departure, Odin had unexpectedly entered the Odinsleep, leaving Loki to claim the throne. Seeking to ensure Thor's absence from Asgard, Loki told Thor that Odin had died, heartbroken by Thor's banishment and the threat of war. Grieving, Thor asked Loki if he could return home, but Loki claimed that a truce with Jotunheim was conditional on his exile. Penitent, Thor accepted this news, blaming himself. After Loki's departure, Selvig visited the compound with a fake driver's license and claimed Thor was a distraught colleague who had overreacted to having his research confiscated. Though S.H.I.E.L.D. Agent Phil Coulson saw through the deception, he let Selvig take Thor, hoping they could learn more by surveilling him; as he left, Thor covertly purloined Foster's notebook to return to her. Thor then bonded with Selvig through drinking and with Foster by telling her of Asgard and the Nine Realms.

FACT SHEET

- BEFORE THE VAULT'S ALARMS INTERRUPTED THE SUCCESSION CEREMONY, THOR SWORE TO GUARD THE NINE REALMS, PRESERVE THE PEACE, CAST ASIDE ALL SELFISH AMBITION, AND PLEDGE HIMSELF ONLY TO THE GOOD OF THE REALMS.
- THOR CAN FLY BY THROWING MJOLNIR AND HANGING ON TO ITS STRAP. WHEN HE THROWS MJOLNIR AWAY FROM HIM, IT AUTOMATICALLY RETURNS TO HIS HAND AFTER STRIKING ITS TARGET.
- SEEKING TRANSPORT TO THE MJOLNIR CRASH SITE, THOR VISITED PUENTE ANTIGUO'S PET STORE AND DEMANDED A HORSE; INFORMED THEY ONLY HAD DOGS, CATS, AND BIRDS, THOR NAIVELY DEMANDED ONE OF THOSE LARGE ENOUGH TO RIDE.
- THE FAKE ID SELVIG PROVIDED FOR THOR USED THE NAME OF FOSTER'S EX-BOYFRIEND DONALD BLAKE, M.D., IDENTIFIED HIM AS 6'3", AND CLAIMED HIS DATE OF BIRTH WAS NOVEMBER 21, 1984.

The next day, disobeying Loki's orders, Sif and the Warriors Three came to Earth and located Thor, exposing Loki's lies. To prevent their return, Loki sent the Destroyer to Puente Antiguo to kill Thor and destroy all. Though aware that in his mortal state he could not hope to help fight the animated armor, Thor heroically risked his life trying to evacuate the town while his Asgardian friends battled their foe. When it defeated them, Thor offered himself to it, appealing to Loki to spare the innocents and apologizing for whatever he had done to offend his brother. The Destroyer struck him down and Thor died in Jane's arms, happy that she was now safe. However, even in the Odinsleep, Odin sensed Thor's sacrifice; Mjolnir flew to its master, once more worthy, and restored his life and powers. After swiftly defeating the Destroyer, Thor informed Coulson, who had witnessed the battle, that they were allies in the common cause of defending Earth and assured that S.H.I.E.L.D. could count him as an ally—so long as Foster's research and equipment were returned. Promising Foster he would soon come back, Thor and his friends returned to Asgard to confront Loki. Learning that Loki had brought Laufey to Asgard to slay the somnolent Odin, Thor raced to save his father, but arrived to find Loki had instead slain Laufey. This had been his plan all along: to slay the giant in a desperate attempt to prove himself the more worthy son. Loki then activated the Bifrost, intending to further prove himself by killing all Jotuns with its full power, and demanded Thor fight him. When Thor refused to fight his brother, Loki angrily threatened to find and hurt Foster. Finally provoked, Thor attacked and, after a brutal battle, defeated Loki. Unable to shut down the Bifrost, Thor smashed the bridge, despite knowing he would be stranded in Asgard. About to fall from its shattered edge into endless space, Thor and Loki were caught by a wakened Odin, but when Odin rebuked him, Loki let go, choosing to fall into a space warp created by Bifrost's destruction. In the aftermath, Odin informed Thor he would make a wise king, but Thor insisted he now knew he still had much to learn.

IN THE COMICS

BORN TO ODIN AND THE EARTH GODDESS JORD (Gaea), Thor grew up in Asgard alongside his adopted brother Loki, whose birth parentage was not a secret. He had other half-brothers, including Frigga's sons Balder, Hermod, and Tyr; the giant Vidar; and a half-sister, Angela, whom he did not learn of until modern times. Odin had dwarves forge the hammer Mjolnir for Thor out of the mystic metal Uru, but when Thor broke a truce between the Asgardians and the Jotuns, Odin banished him to Earth to learn humility, transforming him into the handicapped mortal Dr. Donald Blake, unaware of his true identity. Eventually Odin directed Blake to a Norwegian cave, where he found Mjolnir in the form of a cane. When struck against the ground, the cane transformed him back into Thor, and since then he has defended Asgard and Earth, both solo and as an Avenger, Earth's mightiest super-hero assemblage. Eventually freed of his Blake identity, at different times Thor was briefly merged with the mortals Eric Masterson and Jake Olson. In recent times, Thor became unworthy to wield Mjolnir; Jane Foster secretly took up the hammer to become Thor, Goddess of Thunder, while Thor, now going by Odinson, armed himself with the axe Jarnbjorn.

FIRST APPEARANCE:
JOURNEY INTO MYSTERY #83 (1962)

VOLSTAGG

FIRST APPEARANCE:
Thor (2011)

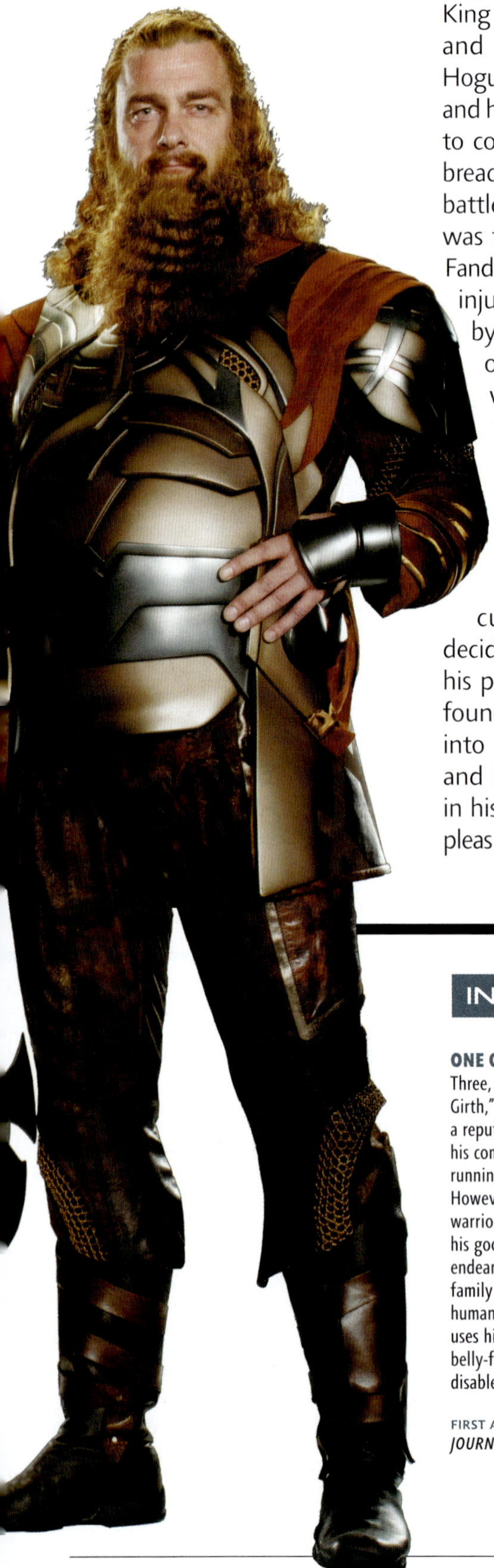

Massive in stature, constantly hungry, and wielding a battle-ax, Volstagg is one of Asgard's heroic Warriors Three and a close friend of Asgardian prince Thor. Against King Odin's commands, Volstagg and fellow warriors Fandral, Hogun, and Sif accompanied Thor and his brother Loki to Jotunheim to confront the Frost Giants for breaching Asgard's defenses. The battle went poorly, and Volstagg was forced to carry a wounded Fandral in retreat, despite a serious injury to his own arm, burned by contact with the icy touch of a Frost Giant. The group was rescued by Odin, who was furious that they had entered Jotunheim. The All-Father subsequently banished Thor to Earth, an action Volstagg and his allies thought rash and unfair. Discussing Thor's fate, they decided to confront Odin and ask his punishment be revoked, but found that Odin had collapsed into his rejuvenating Odinsleep and Loki had taken the throne in his absence. Loki denied their pleas to reverse Odin's banishment. On edge because of Thor's absence and Loki's monarchy, Volstagg drowned his sorrows in food before helping plan a mission to travel to Earth via the Bifrost bridge and find Thor. Their reunion with Thor, however, was short-lived, as Loki sent the powerful Destroyer weapon to kill Thor and destroy all in its path. Volstagg fought valiantly alongside his fellows, but the Destroyer easily defeated them. Volstagg witnessed Thor confront and defeat the Destroyer, proving himself worthy to return to Asgard. The group arrived in Asgard in time for Thor to thwart Loki's scheme to utterly destroy Jotunheim. Later, Volstagg entertained revelers at a party in their honor by recounting the events of their battle.

FACT SHEET

- VOLSTAGG CAN EAT FOUR WILD BOARS, SIX PHEASANTS, A SIDE OF BEEF, AND TWO CASKS OF ALE IN ONE SITTING.
- DESPITE HIS GREAT BULK, VOLSTAGG IS REMARKABLY FAST AND AGILE. WITH A BOOST FROM FANDRAL, HE WAS ABLE TO LEAP A GREAT DISTANCE.
- VOLSTAGG IS QUITE BOISTEROUS AND ENJOYS ENTERTAINING OTHERS WITH EXAGGERATED TALES OF HIS EXPLOITS.

IN THE COMICS

ONE OF ASGARD'S FAMED WARRIORS Three, Volstagg is known as the "God of Girth," possessing great body mass. He gained a reputation for exaggeratedly bragging of his combat skills, but also for occasionally running or hiding when battle erupted. However, he has proven to be a skilled warrior when he engages an enemy, and his good-hearted nature and jovial attitude endear him to his allies. He has a large family with many children, including adopted human youths Kevin and Mick. He often uses his tremendous bulk to his advantage, belly-flopping onto or sitting on enemies to disable them.

FIRST APPEARANCE:
JOURNEY INTO MYSTERY #119 (1965)

PHIL COULSON UPDATE

FIRST APPEARANCE:
Iron Man (2008)

FACT SHEET

- WHEN COULSON FOUND MJOLNIR, IT WAS SURROUNDED BY A PARTY OF PEOPLE TRYING AND FAILING TO LIFT THE OBJECT.
- THOR CALLS COULSON "SON OF COUL."
- WHEN ASKED BY A S.H.I.E.L.D. AGENT IF THE DESTROYER WAS ONE OF TONY STARK'S WEAPONS, COULSON GROUSED THAT STARK NEVER TELLS HIM ANYTHING.

Ordered by S.H.I.E.L.D. Director Nick Fury to investigate an event in the New Mexico desert, Agent Phil Coulson found an immovable hammer-shaped object that fell from the sky, unaware Asgardian king Odin had stripped his son Thor of his hammer Mjolnir and banished both to Earth for Thor's disobedience and arrogance. After clearing the area of bystanders, Coulson set up a quarantine around it, then oversaw the confiscating of the equipment and research of Dr. Jane Foster, who was investigating atmospheric disturbances, deeming her data key to understanding the mysterious object. Seeking his hammer, Thor broke into the secured S.H.I.E.L.D. facility. Coulson directed defensive measures against the intruder, ordering agent Clint Barton into a crane bucket to get eyes up high. Coulson observed as Thor tried and failed to lift Mjolnir.

During a subsequent interrogation, Coulson unsuccessfully attempted to learn Thor's true identity. Thor's new acquaintance Erik Selvig came to Thor's rescue, telling Coulson that Thor was Dr. Donald Blake, a colleague distraught that S.H.I.E.L.D. had confiscated all of their research. Knowing that Selvig was lying, Coulson allowed the two to leave, but had them followed.

After S.H.I.E.L.D. systems monitored a massive energy spike, Coulson scrambled his men to check out the source of the disturbance. Upon arrival, Coulson found the Asgardian Destroyer construct, sent by Thor's brother Loki to destroy Thor. After the Destroyer attacked the grossly overwhelmed S.H.I.E.L.D. agents, Thor sacrificed his life battling the Destroyer, which proved him worthy of his hammer and stature. After being resurrected and defeating the Destroyer, Thor made a deal with Coulson: Thor would be his ally if S.H.I.E.L.D. returned all data and equipment to Foster, whom Thor had fallen in love with; Coulson agreed, offering S.H.I.E.L.D.'s help in continuing her astrophysics research.

NICK FURY UPDATE

FIRST APPEARANCE:
Iron Man (2008)

Following S.H.I.E.L.D. Director Nick Fury's recruitment of Tony Stark as a consultant for S.H.I.E.L.D.'s Avengers Initiative, Fury was briefed about the Asgardian events in New Mexico. Fury summoned witness Dr. Erik Selvig to an underground S.H.I.E.L.D. complex and informed Selvig that his research into dimensional gateways with Dr. Jane Foster had impressed many people. Selvig modestly waived the compliment, deferring credit to Foster, saying her Einstein-Rosen Bridge discovery gave him a lot of material to work with. After Selvig claimed the discoveries they made were unprecedented, Fury implied that wasn't necessarily true. Fury directed Selvig to an armored lockbox, revealing a glowing cube crackling with energy, saying legend and history occasionally intersected. Explaining the cube—later called the Tesseract—was a potentially unlimited source of power, Fury asked Selvig to help determine a way to tap the cube's possibilities. Selvig, expressing interest, agreed, but Fury was unaware the doctor was apparently being mentally manipulated by the Asgardian trickster Loki.

FACT SHEET

- EVEN FURY HIMSELF REQUIRED SPECIAL LEVEL CLEARANCE TO GAIN ACCESS TO S.H.I.E.L.D.'S UNDERGROUND SUBLEVEL G SCIENCE COMPLEX, WHERE THE CUBE WAS STORED.
- WHEN DR. SELVIG JOKED ABOUT FURY SUMMONING HIM TO HAVE HIM KILLED, FURY, WHO HAD AN ARMED S.H.I.E.L.D. GUARD PRESENT, REMAINED STOIC IN HIS NON-RESPONSE.

MARVEL'S *THOR*
BACK-COVER ART BY PASCAL CAMPION

MARVEL'S *CAPTAIN AMERICA: THE FIRST AVENGER*

GUIDEBOOK TO THE MARVEL CINEMATIC UNIVERSE

MARVEL

CAPTAIN AMERICA

THE FIRST AVENGER

PARAMOUNT PICTURES AND MARVEL ENTERTAINMENT PRESENT A MARVEL STUDIOS PRODUCTION A FILM BY JOE JOHNSTON "CAPTAIN AMERICA: THE FIRST AVENGER" CHRIS EVANS TOMMY LEE JONES HUGO WEAVING DOMINIC COOPER NEAL McDONOUGH DEREK LUKE AND STANLEY TUCCI MUSIC BY ALAN SILVESTRI MUSIC SUPERVISOR DAVE JORDAN CO-PRODUCERS STEPHEN BROUSSARD VICTORIA ALONSO COSTUME DESIGNER ANNA B. SHEPPARD EDITORS ROBERT DALVA JEFFREY FORD, A.C.E. PRODUCTION DESIGNER RICK HEINRICHS DIRECTOR OF PHOTOGRAPHY SHELLY JOHNSON, ASC EXECUTIVE PRODUCERS ALAN FINE STAN LEE DAVID MAISEL EXECUTIVE PRODUCERS JOE JOHNSTON LOUIS D'ESPOSITO NIGEL GOSTELOW PRODUCED BY KEVIN FEIGE SCREENPLAY BY CHRISTOPHER MARKUS & STEPHEN McFEELY DIRECTED BY JOE JOHNSTON

Collecting information from Marvel's *Captain America: The First Avenger (2011)*, *Captain America: First Vengeance #1-4 (2011)*, and Marvel's *Captain America: The First Avenger Adaptation #1-2 (2013)*.

HEAD WRITER/COORDINATOR: **MIKE O'SULLIVAN**

COORDINATION: **DARON JENSEN**

WRITERS: **TROY BENJAMIN**, **ANTHONY COTILLETTA**, **PATRICK DUKE**, **DARON JENSEN**, **ROB LONDON**, **CHRIS MCCARVER**, **MARKUS RAYMOND**, **MARC RIEMER**, **JACOB ROUGEMONT**, AND **STUART VANDAL**

ARTISTS: **DICK AYERS**, **MAURO BORRELLI**, **JIM CHEUNG**, **GENE COLAN**, **MIKE DEODATO JR.**, **ANITA DHILLON**, **STEVE EPTING**, **PASCUAL FERRY**, **JACK KIRBY**, **KEVIN MAGUIRE**, **DAVID MARQUEZ**, **RYAN MEINERDING**, **SIYA OUM**, **CARLOS PACHECO**, **JOHN ROMITA JR.**, **DANIEL SIMON**, **JOE SIMON**, **HENRICK TAMM**, **GUS VAZQUEZ**, AND **MIKE ZECK**

COVER ARTIST: **MIKE DEL MUNDO**

SPECIAL THANKS TO DAVE ALTHOFF, SHAWN "KEEBLER" BYERS, JEFF CHRISTIANSEN, MATT DELMANOWSKI, ERIKA DENTON, TIM DILLON, PERCIVAL LANUZA, AMANDA NALLEY, JACQUE PORTE, RYAN POTTER, AND JEPH YORK

CAPTAIN AMERICA CREATED BY JOE SIMON AND JACK KIRBY

BUCKY / JAMES BARNES

FIRST APPEARANCE:
Captain America: The First Avenger [2011]

James Buchanan "Bucky" Barnes met scrawny Steve Rogers in September of 1930 in Hell's Kitchen, New York, when both were young boys, aiding him during a back-alley brawl against several bullies attempting to steal Rogers' money; Barnes had never confronted the bullies until Rogers inspired him to act. In adulthood, Barnes became a three-time YMCA welterweight boxing champ and trained the physically weaker Rogers for military enlistment when the U.S. entered WWII in 1941. Although Rogers was rejected due to ill health, Barnes joined the Army's 107th Infantry Division, attaining a sergeant's rank.

Later, Barnes intervened in another back-alley scuffle between Rogers and a disrespectful moviegoer who had loudly protested the opening wartime newsreel, provoking the confrontation. Learning his friend had tried again to enlist by using a fraudulent form, Barnes reminded Rogers this was illegal, but seemed more offended the New York native claimed he was from New Jersey. Before deploying to England, Barnes convinced Rogers to attend the World Exposition of Tomorrow in Queens, New York, where Rogers slipped away to attempt enlisting again. Concerned for Rogers' well-being, Barnes followed and tried to dissuade him, but ultimately realized his efforts were futile.

Nearly a year later, the 107th was overpowered by the Red Skull's forces near Azzano, Italy, and those captured were imprisoned at Hydra's weapons facility in Krausberg, Austria. Barnes caught a battlefield virus that developed into walking pneumonia, prohibiting him from working efficiently, and he was mercilessly beaten by Hydra's Col. Lohmer; in retaliation, Barnes' cellmates staged an "accident" that killed Lohmer. Barnes was given to Hydra scientist Arnim Zola for experimentation, but Rogers, now the Super-Soldier serum-enhanced Captain America, infiltrated the Hydra base and freed Barnes from Zola's lab table.

Barnes, along with nearly 400 rescued prisoners, accompanied Rogers back to the U.S. Army

WITH CAPTAIN AMERICA

WITH THE HOWLING COMMANDOS

command center, where Barnes led a cheer for Captain America. Soon after, Barnes, Rogers, and their Howling Commandos teammates staged multiple raids, destroying Hydra bases across Europe. Hoping to capture Zola, Barnes and Rogers boarded a speeding train, encountering a Hydra soldier with a powerful energy-based weapon. The weapon ruptured a train car, hurling Barnes through the gaping hole. Barnes grabbed onto a handrail as Rogers attempted to save him, but the rail detached, and Barnes fell into an icy ravine, apparently dying from the massive fall.

FACT SHEET

- WHEN ROGERS ASKED IF BUCKY WOULD FOLLOW CAPTAIN AMERICA AGAINST HYDRA, BARNES INSTEAD STATED HE WOULD FOLLOW "THAT LITTLE GUY FROM BROOKLYN WHO WAS TOO DUMB NOT TO RUN AWAY FROM A FIGHT," REFERRING TO ROGERS BEFORE HIS TRANSFORMATION.
- AS YOUTHS, BARNES MADE ROGERS RIDE THE CYCLONE ROLLER COASTER AT CONEY ISLAND; ROGERS WAS SICK AFTERWARD. WHILE ON MISSION TO CAPTURE ZOLA, BARNES ASKED ROGERS IF MAKING HIM ZIP-LINE ONTO ZOLA'S SPEEDING TRAIN WAS PAYBACK.
- BARNES' PREFERRED WEAPON WAS THE M1928A1 THOMPSON SUBMACHINE GUN, BUT HE ALSO USED A COLT M1911A1 SIDEARM AND A M1941 JOHNSON SCOPED RIFLE, AND EVEN BRIEFLY WIELDED CAPTAIN AMERICA'S VIBRANIUM SHIELD.

IN THE COMICS

JAMES BUCHANAN BARNES WAS orphaned in adolescence but shared his father's love of the military. Poverty-stricken, Barnes lived in Virginia's Camp Lehigh, eventually becoming a special military operative assigned to select missions. There Barnes met Captain America (Steve Rogers) and was assigned to be the Captain's partner, though he continued his special missions in secret; Barnes adopted a costumed identity, and as Bucky, developed a close friendship with Rogers. Active stateside and overseas, they frequently battled the Red Skull (Johann Schmidt) and other costumed criminals. Apart from Rogers, Bucky adventured alongside the Young Allies, and after Pearl Harbor was bombed in 1941, Bucky and Rogers became founding members of the wartime Invaders. Bucky and Rogers foiled numerous Nazi schemes and made powerful enemies, including Baron (Heinrich) Zemo. When Zemo stole a drone plane, Bucky and Rogers jumped onto it just after takeoff. Bucky discovered a bomb onboard and tried diffusing it, but it detonated, casting both men into freezing ocean waters. Rogers went into suspended animation, while Bucky was apparently killed.

FIRST APPEARANCE:
CAPTAIN AMERICA COMICS #1 (1941)

CAPTAIN AMERICA
STEVE ROGERS

FIRST APPEARANCE: ***Captain America: The First Avenger [2011]***

Orphaned, frail, and sickly, Steve Rogers nevertheless burned with a powerful desire to defend the innocent; as a child in Depression-era New York City, he often tried to fight off bullies, persisting despite constant failures. During one such encounter, he met and befriended James "Bucky" Barnes. When the United States entered World War II, Rogers tried repeatedly to enlist, but was rejected on medical grounds every time; the strapping Barnes had no such problems, and soon became a sergeant in the 107th Infantry. Trying to lift Steve's spirits, Barnes took his friend on a double date to the World Exposition of Tomorrow to go dancing and to see inventor Howard Stark demonstrate his Gravitic Reversion technology; however, Steve slipped away and again tried to sign up at the fair's recruiting station, where he was noticed by Project: Rebirth scientist Dr. Abraham Erskine. Erskine needed volunteers for the Strategic Scientific Reserve's attempts to create a Super-Soldier and saw Rogers' indomitable spirit and hidden potential. Rogers was shipped out to Camp Lehigh, where he trained under the disdainful eye of Col. Chester Phillips; Phillips' colleague, British agent Peggy Carter, took a kinder view of him. Ultimately, Rogers' determination, intelligence, and selflessness earned him the chance to be Erskine's first test subject in Project: Rebirth.

PERFORMANCE COSTUME

Before the experiment, Erskine told Rogers of German fanatic Johann Schmidt, leader of Hydra, the Nazi deep-science division, who experimented on himself with an incomplete version of Erskine's formula and was transformed into the maniacal, deformed Red Skull. At a secret facility in Brooklyn, Rogers was injected with the completed Super-Soldier serum and bathed in vita-rays. The experiment was a success, and Rogers was transformed into the pinnacle of human perfection. However, Hydra assassin Heinz Kruger had infiltrated the testing facility and shot Erskine, who died, taking the complete formula to the grave.

Rogers hunted down the assassin, chasing him through the streets of Brooklyn and pulling him from a Hydra escape submarine, only for Kruger to kill himself before he could be questioned. Phillips had wanted an army of Super-Soldiers; unable to use only one, he assigned Rogers to a research lab in Alamogordo, New Mexico, for further study. Desperate to serve, Rogers latched onto an offer from Senator Brandt, who put Rogers on a promotional tour; as the costumed "Captain America," Rogers traveled across the country with a musical revue, promoting war bond sales. Cap was a huge success with children, but when he was sent to the front lines to entertain the troops, the war-weary soldiers taunted him and pelted him with rotten food.

When Rogers visited a camp where Carter was stationed, she tried to bolster Rogers' confidence, but her mention that his unfriendly audience consisted of the remnants of Barnes' division, the majority of whom had been captured or killed by Hydra near Azzano, Italy, spurred him to approach Phillips. Despite Phillips' dismissal of his intent to rescue Barnes' division, Carter and Howard Stark flew Rogers to the Hydra factory in Krausberg, Austria, where the captive 107th were held. After locating Schmidt's factory, Rogers, wearing his Captain America costume and wielding his steel prop shield, stealthily entered and freed all of Hydra's captives, including Barnes and the 107th detainees. As Rogers and Barnes fled the factory, the pair encountered Schmidt, who revealed his red-skinned skull-like appearance to them before retreating. After escaping the self-destructing factory, Rogers, Barnes, and the former captives marched 30 miles back to the command center, to the relief of Phillips and Carter and the cheers of their comrades.

PRE-SERUM

POST-SERUM

RESCUING PRISONERS

Phillips, finally convinced of Rogers' value, set up a task force to proactively attack Hydra with Rogers as field leader. Rogers assembled a team consisting of Barnes and several soldiers he had rescued. Stark developed a bulletproof combat uniform for Rogers based on Rogers' designs and built various substitutes for his damaged shield, but Rogers took a liking to a circular prototype composed of nearly indestructible Vibranium. Rogers and his team, the Howling Commandos, systematically decimated Hydra's facilities and halted Schmidt's research of Asgardian runestones, but their successful capture of a train ferrying Hydra scientist Arnim Zola proved pyrrhic, as Barnes fell off the train during battle, apparently dying in a massive fall down a mountain ravine.

Emboldened by Barnes' death, Rogers and the Howlers assaulted the last of Schmidt's bases, from which Schmidt intended to launch a massive aircraft for an assault on the United States. Rogers boarded the plane as it launched and faced Schmidt in single combat; Schmidt proved his own undoing when he picked up the Tesseract, Hydra's preternatural power source, and was apparently disintegrated. Fearful of the aircraft's destructive payload and with no safe landing sites, Rogers crashed the aircraft into the North Atlantic, despite Carter's tearful pleas over the radio.

Rogers awoke in a room apparently in 1940s New York, but, realizing something was amiss, escaped to find himself in 21st century Times Square, where S.H.I.E.L.D. Director Nick Fury informed him that he had slept for nearly 70 years. Later, finding Rogers at a local boxing gym, Fury presented him with a new mission of global importance.

FACT SHEET

- STEVE ROGERS WAS BORN ON JULY 4, 1918.
- ROGERS' FATHER WAS KILLED WHILE FIGHTING IN WORLD WAR I; HIS MOTHER, A NURSE, DIED OF TUBERCULOSIS.
- DURING HIS MULTIPLE ATTEMPTS TO ENLIST, ROGERS LISTED A NUMBER OF FAKE RESIDENCES, INCLUDING NEW HAVEN, CONNECTICUT, AND PARAMUS, NEW JERSEY.
- AT THE HEIGHT OF HIS POPULARITY, CAPTAIN AMERICA STARRED IN A FILM SERIAL (PLAYING HIMSELF) AND HIS OWN COMIC BOOK.
- THANKS TO HIS ENHANCED METABOLISM, ALCOHOL HAS NO EFFECT ON ROGERS.
- ROGERS IS A GIFTED ARTIST.

IN THE COMICS

WITHOUT SERUM

IN 1941, THE PATRIOTIC YET FRAIL Steve Rogers was recruited into the Army's Super-Soldier program, where an experimental serum enhanced his physique to peak human development. Rogers was thereafter bestowed the guise of Captain America, a figure that would not only combat the Nazi regime but serve as a living symbol of Allied patriotism. Alongside James "Bucky" Barnes and the Invaders, a band of costumed Allied heroes, Cap battled the Nazis throughout the war until falling into the North Atlantic Ocean when he and Bucky sacrificed themselves to stop a Nazi drone plane en route to America.

Cap remained frozen in suspended animation for decades until his rescue by the superhuman heroes, the Avengers, who welcomed him into their ranks. Though initially stymied by modern-day advances, Cap continued his battle against tyranny and terror, alone and with the Avengers and, occasionally, several heroic protégés. Recently, the terrorist Iron Nail neutralized Cap's Super-Soldier enhancements, aging him to his natural, elderly age. Rogers bequeathed the Cap identity to longtime heroic colleague Sam Wilson (formerly the Falcon) and took an advisory position with the Avengers.

FIRST APPEARANCE:
CAPTAIN AMERICA COMICS #1 (1941)

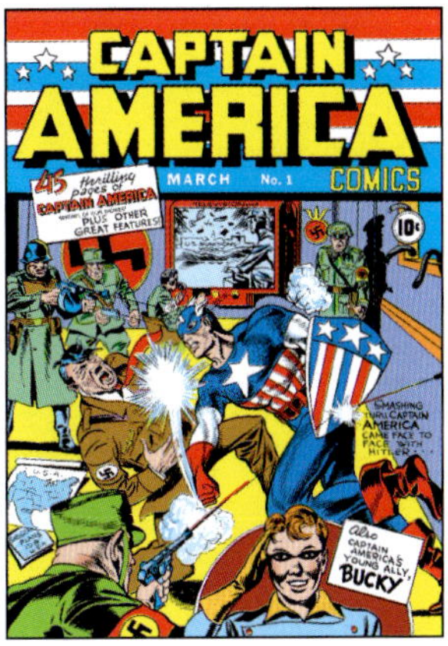

CAPTAIN AMERICA'S COSTUMES & SHIELDS

FIRST APPEARANCE:
Captain America: The First Avenger [2011]

Steve Rogers' original Captain America uniform was little more than a skintight red, white, and blue theatrical costume with a badge-shaped metallic shield in matching colors, designed more to sell war bonds than for combat. When in Europe during World War II to entertain the troops, Rogers defied orders to rescue the captured members of the 107th Infantry from Hydra, Rogers supplemented his performance attire with a bomber jacket and fatigue trousers, plus a helmet from one of his dancing girls' costumes. The shield proved capable of stopping small arms fire, but not the enhanced might of Hydra leader Red Skull, who punched a fist-shaped dent into it.

When Col. Chester Phillips retasked Rogers to head up a new offensive against Hydra, mechanical engineer Howard Stark was assigned to outfit Rogers and his team, the Howling Commandos, with weapons and equipment.

COMBAT UNIFORM

ORIGINAL STEEL SHIELD

MODIFIED PERFORMANCE COSTUME

For Rogers, he developed a battle uniform composed of a bullet-resistant carbon polymer and several models of shields to replace the one damaged by Schmidt. Despite Stark's preference for his more advanced models, Rogers favored a circular prototype composed of vibration-absorbent, nearly indestructible Vibranium. The shield could not only repel much more damage than the original, but also serve as an effective throwing weapon thanks to its circular shape. Rogers became adept over the following months at making uncannily accurate thrown attacks with the shield, even with multiple ricochets.

VIBRANIUM SHIELD

FACT SHEET

- ROGERS, AN ACCOMPLISHED ARTIST, DESIGNED THE OUTWARD APPEARANCE OF HIS BATTLE UNIFORM AS A COMBAT-PRACTICAL VERSION OF HIS THEATRICAL COSTUME.
- IN ADDITION TO HIS SPECIALIZED EQUIPMENT, ROGERS ALSO USED A COLT M1911A1 AUTOMATIC PISTOL AND M1928A1 THOMPSON SUBMACHINE GUN.
- SOME OF THE STARK-DESIGNED SHIELDS THAT ROGERS REJECTED WERE EQUIPPED WITH ELECTRICAL RELAYS AND GUNS; ROGERS CHOSE THE VIBRANIUM SHIELD BEFORE STARK COULD EXPLAIN THEIR PURPOSE.

IN THE COMICS

FIRST APPEARANCE:
(ORIGINAL UNIFORM AND SHIELD)
CAPTAIN AMERICA COMICS #1 (1941)

FIRST APPEARANCE:
(CIRCULAR SHIELD)
CAPTAIN AMERICA COMICS #2 (1941)

WHEN STEVE ROGERS BECAME CAPTAIN AMERICA, THE U.S. GOVERNMENT supplied him with a patriotic red, white, and blue uniform based on Rogers' own design intended to make Cap the antithesis of the Nazi's top agent and living propaganda symbol, the Red Skull. Cap has worn several variations of this uniform over the years, most of which employ a form of woven chain armor. He also employed a powered exoskeleton during periods when his health was deteriorating.

Cap was originally equipped with a badge-shaped steel shield, but President Franklin D. Roosevelt presented Cap with a circular shield made from a unique, nigh indestructible Vibranium-based alloy developed by metallurgist Myron MacLain. During rare occasions where the shield was damaged or lost, Cap has used several replacement shields of varying materials, including replicas of his original shield and a wrist-worn energy shield. After its most recent shattering at the hands of Cul the Serpent, the shield was re-forged by Asgardian dwarves and infused with uru, the metal from which Thor's hammer, Mjolnir, was forged. The shield has been used by others that have served as Captain America in Rogers' stead, including John Walker (now U.S.Agent), James "Bucky" Barnes (now Winter Soldier), and current Cap Sam Wilson (formerly Falcon).

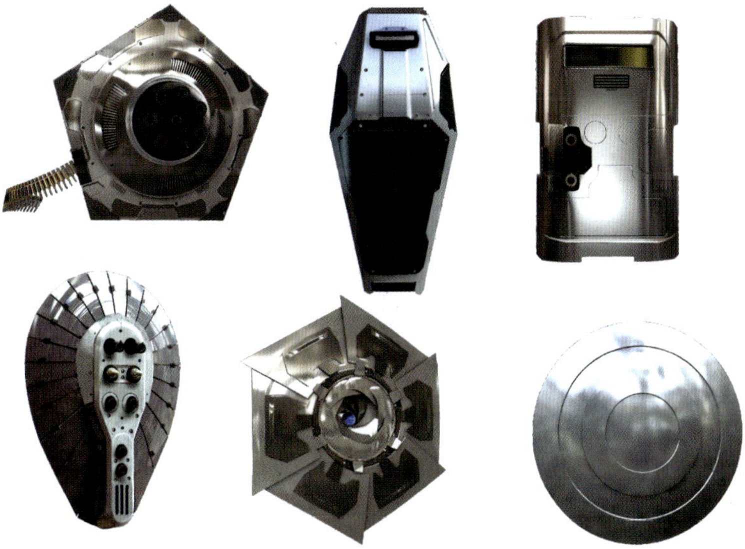

UNPAINTED VIBRANIUM SHIELD

HOWARD STARK'S SHIELD PROTOTYPES

PEGGY CARTER

FIRST APPEARANCE:
Captain America: The First Avenger (2011)

During World War II, British Secret Intelligence's Agent 13 Peggy Carter infiltrated Nazi Germany's advanced weapons division, Hydra, by posing as a servant in Hydra's Bavarian Alps base, Castle Kaufman. After which, she smuggled footage of Hydra weapons deployed in Guernica, Spain, to her superiors, who shared it with the Americans. Their involvement in the war proving increasingly inevitable, America formed the Strategic Scientific Reserve to oppose Hydra, and helped Carter extract scientist Abraham Erskine from Hydra captivity. The SSR recruited Erskine and Carter to help run their Super-Soldier program, Project: Rebirth. The sexism of the 1940s forced Carter to prove herself continuously; assigned to oversee candidates training at Camp Lehigh, Carter quickly asserted her authority by punching candidate Gilmore Hodge for disrespecting her gender and nationality.

Carter took a growing interest in candidate Steve Rogers, who, despite his frailty, impressed Carter with his ingenuity, perseverance, and willingness for self-sacrifice. Carter witnessed Rogers' transformation into a physical powerhouse at the program's hidden Brooklyn laboratory. When Hydra spy Heinz Kruger stole the last vial of Erskine's serum and killed the scientist, Carter pursued and killed Kruger's driver, assisting Rogers' capture of Kruger. Carter had several vials of Rogers' blood taken, hoping that Erskine's formula could someday be replicated. Program commander Col. Chester Phillips assigned Carter to an overseas anti-Hydra offensive, but dismissed Rogers as untested.

In Europe, Carter reunited with Rogers, now a costumed Army mascot known as "Captain America." She attempted to bolster his confidence and explained that a recent unfriendly reception from the soldiers stationed there was due to low morale: Hydra had killed or captured many of their comrades. Learning Rogers' friend James "Bucky" Barnes was among the missing, Carter and SSR engineer Howard Stark defied Phillips' orders and flew Rogers behind enemy lines where the captives were held in a Hydra factory. The next day, Phillips angrily admonished Carter for her actions, but to Carter and Phillips' relief, Rogers returned to the command center with nearly 400 freed prisoners.

Carter and Phillips established an anti-Hydra task force in London with Rogers as leader of their field team, the Howling Commandos. Carter became attracted to Rogers, but was hurt when she found Phillips' secretary kissing him. Her feelings toward Rogers warmed again when, in footage of the team's exploits, she saw he kept a photo of her in his pocket compass. She later comforted Rogers when Barnes was lost in action.

Carter and Phillips led the ground assault on Hydra leader Red Skull's Alpine base. As Schmidt launched his advanced bomber, the *Valkyrie*, Carter and Phillips drove Rogers close enough to board the aircraft, but not before Carter kissed Rogers and wished him luck. After defeating Schmidt on the plane, Rogers contacted Carter and told her the only way to safeguard New York from the *Valkyrie*'s destructive payload was to crash it into the ocean. Knowing they would never see each other again, they nonetheless made a date for the following week as Rogers' transmission was cut off. After the war's end, a mournful Carter helped dismantle the task force's offices. Phillips gave Carter the SSR's file and photos of Rogers, knowing she was mourning his loss.

FACT SHEET

- CARTER WAS AN ACCOMPLISHED MARKSMAN; SHE FATALLY SHOT HEINZ KRUGER'S GETAWAY DRIVER IN THE HEAD FROM SEVERAL YARDS AWAY. HER SERVICE WEAPON WAS A WALTHER PPK.
- CARTER WAS BOTH BEMUSED AND SOMETIMES INFURIATED BY ROGERS' INEXPERIENCE WITH WOMEN.
- AFTER CATCHING ROGERS WITH PHILLIPS' SECRETARY, CARTER TESTED THE RESILIENCE OF ROGERS' VIBRANIUM SHIELD BY ABRUPTLY FIRING THREE BULLETS INTO IT WHILE HE WAS HOLDING IT.

IN THE COMICS

MARGARET "PEGGY" CARTER WAS a resistance fighter during World War II who frequently encountered American hero Captain America (Steve Rogers), a relationship that eventually became romantic. Carter and Cap were separated toward the war's end, and each mistakenly thought the other dead. They reunited in modern times, but because Cap had spent decades in suspended animation, Carter was now physically much older than him. Cap gently refused Carter's attempts to resume their relationship, partially because, initially unaware of the family connection, he had begun a romance with Carter's niece Sharon. She thereafter joined S.H.I.E.L.D. and later accepted Cap's friendship and offer to become the Avengers' communications officer. Carter later died of natural causes.

FIRST APPEARANCE:
TALES OF SUSPENSE #77 (1966)

JACQUES DERNIER

FIRST APPEARANCE:
Captain America: The First Avenger (2011)

Jacques Dernier, an explosives expert, fought with the French Resistance in occupied France until he was captured by Hydra forces in Marseilles and imprisoned in Hydra's weapons facility in Krausberg, Austria, where he was used as slave labor. Coordinating with other prisoners, Dernier mixed chemicals to corrode machinery, staging an accident which killed the torturing Col. Lohmer; the prisoners were punished by having rations withheld for a week, but a bond formed between them. Later, Captain America attacked the weapons facility and freed the prisoners. Dernier was surprised to see the effects of the weapons he had helped build, and joined with his new comrades in leading the prisoners' attack against the Hydra guards. Dernier then marched 30 miles to the nearest U.S. Army command center along with the other survivors.

Soon after, Captain America approached Dernier and his friends in a London pub and recruited them to a strike force specialized to attack Hydra bases in Europe for the Strategic Scientific Reserve. Dernier immediately agreed, but Gabe Jones had to translate for him, since Dernier's impassioned reply was in French. Naming themselves the Howling Commandos, they assisted Captain America in destroying several Hydra facilities, and clashed with Hydra's leader the Red Skull, interrupting his research into Asgardian runestones. Later, the Howlers apprehended the Red Skull's lead scientist Arnim Zola near the Danube River, but lost Howler James "Bucky" Barnes in the process.

Learning from Zola that the Red Skull planned to attack America's eastern seaboard, the Howling Commandos attacked Hydra's last remaining base in the Swiss Alps. As Captain America fought the Red Skull, the Howlers and the SSR battled the Hydra troops. Captain America seemingly sacrificed his life downing Hydra's attack plane. On Victory in Europe Day, the Howling Commandos quietly celebrated the end of the war by toasting to the memory of Captain America and Bucky. ✪

IN THE COMICS

JACQUES "FRENCHIE" DERNIER was a member of the French Resistance against the Nazis in occupied France during WWII. Dernier first met Sgt. Nick Fury and his Howling Commandos when they were rescuing a prisoner from the former Czechoslovakia (at the time part of Germany); Dernier and the French Resistance gave the Howlers transportation to Paris. Subsequently, Dernier occasionally crossed paths with the Howlers: They rescued Dernier when he was captured by the Nazis and Dernier helped Gabe Jones rescue captured American jazz singer Carla Swain. The French Resistance rescued the Howling Commandos from Adolf Hitler's order of execution the day before D-Day.

FIRST APPEARANCE:
SGT. FURY AND HIS HOWLING COMMANDOS #21 (1965)

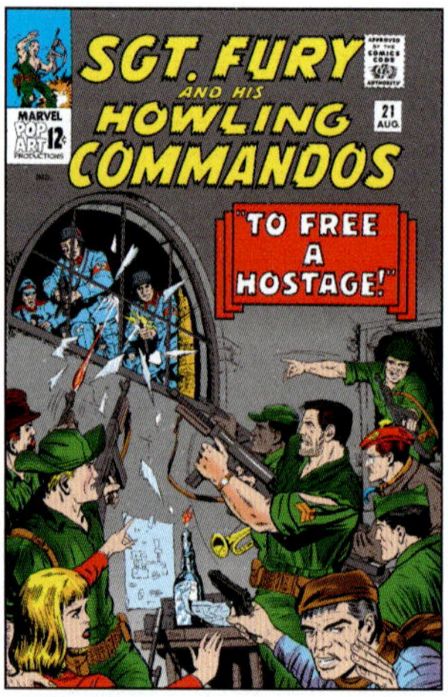

FACT SHEET

- DERNIER WAS PRISONER #03691 IN THE KRAUSBERG, AUSTRIA, WEAPONS FACILITY. WHILE IMPRISONED THERE, "DUM DUM" DUGAN GOADED DERNIER ABOUT PERCEIVED FRENCH COWARDICE; DERNIER PROVED HIS COURAGE DURING THE BREAKOUT AND LATER AS A HOWLING COMMANDO.
- DERNIER USED A STEN MARK II SUBMACHINE GUN AS HIS PRIMARY WEAPON, AS WELL AS VARIOUS EXPLOSIVE DEVICES.

IN THE COMICS

TIMOTHY "DUM DUM" DUGAN was a former circus strongman who joined the armed forces during WWII. After the Japanese attacked Pearl Harbor, Lt. Sam Sawyer and Sgt. Nick Fury assembled a special Rangers unit, the First Attack Squad (later known as the Howling Commandos) and enlisted Dugan, whom they had met previously in Europe. Dugan became close friends with Fury; he served with the Howlers through the war and briefly led the Deadly Dozen, a squad comprised mostly of criminals.

In modern times, Dugan was recruited into S.H.I.E.L.D. by new director Col. Nick Fury. Dugan died on an early S.H.I.E.L.D. mission; Fury couldn't bear losing his friend, so he secretly replaced Dugan with a series of Life Model Decoys, discreetly replacing them as they occasionally died on missions. Unaware of his own death, "Dugan" served with S.H.I.E.L.D. over the years and was briefly the organization's director. Dugan has since learned of his death and is unhappy with being trapped in a form that cannot permanently die.

FIRST APPEARANCE:
SGT. FURY AND HIS HOWLING COMMANDOS #1 (1963)

DUM DUM DUGAN

FIRST APPEARANCE:
Captain America: The First Avenger (2011)

New York City's Sgt. Timothy "Dum Dum" Dugan joined the Army during World War II. Enlisted in the 107th Infantry, Dugan became friends with James "Bucky" Barnes. The 107th was captured by Hydra forces near Azzano, Italy, and imprisoned in Hydra's Krausberg, Austria, weapons facility, where Dugan was used as slave labor. When Barnes was tortured by Hydra's Col. Lohmer, Dugan and other prisoners covertly killed Lohmer. They were punished by having rations withheld for a week, but a bond formed between them. Later, Captain America attacked the weapons facility and freed the prisoners. Dugan yelled his signature "yahoooooo!" while commandeering a Hydra tank during the prisoners' attack against the Hydra guards and later drove it 30 miles back to the nearest U.S. Army command center.

Soon after, Captain America recruited Dugan and his friends to a specialized strike force to attack Hydra bases in Europe for the Strategic Scientific Reserve. Naming themselves the Howling Commandos, they assisted Captain America in destroying several Hydra facilities, and clashed with Hydra's leader the Red Skull, halting his research into Asgardian runestones. On a mission to apprehend the Red Skull's lead scientist Arnim Zola, Barnes was lost and apparently killed.

During interrogation, Zola revealed that the Red Skull intended to destroy America's eastern seaboard. Attacking Hydra's last remaining base in the Swiss Alps, the Howling Commandos and SSR battled the Hydra troops, while Captain America pursued the fleeing Red Skull and seemingly sacrificed himself to stop the bombings. On Victory in Europe Day, the Howling Commandos quietly celebrated the end of the war by toasting to the memory of Captain America and Bucky. ⍟

FACT SHEET

- WHILE IMPRISONED IN KRAUSBERG, DUGAN EARNED THE NICKNAME "DUM DUM" FROM BUCKY WHEN DUGAN MISTAKENLY CALLED HIM "JIMMY."
- WHILE THE OTHER HOWLERS IMMEDIATELY AGREED TO CAPTAIN AMERICA'S OFFER TO ATTACK HYDRA BASES, DUGAN DEMANDED HE BUY THEM UNLIMITED DRINKS FIRST.
- DUGAN USED A WINCHESTER 1897 TWELVE GAUGE SHOTGUN AS HIS PRIMARY WEAPON, CARRIED A COLT M1917 .45 ACP REVOLVER AS A BACKUP, AND ALMOST ALWAYS WORE A BOWLER HAT.

ABRAHAM ERSKINE

FIRST APPEARANCE:
Captain America: The First Avenger (2011)

Born in the Bavarian town of Augsburg, Germany, Dr. Abraham Erskine and his scientific research attempts to turn a simple man into a super human caught the eyes of Adolf Hitler and Hydra's Johann Schmidt, who took Erskine and his family hostage as they tried to flee to Switzerland in 1935. Schmidt held the scientist at gunpoint and injected himself with the untested, incomplete formula; he was immediately enhanced to peak physical condition, but grotesquely disfigured. Erskine learned his family was dead when he was rescued by British Secret Intelligence Agent Peggy Carter. He was then taken to the United States and placed under the Strategic Scientific Reserve's protection, continuing his research under their watchful eye.

Convinced Schmidt's transformation was the serum's reaction to Schmidt's negative personality, Erskine rejected the aggressive candidates the U.S. Army kept offering him. Attending the 1943 World Exposition of Tomorrow hoping to find better subjects, Erskine overheard the small, sickly Steve Rogers express his devotion to serving his country, despite being deemed unfit to serve because of his health. Deeply impressed, Erskine approved the oft-rejected Rogers' application to enlist. Rogers' spirit ultimately proved him worthy of Erskine's complete serum, and he was chosen as the first true subject for Project: Rebirth. In the evening prior to Rogers' procedure, Erskine shared a warm conversation with him in the barracks, stating that he had picked Rogers because a weak man understood the value of strength and compassion.

Within the confines of a secret laboratory, Erskine supervised the process to turn Rogers into the ultimate Super-Soldier. After a tense procedure, Rogers was successfully transformed from a scrawny weakling into a muscular soldier. A sudden explosion triggered by Hydra assassin Heinz Kruger cut the celebration short; Kruger shot Erskine twice, preventing the replication of Roger's procedure, then fled with a vial of the serum. When Rogers rushed to the doctor's side, Erskine pointed to Rogers' heart to remind him to be a good man—not the perfect soldier—then drew his last breath. Rogers subsequently stopped Kruger from escaping with the serum.

IN THE COMICS

GERMAN DOCTOR ABRAHAM Erskine tirelessly worked to end infirmity and, sickened by Nazi atrocities during WWII, assisted the FBI and U.S. military in using his research to create the serum that transformed Steve Rogers into the peak-human Captain America. Immediately following this success, Erskine was murdered by a member of Hitler's Gestapo to prevent a U.S. Super-Soldier army. To protect the serum from abuse, Erskine only recorded partial copies of his equations, so his crowning accomplishment was never duplicated despite multiple attempts by friend and foe.

FIRST APPEARANCE:
CAPTAIN AMERICA COMICS #1 (1941)

FACT SHEET

- TO PREVENT HIS FORMULA FROM FALLING INTO THE WRONG HANDS, ERSKINE REFUSED TO COMMIT HIS COMPLETE RESEARCH TO PAPER.
- ERSKINE'S WIFE, GRETA, AND CHILDREN, KLAUS AND MARLENE, DIED OF TYPHUS IN 1937 IN THE DACHAU CONCENTRATION CAMP.
- ERSKINE'S PROCEDURE, INVOLVING MICRO-INJECTIONS OF HIS FORMULA INJECTED INTO MUSCLE GROUPS AND VITA-RAY SATURATION, CONSUMED SO MUCH ELECTRICITY IT HAD THE POTENTIAL TO CAUSE POWER FAILURES ACROSS THE ENTIRE BROOKLYN BOROUGH.

JAMES MONTGOMERY FALSWORTH

FIRST APPEARANCE:
Captain America: The First Avenger [2011]

An expert strategist, James Montgomery Falsworth of the Birmingham Falsworths served in His Majesty's Third Independent Parachute Regiment. In October 1943, several of his company were captured by Hydra, the Nazi deep-science division, and held in a facility in Krausberg, Austria. They shared a cell with Allied prisoners from widely differing backgrounds, a practice designed to ensure that internal rivalries kept the captives too busy fighting one another to think about turning against their captors. At first this succeeded—but amid concerns that a particularly brutal overseer, Col. Lohmer, would use the ill health of cellmate James "Bucky" Barnes as an excuse to murder him, the cellmates put aside their differences. Working together using a plan Falsworth devised, the captives arranged a fatal "accident" for Lohmer.

A month after Falsworth's capture, the prisoners were rescued from their cells by Bucky's friend Captain America and fought alongside one another to escape from Krausberg. Falsworth manned the guns of a tank commandeered by Gabe Jones and Timothy "Dum Dum" Dugan, providing cover for other escapees. Impressed with their bravery and teamwork, Captain America later handpicked the six cellmates for his personal squad, the Howling Commandos, leading Strategic Science Reserve forces in attacking Hydra bases across occupied Europe over the next several months. In April 1944, the Howlers confronted Hydra leader the Red Skull, halting his research into Asgardian runestones. Barnes was lost while capturing Hydra's lead scientist, Arnim Zola, and Cap apparently sacrificed himself to stop Hydra from attacking America. On Victory in Europe Day, the now Brigadier Falsworth toasted their memories with the surviving squad members.

IN THE COMICS

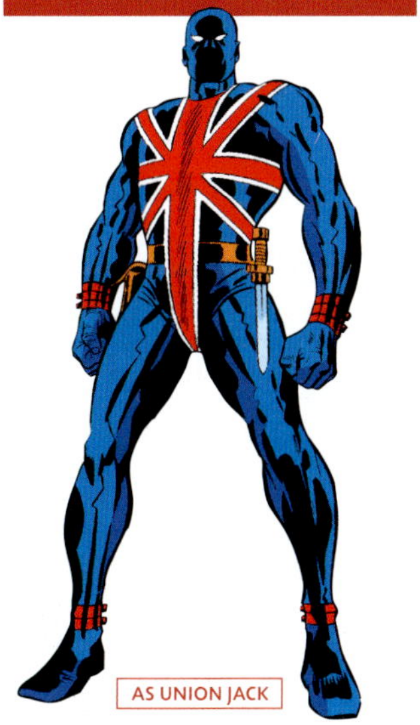

AS UNION JACK

IN THE COMICS, JAMES MONTGOMERY, Lord Falsworth, was Union Jack, a costumed hero who fought in World War I. He came out of retirement during World War II to assist the Invaders, but was crippled by his vampiric brother, Baron Blood. His son, John Falsworth, replaced him as Union Jack. Outliving John, who died in a car crash in 1953, an increasingly infirm Montgomery Falsworth held on determinedly to life until he could assist Captain America in finally slaying Baron Blood.

FIRST APPEARANCE:
INVADERS #7 (1976)

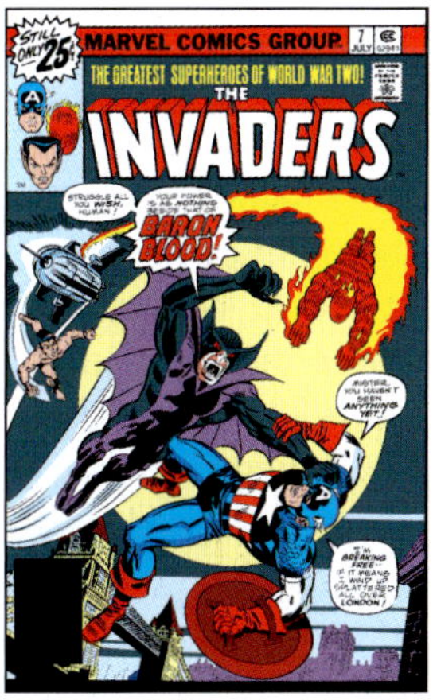

FACT SHEET

- FALSWORTH WAS PRISONER #49275 IN THE AUSTRIAN HYDRA BASE.
- FALSWORTH WAS THE FIRST OF THE FORMER PRISONERS TO AGREE TO JOIN CAP'S HOWLING COMMANDOS, CLAIMING THAT THEIR NEAR-SUICIDAL MISSION SOUNDED "RATHER FUN."
- BY THE END OF THE WAR, FALSWORTH HAD EARNED SEVERAL SERVICE RIBBONS, INCLUDING THE ORDER OF BURMA, AFRICA STAR, DEFENCE MEDAL, AND THE WAR MEDAL.

HYDRA

FIRST APPEARANCE:
Captain America: The First Avenger [2011]

Supported by Schutzstaffel (S.S.) leader Heinrich Himmler, Johann Schmidt became leader of the S.S.-associated deep-science division Hydra. In June 1934, the S.S. took over the Special Weapons Division of the Sturmabteilung (S.A.) following S.A. leader Ernst Kaufmann's assassination at Schmidt's hand. During the brutal takeover, the S.S. slaughtered Kaufmann's followers at the S.A.'s Weapons Testing Ground in Kummersdorf and recruited Dr. Arnim Zola, who chose to continue his work under Schmidt—though Schmidt was more interested in human Super-Soldiers than Zola's exoskeletons.

In September 1935, Schmidt prevented Dr. Abraham Erskine's escape from Nazi Germany and forced him to continue work on a Super-Soldier serum within Hydra's ranks, using Erskine's family as leverage. While Erskine continued working on the serum, Zola's weapons systems were already in use in the late 1930s when Hitler sent Hydra to Spain to level the rebel-held town Guernica to aid Generalissimo Francisco Franco during the Spanish Civil War. When U.S. officials learned of these events from undercover British agent Peggy Carter in February 1940, they formed the Strategic Scientific Reserve to counteract Hydra.

In November 1940, Schmidt tested Dr. Erskine's incomplete serum on himself. Though it amplified his physical abilities, it left him massively deformed, and he became known as the Red Skull. Schmidt imprisoned Erskine for his failure. Having infiltrated Hydra's ranks, Carter freed Erskine and took him to the United States. Erskine joined the SSR to continue his research into the Super-Soldier serum. Meanwhile, Hitler provided Schmidt with a new headquarters for Hydra hidden in the Swiss Alps. Schmidt saw the move for what it was: He had been exiled, as he no longer reflected Hitler's image of Aryan perfection. Hydra became a cult, worshiping the Skull, and stopped providing the Nazis with weaponry. Unsanctioned by the Nazis, Hydra invaded Tønsberg, Norway, in March 1942 in search of the Tesseract, a powerful alien artifact once the alleged crown jewel of Asgardian King Odin's treasure room. The Red Skull found it hidden in a church and took it to Arnim Zola, who had become the Skull's second-in-command. Zola harnessed the Tesseract's energies to power his inventions. When Hydra located Erskine in the United States, the Red Skull sent Hydra agent Heinz Kruger to assassinate him. Though Kruger succeeded, successful Super-Soldier subject Steve Rogers prevented Kruger from escaping with the sole remaining vial of serum, and Kruger committed suicide to avoid capture.

Hydra became a cult, worshiping the Skull, and stopped providing the Nazis with weaponry.

Growing tired of Hydra's actions, Hitler sent three S.S. officers to put the Skull in his place, but Schmidt used a Tesseract-energized cannon to vaporize them. Declaring Hydra could grow no further

under Hitler's rule, the Skull began a military build-up in bases across Europe. Soldiers caught by Hydra were forced to work in his weapons facilities. Hydra's base in Krausberg, Austria—where parts of the immense *Valkyrie* plane was built—became the first such facility to fall when Captain America invaded the base and freed the captured soldiers. Realizing his men were outmatched, the Red Skull activated the facility's self-destruct sequence and fled. Remembering the Hydra bases' locations from a map in Krausberg, Captain America and his Howling Commandos slowed Hydra's progress by taking out facilities in France, Belgium, the former Czechoslovakia, and Liechtenstein, as well as on an island in the Danish Straits. In March 1945, Zola set a trap for Captain America on a train; though Cap's longtime friend James "Bucky" Barnes apparently lost his life during the mission, Zola was captured and taken to the SSR's headquarters for interrogation. Unwilling to die for Hydra, Zola revealed the location of the organization's main base to the SSR. Meanwhile, the Skull readied Hydra to launch a worldwide attack, beginning with the United States, within the next 24 hours. Captain America, the Howling Commandos and the SSR raided Hydra's mountain base; while the battle on the ground continued, the Red Skull took off in the *Valkyrie*; Cap managed to stowaway on the plane before takeoff. After dispatching the Hydra agents on board, Cap attacked the Red Skull, who apparently perished when he grabbed the unshielded Tesseract. Unable to change the plane's course, Captain America forced it to crash, sacrificing himself and ending Hydra's plan for world domination.

FACT SHEET

- HYDRA AGENTS WERE SO FANATICAL THAT THEY TYPICALLY COMMITTED SUICIDE UPON CAPTURE, USUALLY USING A CAPSULE OF CYANIDE HIDDEN IN A FALSE TOOTH.
- HYDRA USED A MODIFIED NAZI SALUTE; BOTH ARMS WERE HELD ALOFT, FORMING THE BODY INTO AN H-SHAPE.
- THE HYDRA OATH IS "CUT OFF ONE HEAD, TWO MORE SHALL TAKE ITS PLACE! HAIL HYDRA!"

IN THE COMICS

THE MODERN INCARNATION OF Hydra started as a Japanese secret society that was infiltrated and usurped by Nazi fanatic Baron (Wolfgang) von Strucker during World War II. Hydra grew into a massive subversive organization, with its efforts at world domination frequently opposed by Captain America (Steve Rogers) and S.H.I.E.L.D. Over the years, Hydra has employed a number of notorious agents—including the nihilistic terrorist Viper (Ophelia Sarkissian), the enigmatic armored Kraken (Daniel Whitehall) and future Avenger Spider-Woman (Jessica Drew). Left without Strucker's leadership after his death in recent times, a revitalized Hydra has taken aim at the new Captain America (Sam Wilson).

FIRST APPEARANCE:
STRANGE TALES #135 (1965)

WEAPONS & TECHNOLOGY

Designed by the brilliant Arnim Zola, Hydra's advanced weapons would have remained the stuff of science fiction were it not for the Tesseract, whose energies were used to power them. Hydra's technology was decades beyond that of the Allies, but Hydra's ability to produce weaponry was impeded as the war progressed by Captain America's continued destruction of its factories.

FIESER DORSCH — A one-man escape craft, this sleek and stealthy sub was intended to be assassin Heinz Kruger's escape vehicle until Captain America smashed its cockpit and tossed Kruger back to dry land.

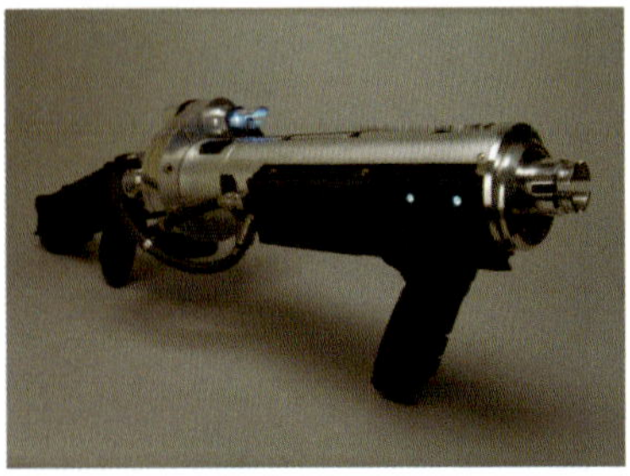

ENERGY WEAPONS — Ranging in size from the Red Skull's sidearm pistol to the standard-issue Hydra rifle to the main cannons of Hydra's tanks, Hydra's Tesseract-powered weapons fired energy blasts that could vaporize anything or anyone they hit.

HYDRA UBER TANK — The size of a house, this lumbering colossus packed a powerful punch, but proved vulnerable to attack from within: Captain America destroyed one by tossing a bomb into its entry hatch.

HYDRA MINI TANK — Though a light armored vehicle, the Mini-Tank was still armed with deadly energy blasters; the Howling Commandos turned those weapons against Hydra when they hijacked a Mini-Tank while escaping from captivity.

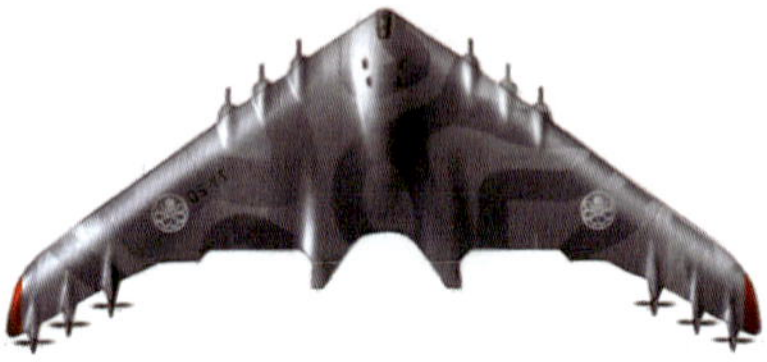

VALKYRIE — A massive bomber loaded with the FliegerParasit flying bombs bound for major cities, the *Valkyrie* launched from Hydra's base in the Alps under the command of the Red Skull. Captain America hijacked the craft while en route to America and crashed it into the icy North Atlantic, where it—and a dormant Captain America—was discovered decades later.

TRIEBFLÜGEL — A wingless aircraft with three propeller-mounted ramjets, the *Triebflügel* was used as an escape craft by the Red Skull when Captain America stormed his factory in Austria.

HYDRA BIKE— These high-speed motorcycles were armed with dual energy blasters and protected by an armored shell, but Captain America outmaneuvered and destroyed them en route to the Red Skull's alpine stronghold.

GABE JONES

FIRST APPEARANCE:
Captain America: The First Avenger (2011)

A student at Howard University until joining the U.S. Army during World War II, the multilingual Gabe Jones enlisted in the all-black 92nd Infantry, but was captured by Hydra forces and forced to work in Hydra's weapons facility in Krausberg, Austria. Jones coordinated with some of his fellow prisoners to arrange a fatal "accident" for brutal overseer Col. Lohmer; they were punished by having rations withheld for a week, but a bond formed between them. Later, Captain America attacked the weapons facility and freed the prisoners. Jones joined with his new comrades in leading the prisoners' attack against the Hydra guards and marched 30 miles back to the nearest U.S. Army command center.

Soon after, Captain America recruited Jones and his friends for a specialized strike force targeting Hydra bases in Europe for the Strategic Scientific Reserve. As the Howling Commandos, they helped Captain America destroy several Hydra facilities and clashed with Hydra's leader, the Red Skull, interrupting his research into Asgardian runestones. On a mission to apprehend the Red Skull's lead scientist, Arnim Zola, fellow Howler James "Bucky" Barnes was apparently killed, but Jones was able to capture Zola.

Learning from Zola that the Red Skull planned to attack America's eastern seaboard, the Howling Commandos raided Hydra's last remaining base in the Swiss Alps. As Captain America fought the Red Skull, the Howlers and the SSR battled the Hydra troops. Captain America sacrificed himself to prevent Hydra's attack plane from reaching the U.S. On Victory in Europe Day, the Howling Commandos solemnly celebrated the end of the war by toasting the memory of Captain America and Bucky. ⍟

IN THE COMICS

AS S.H.I.E.L.D. AGENT

AN ACCLAIMED JAZZ TRUMPETER from Harlem, Gabe Jones joined the Army during World War II. Army units were not racially integrated at the time, but Jones' military proficiency and skill drew the attention of Lt. Sam Sawyer, who recruited Jones into the special Rangers unit he was assembling with Sgt. Nick Fury—the First Attack Squad, later known as the Howling Commandos. Jones served with the Howlers through the war, keeping his trumpet with him.

In modern times, Jones worked for military intelligence and helped Captain America (Steve Rogers), thought dead at the end of WWII but then recently revived, acclimate to modern times. Jones was recruited into S.H.I.E.L.D. by its new director, Col. Nick Fury. Over the years, Jones served as one of Fury's closest confidantes and often headed specialized S.H.I.E.L.D. task forces. Jones was killed in a battle with Hydra, but remained defiant to the last.

FIRST APPEARANCE:
SGT. FURY AND HIS HOWLING COMMANDOS #1 (1963)

IN WWII

FACT SHEET

- JONES, FROM MACON, GEORGIA, STUDIED GERMAN FOR THREE SEMESTERS BEFORE TRANSFERRING TO FRENCH "BECAUSE THE GIRLS WERE PRETTIER."
- AS THE HOWLERS' HEAVY ARTILLERIST, JONES USED A BROWNING M1919A4 30-CALIBER MACHINE GUN. ALTHOUGH THE GUN IS NORMALLY MOUNTED ON VEHICLES, JONES USED A SHOULDER STRAP TO STABILIZE IT AS HE FIRED FROM THE CHEST.

JIM MORITA

FIRST APPEARANCE:
Captain America: The First Avenger (2011)

Captured by rogue Nazi science division Hydra, Japanese-American soldier Jim Morita was caged with other Allied prisoners and forced to work at Hydra's Krausberg weapons facility in Austria. On an unsanctioned mission, Captain America freed the captives; although outgunned, Morita was among the first to bravely engage the base's troops as the Allied soldiers fought their way to freedom. He was at the head of the column as they marched 30 miles to the safety of the nearest U.S. Army command center. Initially suspicious because of Morita's Japanese ethnicity, Timothy "Dum Dum" Dugan eventually welcomed him as a compatriot. Morita subsequently joined Captain America's strike force, the Howling Commandos, tasked with destroying further Hydra installations. One such mission in Nazi-occupied Denmark saw Morita and the other Howling Commandos first directly encounter Hydra's leader, the Red Skull. After taking part in the mission that captured the Red Skull's chief scientist, Arnim Zola, Morita attended the strategy meeting back in London. Learning that the Red Skull intended to bomb the U.S. East Coast, they devised a plan to stop the Hydra leader.

Morita joined a multipronged assault on Hydra's last base in the Swiss Alps. Once in, Morita radioed Col. Chester Phillips that he could begin his attack. With the base soon in Allied hands after a heated battle, Morita worked the radio used for communication between Rogers and his paramour, Peggy Carter. Phillips and Morita left Carter to her final conversation with Rogers as he sacrificed himself by intentionally crashing the Red Skull's attack plane. After the Allied victory over Nazi Germany, Morita joined the other Howling Commandos in a toast to the lost Captain America and other teammates. ✪

IN THE COMICS

A SECOND-GENERATION JAPANESE-American, Pvt. Jim Morita formed part of the Nisei commando squad stationed alongside the Howling Commandos in England during WWII. A karate expert, Morita fought with the Howlers against Nazi soldiers and the Blitzkrieg Squad. Sgt. Nick Fury vouched for him when his loyalty was questioned after he escaped a German prison camp.

FIRST APPEARANCE:
SGT. FURY AND HIS HOWLING COMMANDOS #38 (1967)

FACT SHEET

- JIM MORITA PROUDLY HAILS FROM FRESNO, CALIFORNIA.
- MORITA IS A SKILLED RADIO OPERATOR AND CAN ADAPT QUICKLY TO NEW EQUIPMENT.
- ALTHOUGH HE HAD ACCESS TO ADVANCED HYDRA WEAPONS, MORITA PREFERS USING M3A1 SUBMACHINE GUNS ("GREASE GUNS") WHEN ATTACKING NAZI STRONGHOLDS.

CHESTER PHILLIPS

FIRST APPEARANCE:
Captain America: The First Avenger (2011)

In 1940, after footage of advanced Nazi weapons created by their scientific division, Hydra, was smuggled out of Germany, President Roosevelt authorized the secret creation of the Strategic Scientific Reserve under the gruff, no-nonsense U.S. Army Col. Chester Phillips' command. One of Phillips' first recruits, on Roosevelt's personal orders, was scientist Howard Stark. By 1942, SSR was running Project: Rebirth, a program to develop Super-Soldiers. Initially objecting when Dr. Abraham Erskine chose asthmatic, underweight Steve Rogers for the project's first test subject, Phillips conceded when Rogers threw himself on a dummy grenade to protect fellow soldiers while Phillips' preferred choice fled for cover with all the other candidates. Phillips attended Erskine and Stark's experiment in a secret SSR base in Brooklyn, unaware that a Hydra spy, Heinz Kruger, had infiltrated the assembled witnesses gathered for the occasion. When the experiment succeeded, Kruger assassinated Erskine, and the last serum sample was destroyed during his attempted escape. With Erskine dead and no sample of the serum remaining, Project: Rebirth stalled. After a talk with the President, the SSR and Phillips were tasked with defeating Hydra. Thinking him more of a showpiece than a soldier, Phillips rejected Rogers' request to be part of his force, relegating him to laboratory experimentations, but Rogers was instead recruited by Senator Brandt for propaganda purposes.

While pursuing Hydra in Italy, Phillips encountered Rogers again when his entertainment tour arrived to perform for troops. Learning that members of the 107th division had been slaughtered by Hydra, Rogers asked Phillips if longtime friend Sgt. James Barnes was among the casualties. Believing they'd lose more men than they'd save, Phillips denied Rogers' request to launch a rescue mission deep behind enemy lines. Going AWOL with Agent Peggy Carter and Howard Stark's aid, Rogers was believed killed in action. Phillips blamed Carter—until Rogers returned, accompanied by nearly 400 rescued prisoners and confiscated Hydra weaponry. Rogers surrendered for disciplinary action, but Phillips instead tasked him with taking down Hydra installations throughout Europe. When Rogers captured lead Hydra scientist Arnim Zola, Phillips questioned him, preying on Zola's fear of retribution from Hydra leader, the Red Skull, and learned the location of Hydra's primary base in the Alps. Phillips personally led the ground assault on the base while Rogers confronted the Skull. Leaving in an aircraft armed with weaponry powered by the cosmically-powered Tesseract, the Skull intended to destroy America's East Coast. Phillips confiscated the Skull's personal automobile, getting Rogers close enough to grab and enter the taxiing plane; Rogers ultimately sacrificed himself to prevent the Skull's plans. ⍟

IN THE COMICS

GEN. CHESTER PHILLIPS WAS AN Army liaison to Operation: Rebirth, the government project that created the Super-Soldier serum, and personally chose Steve Rogers to become Captain America. Besides assigning missions to Rogers, Phillips also oversaw such diverse projects as the creation of the robots Electro and Project: TESS, intending to use them to help control any future Super-Soldiers.

FIRST APPEARANCE:
CAPTAIN AMERICA COMICS #1 (1941)

FACT SHEET

- BEFORE ROGERS WAS CHOSEN, PHILLIPS' CHOICE FOR PROJECT: REBIRTH WAS PHYSICALLY CAPABLE BULLY PVT. GILMORE HODGE.
- AS PART OF HIS PSYCHOLOGICAL WARFARE WHILE INTERROGATING ARNIM ZOLA, PHILLIPS CASUALLY ENJOYED A STEAK DINNER IN FRONT OF THE HUNGRY VEGETARIAN PRISONER.

RED SKULL
JOHANN SCHMIDT

FIRST APPEARANCE:
Captain America: The First Avenger (2011)

A German scientist obsessed with Norse mythology and cosmic power, Johann Schmidt met Adolf Hitler in 1934. Hitler was intrigued by Schmidt, but Ernst Kaufmann, head of the Special Weapons Division of the Sturmabteilung (S.A.), warned Schmidt to stay away from the Fuehrer because Kaufmann did not want Hitler distracted by Schmidt's "fairy tales." Schutzstaffel (S.S.) head Heinrich Himmler saw Schmidt's potential and took him under his wing. Soon, Schmidt had risen high enough in the Nazi ranks to be allowed to kill Kaufmann himself during a Nazi purge and take over his weapons program. Schmidt was later promoted to head of Hydra, the Nazi deep-science division. In September 1935, he arrested Dr. Abraham Erskine, sending his wife and children to a concentration camp, to force Erskine to continue his research into biological human enhancement for Schmidt. Erskine's family soon died in a typhus outbreak at the camp, but Schmidt kept Erskine in the dark to maintain his hold over the scientist. When Erskine had believed he had perfected his experimental Super-Soldier serum in November 1940, Schmidt tested it on himself, believing only a superior man could claim the power of the gods. He was granted superhuman strength and endurance, but the formula enhanced the evil within Schmidt, leaving him with a drastically disfigured

physical form, his face transformed into a crimson death's-head. Schmidt concealed his monstrous features behind a realistic mask, but the grotesque scientist no longer fit Hitler's ideal of Aryan perfection. As a reward for his services, but to keep him isolated from the rest of the Nazi war effort, Schmidt—now known as the Red Skull—was given command of a fortress buried deep within the Alps. He soon indoctrinated Hydra's members into his beliefs, making Hydra both his personal army and a fanatical cult.

The Skull did not share Hitler's dreams of racial purity and nationalistic pride—he saw a world without flags, ruled by self-made supermen. To achieve that world, he sought out the power of the Norse gods, whom Schmidt believed to be not mythological, but advanced otherworldly beings. Seeking the Tesseract, a powerful Asgardian artifact, the Skull led Hydra into Norway. In March 1942, he finally found the Tesseract hidden in a church in Tønsberg; he stole it, then had Tønsberg razed. He handed the Tesseract over to his chief scientist, Dr. Arnim Zola, who used the artifact's energies to power an array of advanced weapons and vehicles. The Skull soon had factories across Europe producing Tesseract-powered war material. Eventually, the Skull's spies found Erskine, who had escaped custody, fled Germany, and joined the American war effort, in New York City. Schmidt dispatched an assassin, Heinz Kruger, to kill him. Kruger was successful, but not before Erskine's completed formula had successfully empowered one test subject: Steve Rogers.

Soon, the Skull's ambitions outpaced even Hitler's. His ultimate plan hinged on the *Valkyrie*, a massive bomber that would drop

The Skull did not share Hitler's dreams of racial purity and nationalistic pride—he saw a world without flags, ruled by self-made supermen.

IN THE COMICS

A SIMPLE BELLHOP, JOHANN SCHMIDT was chosen by Adolf Hitler himself to become his ultimate Nazi operative when the German leader saw the evil burning in Schmidt's eyes. Schmidt became the costumed Red Skull and waged a campaign of terror across Europe. He frequently clashed with his opposite number, the super-soldier Captain America (Steve Rogers). At war's end, the Skull was buried alive in a collapsing bunker but kept in suspended animation by an experimental gas. When he was discovered in the modern day, he resumed his war on freedom and his old nemesis, Captain America, who had survived the intervening decades frozen in ice. Just as he had during the war, the Skull met defeat repeatedly, even when he wielded the all-powerful Cosmic Cube.

Eventually, the Skull succumbed to old age and died, only for his loyal operative Arnim Zola to transfer his mind into a clone of Steve Rogers' youthful body. While battling the real Rogers, the Skull's poisons backfired and turned his new face into a literal red skull. Later assassinated by the Winter Soldier (James "Bucky" Barnes), the Skull's mind survived in oligarch Aleksander Lukin's body, thanks to the Cosmic Cube. He then orchestrated a complex plan to fake Captain America's assassination and usurp Cap's body. He ultimately failed, and the Skull's bodiless consciousness faded into oblivion. The Red Skull's evil would not remain dormant for long, however — a clone of the Skull, created during WWII, awoke and had the late telepath Professor Charles Xavier's brain grafted to his own, granting him psychic powers to wage a global war on mutants, whom the Skull saw as aberrations. The Skull's diabolical daughter, Sinthea "Sin" Schmidt, has also adopted the mantle of the Red Skull and bedeviled Captain America.

FIRST APPEARANCE:
CAPTAIN AMERICA COMICS #1 (1941)

huge Tesseract-powered bombs on major cities across the globe, leaving the Skull as master of the world that remained. As he pursued his mad dreams, the Skull neglected his stated mission of producing weapons for the Nazis. When the Germans learned of his incursion into Norway, they were furious. Hitler sent several S.S. officers to report back on his progress; the Skull dismissed their concerns, but when they saw that the Skull's targets included Berlin, he vaporized them with a Tesseract-powered cannon. In 1943, he was visiting one of Hydra's factories in Austria when it was raided by Rogers, now the costumed Super-Soldier Captain America. As Cap freed Hydra's prisoners and tore through the base, the Skull set it to self-destruct. While escaping, he briefly battled Captain America. To show Cap the price he had paid for his power, Schmidt tore off his mask, revealing his true form. Over the ensuing months, Captain America and his Howling Commandos ravaged Hydra during raids on its bases, enraging the Skull but never swaying him from his mission of conquest. In Denmark, Schmidt tried to unlock the mystical power of an Asgardian runestone, but destroyed it to escape Captain America.

RED SKULL'S COUPE

Before long, the Skull's Alps headquarters was Hydra's only remaining outpost. With the *Valkyrie* bomber nearly ready for launch, the Skull's men captured Captain America as he embarked on a daring raid on the base. The Skull had Cap brought to him, only to learn that Cap's capture was only the first stage of a full-scale assault on his mountain redoubt by the Strategic Scientific Reserve's troops and Cap's Howling Commandos teammates. The Howlers soon took the base, but the Skull escaped in the *Valkyrie* with the Tesseract, unaware Cap had stowed away in the landing gear. The two battled in the plane's cockpit as it streaked toward its first target: New York City. In the course of their battle, Cap damaged the Tesseract's containment unit. The Skull grabbed the Tesseract and tried to unleash its power, but was apparently destroyed by the cube's energies. Cap subsequently sacrificed himself to crash the plane before it could reach America.

RED SKULL'S MODIFIED LUGER

FACT SHEET

- MUCH LIKE HITLER, THE SKULL ENJOYED THE MUSIC OF RICHARD WAGNER.
- THE RED SKULL CARRIED A TESSERACT-POWERED LUGER P.08 AS HIS SIDEARM.
- THE SKULL DISMISSED HITLER'S OWN OCCULT RESEARCH AS "DIGGING FOR TRINKETS IN THE DESERT."
- THE SKULL WAS MERCILESS TO BOTH ALLIES AND ENEMIES, AND EXECUTED UNDERPERFORMING SUBORDINATES WITHOUT HESITATION.

HOWARD STARK
UPDATE

FIRST APPEARANCE: ***Iron Man (2008)*** **(PHOTO);** ***Iron Man 2 (2010)*** **(FULL APPEARANCE)**

Known as a ladies' man, Howard Stark was the inventor head of Stark Industries and a primary weapons contractor for the U.S. military. Following a 1940 presentation on the vibration-absorbing metal Vibranium, Stark was asked to join the secret Strategic Scientific Reserve by Col. Chester Phillips, who showed Stark footage of advanced weapons used by Nazi deep-science division Hydra in Guernica, Spain. Stark remained unsure until Hydra agents tried unsuccessfully to assassinate Phillips and him. Declaring the incident the most fun he'd had in months, Stark joined the SSR. Later that year, he helped British agent Peggy Carter extract Dr. Abraham Erskine from Germany. In 1943, after a partially successful demonstration of his Gravitic Reversion Technology automobile at the World Exposition of Tomorrow, Stark aided Dr. Erskine in attempting to create a Super-Soldier. After Pvt. Steve Rogers was injected with Erskine's Super-Soldier serum, Howard saturated him with vita-rays to stimulate muscle growth, briefly lowering the power when Rogers howled in pain, then continuing at Rogers' insistence. Moments after the successful experiment, a Hydra spy killed Erskine but Rogers ultimately prevented his escape. Stark examined the spy's escape vehicle, a mini-submarine, but despite his mechanical prowess and technical knowledge, was unable to determine how it worked and what powered it before he was sent to London on a SSR mission.

When Rogers—who had gained celebrity as Captain America—and Carter mounted a mission to rescue the captured 107th Infantry, Stark agreed to pilot a Stark plane into Austria. Stark followed Captain America's orders and turned the plane around when it came under fire and Cap jumped from the plane for his mission. Following Captain America's rescue of the 107th, Stark began experimenting with synthesizing a new element and designed combat gear for Captain America, including carbon polymer armor and various types of shields. Rogers chose Stark's prototype Vibranium shield and Howard agreed to modify the Captain America uniform per Rogers' specifications. Stark continued aiding Captain America's missions via radio and remained with the SSR while Captain America led a frontal assault on the base of the Hydra leader Red Skull. When the Red Skull was apparently killed trying to access the energy of the cosmically-powered Tesseract and Captain America sacrificed himself to crash the Skull's attack plane before it could reach America, Howard Stark led missions to find the plane's wreckage, but found only the Tesseract.

FACT SHEET

- THE SSR'S AGENT PEGGY CARTER CONSIDERED STARK THE BEST CIVILIAN PILOT SHE HAD EVER SEEN.
- DESPITE GOING AGAINST MILITARY ORDERS BY HELPING CAPTAIN AMERICA, HOWARD STARK WAS NOT PUNISHED BY COL. CHESTER PHILLIPS DUE TO HIS WEALTHY STATUS AS A WEAPONS CONTRACTOR.
- STARK LIKED "KEEPING THE BEST TOYS FOR HIMSELF," SECRETING BOTH A WET BAR AND MISSILE LAUNCHERS IN HIS CAR.

PRESENTING ROGERS WITH SHIELD PROTOTYPES

WORLD EXPOSITION OF TOMORROW

FIRST APPEARANCE: ***Captain America: The First Avenger [2011]***

A precursor to Howard Stark's Stark Expos, the 1943 World Exposition of Tomorrow took the place of the planned World's Fair (which was canceled because of World War II). A symbol of hope during wartime, the Exposition was an outlet for the greatest minds of the world—scientists, inventors and futurists—to give America a glimpse of its potential. Attendees of the fair were greeted by fireworks high above a grand statue of a globe, surrounded by flags of the world. A futuristic floating tram transported guests around the fairgrounds to the centrally located "Modern Marvels" exhibition.

Within the halls of the Modern Marvels attraction were stages for "The Engine of the Future," an exhibit that boasted a large and powerful engine about the size of a jet airliner's turbine; "The Earth's Treasures," that presented a cross-section of the Earth showing its core and the valuable assets under the ground; and "Smell-O-Vision," which, true to its namesake, presented a whole new audience experience wherein a third

A MODERN MARVEL: THE SYNTHETIC MAN

sense was added to movie viewing. Also touted was "The Synthetic Man," presented by Dr. Phineas Horton, in which what appeared to be a red jumpsuit-clad cybernetic humanoid was encased in a containment chamber adorned with high voltage electrodes.

The main attraction of the exhibit hall was a centrally located stage for Stark Industries which featured a cherry red 1941 Cadillac Series 62. Steve Rogers, James "Bucky" Barnes and their dates Bonnie and Connie watched as Howard Stark took the stage. Stark informed the audience that in just a few short years, automobiles would never have to touch the ground again, then proceeded to have his assistant Mandy lead the charge to remove the wheels of the automobile, revealing Stark Industries' Gravitic Reversion Technology hidden within the wheel wells. The audience was amazed as Stark rotated a knob and the Cadillac levitated a few feet before shorting out and crashing back to the stage below. With a knowing smirk Stark reminded the audience he did say the flying car was still a few years away.

At the conclusion of Stark's presentation, Rogers, Barnes and their dates exited to find a place to dance, but a recruitment booth on the fairgrounds caught the eye of the eager to enlist Rogers. Barnes was concerned for his friend's well-being in yet another application to serve his country and, as the two argued, their conversation was overheard by Dr. Abraham Erskine, who subsequently offered Rogers a once-in-a-lifetime opportunity to become a better man, ultimately leading to Rogers becoming Captain America.

STEVE ROGERS AT THE RECRUITMENT CENTER

FACT SHEET

- THE STARK EXPO THEME "MAKE WAY FOR TOMORROW TODAY" WAS PLAYED DURING HOWARD STARK'S CENTER STAGE PRESENTATION.
- THE 1942 WORLD EXPOSITION OF TOMORROW WAS HIGHLY ADVERTISED, INCLUDING ADS IN NEW YORK NEWSPAPERS FEATURING THE GLOBE STATUE AND FIREWORKS DISPLAY.

ARNIM ZOLA

FIRST APPEARANCE:
Captain America: The First Avenger [2011]

Third Reich scientist Dr. Arnim Zola was working on exoskeletons at the Sturmabteilung (S.A.) Weapons Testing Ground in Kummersdorf, Germany when Johann Schmidt and the Schutzstaffel (S.S.) violently took over operations in July 1934. Zola avoided execution by agreeing to continue his work under Schmidt's command in the Nazi deep-science division, Hydra. After Dr. Abraham Erskine's prototype Super-Soldier serum mutated Schmidt into the hideous Red Skull in November 1940, Zola became Schmidt's second-in-command, providing the Skull with a technological response to the Super-Soldier program.

To power all the advanced weaponry he had designed for Hydra, Zola successfully collected some of the vast energies of the Tesseract, an alien artifact acquired by the Red Skull in March 1942. When the Red Skull turned his back on the Third Reich, Zola remained loyal out of self-preservation and used captured Allied soldiers as a workforce at Hydra's Krausberg, Austria, facility, which Captain America infiltrated in November 1943. Freeing the soldiers, Captain America led an attack on Hydra, forcing the Red Skull to abandon and self-destruct the base. Over the next number of months, Captain America and the Howling Commandos continued their attacks on Hydra bases. The Red Skull put Zola in charge of stopping them, but he repeatedly failed. After losing another outpost in the Danish Straits in April 1944, Zola set a trap for Captain America on a train near the Danube River that apparently cost the life of Cap's longtime friend James "Bucky" Barnes but also led to Zola's capture.

Brought to the Allies' Strategic Scientific Reserve headquarters for interrogation, Zola—unwilling to commit suicide like other Hydra agents and fearing for his life—cooperated and revealed the location of Hydra's last remaining base in the Alps. Zola's information enabled Captain America and the SSR to stop the Red Skull's plot for world domination.

IN THE COMICS

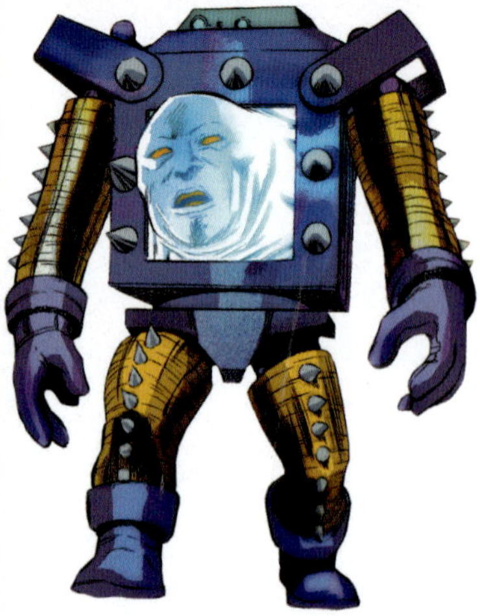

SWISS GENETICIST ARNIM ZOLA worked for the Nazis throughout World War II and ensured his own survival after the war by transferring his consciousness between different robotic bodies. Allied with the likes of the Red Skull (Johann Schmidt) up to the modern era, Zola—A.K.A. the Bio-Fanatic—became the creator of countless genetic monstrosities. He eventually became ruler of Dimension Z, where he created a mutate army to invade Earth. Zola's own children—Jet Black and Ian, the latter of whom was raised by Captain America (Steve Rogers) in Dimension Z—ultimately aided Earth's heroes to thwart his invasion plans. Escaping to Dimension Z, Zola surprisingly convinced Jet to return with him.

FIRST APPEARANCE:
CAPTAIN AMERICA #208 (1977)

FACT SHEET

- ARNIM ZOLA IS A NATIVE OF SWITZERLAND.
- HIS WILLINGNESS TO SWITCH LOYALTIES AS NEEDED AND GENERAL COWARDICE SAVED HIS LIFE ON NUMEROUS OCCASIONS.
- ZOLA WORKED ON AN ADVANCED EXOSKELETON, WHOSE BLUEPRINTS HE REGULARLY KEPT WITH HIM.
- HE IS A VEGETARIAN.

SENATOR BRANDT

FIRST APPEARANCE:
Captain America: The First Avenger [2011]

A patron of Project: Rebirth, U.S. Senator Brandt attended Dr. Abraham Erskine's transformation of Steve Rogers into a Super-Soldier at a secret lab in Brooklyn. Witnessing Heinz Kruger's assassination of Erskine, Brandt admired Rogers' heroic efforts in preventing the Hydra spy from escaping. When U.S. Army Col. Chester Phillips denied Rogers active service as Project: Rebirth's lone success, Brandt encouraged Rogers to serve his country in another way, dressing him in a U.S. flag-inspired costume and taking him on a national stage-show tour to promote war bonds, each appearance boosting sales. Eventually Rogers became disillusioned with his role and instead pushed his way into frontline combat. Keen for the public spotlight, Brandt later headed an award ceremony for Captain America, but the hero was too busy fighting the war to attend.

FACT SHEET

- BRANDT SERVED ON A NUMBER OF POLITICAL MILITARY COMMITTEES AND WIELDED CONSIDERABLE POLITICAL INFLUENCE.
- BRANDT UNWITTINGLY ACCOMPANIED THE UNDERCOVER HYDRA AGENT TO ERSKINE'S LAB.

IN THE COMICS

SENATOR BRANDT HAS NO DIRECT comic counterpart, but his role is similar to Emil Gruber, a civilian who was the U.S. Army's Director of Information in 1941. Immediately after Steve Rogers became Captain America, Gruber used him as propaganda to marshal local support with bond rallies, radio shows and media displays, garbed in a signature patriotic costume.

FIRST APPEARANCE:
ADVENTURES OF CAPTAIN AMERICA #1 (1991)

SERGEANT DUFFY

FIRST APPEARANCE:
Captain America: The First Avenger [2011]

Duffy, a U.S. Army drill sergeant, had 17 years' experience training new recruits at Camp Lehigh when his latest commander, Col. Chester Phillips, assigned him to instruct a special group of candidates for the Strategic Scientific Reserve's Super-Soldier program. While training the group, Sgt. Duffy was especially aggressive toward the frail Steve Rogers, but was dumbfounded when Rogers successfully won a capture the flag exercise by dismantling the flagpole rather than trying to climb it, like the other recruits. No other soldier had completed the task during Duffy's tenure. When Col. Phillips threw a dummy grenade at the candidates as a test in courage, Sgt. Duffy and the other soldiers ran for cover while Rogers was the only one who tried to smother the grenade with his own body.

FACT SHEET

- CAMP LEHIGH WAS ESTABLISHED IN 1914.
- CAMP LEHIGH'S MOTTO WAS NULLI SECUNDUS, LATIN FOR "SECOND TO NONE."

IN THE COMICS

SGT. MIKE DUFFY WAS A U.S. ARMY drill sergeant at Camp Lehigh. Often bullheaded and temperamental, he was unaware that Pvt. Steve Rogers and "camp mascot" James Barnes were actually government agents Captain America and Bucky. When he became aggravated with the pair, Sgt. Duffy would often assign them menial tasks, such as peeling potatoes. Sgt. Duffy was attracted to FBI agent Betty Ross, unaware she had affections for Steve Rogers. Duffy died holding the rank of sergeant, and is buried at Arlington National Cemetery.

FIRST APPEARANCE:
CAPTAIN AMERICA COMICS #1 (1941)

NICK FURY UPDATE

FIRST APPEARANCE: *Iron Man [2008]*

When Steve Rogers was found frozen but alive in the Arctic, Nick Fury made arrangements to ease the revived Captain America into modern society. S.H.I.E.L.D. prepared an elaborate hospital set inside its New York City facility, complete with 1940s technology, a fake New York City skyline outside the windows and a baseball game from May 1941 playing on the radio. When Captain America awoke, he was greeted by a S.H.I.E.L.D. agent posing as a nurse, but he immediately saw through the ruse. Believing he was being held by enemy forces, he swiftly broke free, but was shocked when he emerged into current-day Times Square.

S.H.I.E.L.D. cars quickly surrounded the confused hero, but Fury ordered his men to stand down and apologized for the deception, explaining to Captain America he hoped to break the news slowly. When Rogers demanded to know what the news was, Fury told him he had been asleep for almost seven decades.

After giving Rogers a place to live and time to acclimate to his new life, Fury approached him during a workout. Rogers asked whether Fury had a mission for him to get him back to work; Fury said he did—and that the mission was to save the world. ⍟

FACT SHEET

- FURY'S VINTAGE PHILLIES VS. DODGERS RADIO BROADCAST FAILED TO DECEIVE ROGERS BECAUSE HE RECOGNIZED IT—HE HAD ATTENDED THE BASEBALL GAME AT EBBETS FIELD IN 1941.
- WHEN CAPTAIN AMERICA BROKE FREE FROM THE S.H.I.E.L.D. FACILITY, CODE 13 WAS SOUNDED AS AN ALARM.
- WHEN FURY TOLD CAPTAIN AMERICA HOW LONG HE HAD BEEN IN SUSPENDED ANIMATION, ROGERS LAMENTED THAT HE WAS LATE FOR A DATE.

HEINZ KRUGER

FIRST APPEARANCE:
Captain America: The First Avenger [2011]

The Red Skull, leader of Nazi sub-group Hydra, sent Heinz Kruger to steal the Super-Soldier serum from the United States' Strategic Scientific Reserve and assassinate head scientist Dr. Abraham Erskine. Using the identity of State Department employee Fred Clemson, Kruger infiltrated the SSR's experiment and witnessed the successful transformation of Steve Rogers into the first Super-Soldier. Kruger blew up the observation room as a distraction, enabling him to steal the last vial of the serum and fatally shoot Erskine. Despite being shot in the arm by Agent Peggy Carter, Kruger fled with the serum, leaving behind a trail of death on his way to his escape car. Forced to steal a taxi when Carter shot his driver, he was pursued to the harbor by Steve Rogers, who caught up to the agent just after Kruger reached his hidden mini-submarine and reported his mission's success. Rogers dove into the water and pulled him out the vessel; during their subsequent struggle back on land, the serum was destroyed. Kruger avoided interrogation by committing suicide via a cyanide capsule hidden in a tooth. ⍟

FACT SHEET

- KRUGER SWORE LOYALTY TO HYDRA EVEN AS HE DIED.
- KRUGER WAS ARMED WITH A WALTHER P38 PISTOL.

IN THE COMICS

NAZI SPY HEINZ KRUGER INFILTRATED Operation: Rebirth to assassinate chief scientist Dr. Abraham Erskine. Future test subject Steve Rogers thwarted an attempt by Kruger to steal part of the Super-Soldier formula. At the experiment that transformed Rogers into the first Super-Soldier, Kruger fatally shot Erskine, then was electrocuted when he accidentally touched some loose wires.

FIRST APPEARANCE:
CAPTAIN AMERICA COMICS #1 (1941)

TESSERACT

FIRST APPEARANCE: *Thor [2011]*

A crystalline cube containing seemingly unending energy, the Tesseract was allegedly once the jewel of Asgardian ruler Odin's treasure room. Myths claimed it was concealed beneath the Earth by the gods for a superior man to find. It was hidden in a church in the Norwegian town of Tønsberg until Hydra leader the Red Skull forcibly acquired it in March 1942. Hydra's top scientist Arnim Zola collected some of the cube's vast energy to power his advanced weapons designs. When Captain America led a raid on Hydra's Alpine base, the Skull fled in a jet with the Tesseract, but Captain America boarded the vehicle. Fighting above the Atlantic, the Skull snatched the Tesseract with his bare hands, and its energies seemingly destroyed him. Burning its way through the cabin floor, the cube fell into the ocean, where it was later retrieved by Howard Stark. In modern times, S.H.I.E.L.D.'s Director Nick Fury asked astrophysicist Dr. Erik Selvig to examine it as a potential unlimited power source. ⍟

FACT SHEET

- THE TESSERACT'S GUARDIANS USED A POWERLESS DUPLICATE HIDDEN IN A CHURCH SEPULCHER AS A DECOY. THE REAL TESSERACT WAS CONCEALED IN A BAS-RELIEF OF THE ASGARDIAN WORLD TREE, YGGDRASIL.
- ANCIENT ARTWORK DEPICTED THE TESSERACT BEING WIELDED BY VIKING WARRIORS, SLAYING SERPENTINE MONSTERS WITH BEAMS OF ENERGY EMANATING FROM THE DEVICE.

IN THE COMICS

THE COSMIC CUBE IS AN ARTIFICIAL matrix created by A.I.M. (Advanced Idea Mechanics), containing reality-warping energies originating from the mysterious Beyonders race. The Cube's many users included the Red Skull (Johann Schmidt), but it later evolved into the humanoid Kubik. Other alien Cubes pre-dated it, and subsequent man-made ones have been created since, some more successful than others.

FIRST APPEARANCE:
TALES OF SUSPENSE #79 (1966)

YGGDRASIL

FIRST APPEARANCE: *Thor [2011]*

Yggdrasil, the "World Tree," is the Asgardian name for a branching cosmic network connecting Asgard to other worlds of the "Nine Realms," which include Midgard (Earth's realm) and the realm of giants, Jotunheim, along with Alfheim, Vanaheim, Niflheim, Nornheim and others. Knowledge of Yggdrasil brought by Asgardians visiting Earth in times past influenced Norse mythology and is conceptualized as a large tree.

The Tesseract, an immensely powerful energy source left behind on Earth by Odin, was hidden in a church in Tønsberg, Norway, behind a large engraving of Yggdrasil, before the cube was stolen by the Red Skull. ⍟

FACT SHEET

- AMONG NAMES GIVEN TO YGGDRASIL ARE "TREE OF THE WORLD," "GUARDIAN OF WISDOM" AND "GUARDIAN OF FATE."
- WHEN THE ASGARDIAN THOR WAS SENT TO EARTH AS PUNISHMENT FOR DISOBEYING HIS FATHER AND KING, ODIN, THOR DREW A SKETCH OF YGGDRASIL IN A NOTEPAD AS HE EXPLAINED THE CONCEPT OF THE LINKED NINE REALMS TO HUMAN JANE FOSTER.
- ACCORDING TO THOR, HUMANS HAVE SEEN PORTIONS OF YGGDRASIL VIA THE HUBBLE TELESCOPE, BUT FAIL TO UNDERSTAND WHAT THEY'VE SEEN.

IN THE COMICS

YGGDRASIL, THE WORLD TREE, is a massive ash tree in the center of the Asgardian dimension with roots that reach out into each of the Ten Realms. Numerous creatures from Norse myth have their homes in or otherwise use the World Tree, including the dragon Nidhogg who feeds on its roots, the eagle Lerad, who guards its fruits, and the squirrel Ratatoskr, who couriers messages between the dragon and eagle.

FIRST APPEARANCE:
JOURNEY INTO MYSTERY #97 (1963)

MARVEL'S THE AVENGERS

GUIDEBOOK TO THE MARVEL CINEMATIC UNIVERSE

MARVEL

THE AVENGERS

MARVEL STUDIOS PRESENTS IN ASSOCIATION WITH PARAMOUNT PICTURES A MARVEL STUDIOS PRODUCTION A JOSS WHEDON FILM ROBERT DOWNEY JR. "MARVEL'S THE AVENGERS" CHRIS EVANS MARK RUFFALO CHRIS HEMSWORTH SCARLETT JOHANSSON JEREMY RENNER TOM HIDDLESTON CLARK GREGG COBIE SMULDERS WITH STELLAN SKARSGÅRD AND SAMUEL L. JACKSON AS NICK FURY MUSIC BY ALAN SILVESTRI MUSIC SUPERVISOR DAVE JORDAN VISUAL EFFECTS SUPERVISOR JANEK SIRRS VISUAL EFFECTS AND ANIMATION BY INDUSTRIAL LIGHT & MAGIC COSTUME DESIGNER ALEXANDRA BYRNE EDITORS JEFFREY FORD, A.C.E. LISA LASSEK PRODUCTION DESIGNER JAMES CHINLUND DIRECTOR OF PHOTOGRAPHY SEAMUS MCGARVEY, ASC, BSC EXECUTIVE PRODUCERS ALAN FINE JON FAVREAU STAN LEE EXECUTIVE PRODUCERS LOUIS D'ESPOSITO PATRICIA WHITCHER VICTORIA ALONSO JEREMY LATCHAM PRODUCED BY KEVIN FEIGE STORY BY ZAK PENN AND JOSS WHEDON SCREENPLAY BY JOSS WHEDON DIRECTED BY JOSS WHEDON MARVEL

Collecting information from *Marvel's The Avengers (2012)*, *Marvel's The Avengers #1-2 (2014)*, *Marvel's The Avengers: Black Widow Strikes #1-3 (2012)*, and *Marvel's The Avengers Prelude: Fury's Big Week #1-4 (2012)*.

HEAD WRITER/COORDINATOR: **MIKE O'SULLIVAN**

COORDINATION: **DARON JENSEN**

WRITERS: **AL AVISON**, **TROY BENJAMIN**, **CHRIS BUCHNER**, **ANTHONY COTILLETTA**, **PATRICK DUKE**, **MIKE FICHERA**, **DARON JENSEN**, **ROB LONDON**, **CHRIS MCCARVER**, **MARKUS RAYMOND**, AND **JACOB ROUGEMONT**

ARTISTS: **ARTHUR ADAMS**, **RICK BURCHETT**, **OLIVIER COIPEL**, **GABRIELE DELL'OTTO**, **BEN EDELBERG**, **DAVID FINCH**, **JOSH HERMAN**, **BRYAN HITCH**, **AMANDA HUNTER**, **JACK KIRBY**, **LEONARD KIRK**, **ED MCGUINNESS**, **COLIN MCNEIL**, **RYAN MEINERDING**, **PAUL NEARY**, **JOHN ROMITA SR.**, **JOE SIMON**, **GREGORY SMITH**, **JOHN STANISCI**, AND **JIM STERANKO**

COVER ARTIST: **MIKE DEL MUNDO**

SPECIAL THANKS TO DAVE ALTHOFF, SHAWN "KEEBLER" BYERS, JEFF CHRISTIANSEN, MATT DELMANOWSKI, ERIKA DENTON, TIM DILLON, PERCIVAL LANUZA, JACQUE PORTE, AND RYAN POTTER.

THE AVENGERS CREATED BY STAN LEE AND JACK KIRBY

AVENGERS

FIRST APPEARANCE:

***Iron Man* [2008]** [CONCEPT]; ***Marvel's The Avengers* [2012]** [ACTUAL]

The Avengers were originally conceptualized as the world peacekeeping agency S.H.I.E.L.D.'s Avengers Initiative, but the overseeing World Security Council shut the program down before it could be realized. Later, a number of the Initiative's potential candidates were gathered together when the Asgardian trickster Loki stole the extremely powerful Tesseract from S.H.I.E.L.D. Once gathered on S.H.I.E.L.D.'s Helicarrier base, these candidates—the armored genius Iron Man; World War II Super-Soldier Captain America; scientist Bruce Banner, who could become the monstrous Hulk; the Asgardian thunder god Thor; and super-spy S.H.I.E.L.D. Agent Natasha Romanoff (Black Widow)—were unknowingly influenced by Loki's mind-controlling scepter into mistrusting and arguing with one another. However, when Loki's troops and the mind-controlled S.H.I.E.L.D. Agent Clint "Hawkeye" Barton attacked the Helicarrier, Loki's hopes that the Hulk would destroy his potential enemies were derailed when the heroes instead focused on battling the attackers. When S.H.I.E.L.D. Agent Phil Coulson was killed by Loki, the heroes were left demoralized, but S.H.I.E.L.D. Director Nick Fury used Coulson's death to manipulate them into unifying to defeat Loki.

In New York City, Loki directed the mind-controlled Dr. Erik Selvig to set up Tesseract-powered equipment to open a portal in space, allowing biomechanical Chitauri aliens to invade and begin mass destruction. The former Initiative candidates and the freed Hawkeye, now calling themselves the Avengers, arrived and began battling the invaders. The powerful Chitauri brought with them an army of flying Leviathan monsters; needing tactical leadership, the team immediately deferred to Captain America. Under Cap's orders, the group quickly became a unified fighting unit.

Despite the Avengers' increasing success in one-on-one battles, Black Widow realized that the fight could not end until the portal was closed, so she commandeered an enemy vessel and returned to Selvig's machinery. Simultaneously, the Council

BLACK WIDOW, CAPTAIN AMERICA, HAWKEYE, HULK, IRON MAN, THOR Active: *Marvel's The Avengers (2012)*

ordered a nuclear strike against Manhattan, despite Fury's protests, and the Hulk gave Loki a severe beating, leaving the Asgardian incapacitated. Dr. Selvig revealed to Widow that he had programed a safeguard into the equipment: Loki's scepter could destroy the machinery. When Fury warned Iron Man that the nuclear missile was en route, Iron Man steered it through the portal and redirected it into the massive Chitauri mothership in deep space, destroying it and deactivating the Chitauri forces on Earth. Widow destroyed Selvig's equipment, closing the portal just as Iron Man returned through it.

As he regained his senses, Loki was confronted by the assembled Avengers and promptly surrendered. Afterward, at Iron Man's suggestion, the team took a well-deserved break at a local eatery where, quiet and exhausted, they ate shawarma. Earth's newscasts widely reported the events in New York City, making the Avengers a household name.

Some time later, Thor used the Tesseract's power to take it and Loki back to Asgard, and the teammates went their separate ways. While being debriefed by the Council, Fury confidently stated that all worlds now knew that the Earth was protected by a higher power, and later claimed the team would reassemble whenever they were needed.

FACT SHEET

- S.H.I.E.L.D. DIRECTOR NICK FURY ASSEMBLED THE AVENGERS INITIATIVE CANDIDATES WITHOUT THE COUNCIL'S KNOWLEDGE OR APPROVAL BECAUSE THE COUNCIL DEEMED THE PROGRAM TOO VOLATILE A CONCEPT.
- THE TEAM WAS FIRST IDENTIFIED BY NAME WHEN TONY STARK THREATENED LOKI PRIOR TO THE CHITAURI INVASION. STARK ALSO REFERRED TO THE GROUP AS "EARTH'S MIGHTIEST HEROES."
- FOLLOWING THE ATTACK ON NEW YORK, THE WORLD EXPRESSED ITS GRATITUDE TO THE AVENGERS IN A NUMBER OF WAYS—INCLUDING GRAFFITI MURALS, AND HAIRCUTS AND BEARDS MIMICKING TONY STARK'S. ONE WOMAN, IDENTIFIED AS BETH, GAVE A SIMPLE BUT PLAINTIVE THANK YOU DURING A TV INTERVIEW AFTER BEING SAVED BY CAPTAIN AMERICA.

FIRST ROSTER

IN THE COMICS

THE ORIGINAL AVENGERS WERE INITIALLY gathered when Asgardian trickster Loki tried to manipulate a battle between his hated adoptive brother Thor Odinson and the Hulk (Bruce Banner). Iron Man (Tony Stark), the Wasp (Janet Van Dyne), and Ant-Man (Hank Pym) were also drawn into the conflict, but quickly joined forces to defeat Loki, then stayed together as the Avengers. Soon after forming, the team discovered World War II hero Captain America (Steve Rogers) in suspended animation and recruited him as a retroactive founding member and team leader. Over the years, the team has welcomed over 200 superhumans in their ranks. Through victories and tragedies, deaths and triumphs, the Avengers remained the Earth's mightiest heroes and protectors, assembling whenever humankind was in danger.

FIRST APPEARANCE: *AVENGERS #1 (1963)*

BLACK WIDOW
UPDATE

FIRST APPEARANCE: *Iron Man 2 [2010]*

Following her mission to evaluate Tony Stark (Iron Man) for the Avengers Initiative, the highly trained combatant, gymnast, and S.H.I.E.L.D. Agent Natasha Romanoff, a.k.a. Black Widow, was tasked to surveil fugitive physicist Bruce Banner, who could transform into the super-strong Hulk when in an emotional state. During her surveillance, she captured Banner's erstwhile colleague Samuel Sterns for S.H.I.E.L.D. study after his own gamma radiation-induced mutation. Widow's next mission, to shadow Russian arms dealer Mikhail Fjodorov, was complicated by Ten Rings assassin Sofia, a twisted admirer of the Widow's Russian espionage career. Widow pursued Sofia across Russia and stopped the Rings' plan to launch a replica Stark Industries' Jericho missile at a Korean demilitarized zone.

When the Asgardian Loki stole the Tesseract power source from S.H.I.E.L.D., Agent Phil Coulson called in Agent Romanoff to assist in the search. She was reluctant to abort her ongoing mission to interrogate arms dealer Georgi Luchkov, having allowed herself to be captured in order to reach Luchkov, but she changed her mind

and quickly subdued her captors when Coulson mentioned that her longtime colleague Agent Clint "Hawkeye" Barton had been mind-controlled by Loki. She located gamma-radiation expert Bruce Banner in Kolkata, India, and enlisted his aid in the search despite her fear of his gamma-powered Hulk alter ego. After transporting Banner to a S.H.I.E.L.D. Helicarrier, Romanoff and World War II hero Captain America flew to Stuttgart, Germany, to capture Loki; they succeeded with Iron Man's aid.

Agent Romanoff interviewed Loki aboard the Helicarrier and tricked him into revealing he had manipulated events to amass his potential enemies aboard the Helicarrier, where he intended to force Banner into a Hulk transformation and eliminate the heroes and S.H.I.E.L.D. by proxy. When the Loki-controlled Hawkeye disabled the Helicarrier with an exploding arrow, he triggered Banner's transformation; Romanoff barely escaped the rampaging Hulk. Despite being shaken by the encounter with the Hulk, Romanoff broke Loki's control with a blow to Hawkeye's head while the two friends battled.

Upon the arrival of Loki's extraterrestrial Chitauri invasion force in New York City, Romanoff, alongside Hawkeye and Captain America, journeyed there to battle the invaders and were joined by the Asgardian thunder god Thor (Loki's adoptive brother), the Hulk, and Iron Man. During the ensuing hostilities, Black Widow commandeered a Chitauri aircraft and flew to the device atop Stark Tower, where Loki was generating the deep-space portal for the Chitauri invasion. Using Loki's scepter, which doubled as the device's failsafe, Widow force-closed the portal after Iron Man steered an inbound nuclear missile into it, devastating the Chitauri armada and ending the invasion. Following Loki's capture, the six heroes enjoyed a shawarma meal before watching Thor return to Asgard with the captive Loki.

IN THE COMICS

BLACK WIDOW (NATASHA Romanoff) initially worked with the Avengers as an unofficial ally after Hawkeye (Clint Barton) helped her overcome KGB brainwashing, but only officially joined the team for short stints. She led the team during one such tenure, but when her team seemingly died in battle with the psionic entity Onslaught, she regretted taking leadership. Even after her team was found to have survived, Widow was reluctant to rejoin the team. Eventually, she served again with both the team's primary roster and their covert-ops teams.

FIRST ACTIVE WITH THE AVENGERS:
AVENGERS #111 (1973)

FACT SHEET

- BLACK WIDOW WAS BORN IN STALINGRAD (NOW VOLGOGRAD).
- WIDOW REFERS TO HER PAST AMORAL ACTIVITIES AS A RUSSIAN AGENT AS HAVING "RED IN HER LEDGER."
- HAWKEYE DEFIED ORDERS TO KILL BLACK WIDOW AND INSTEAD RECRUITED HER INTO S.H.I.E.L.D.
- ONE OF BLACK WIDOW'S INTERROGATION TECHNIQUES IS FEIGNING SUBMISSIVENESS TO INSTILL OVERCONFIDENCE IN A SUBJECT SO THAT THEY INADVERTENTLY VOLUNTEER INFORMATION.
- BLACK WIDOW LIKENED THE AVENGERS' BATTLE WITH THE CHITAURI TO A MISSION SHE AND HAWKEYE WORKED IN BUDAPEST, HUNGARY; HAWKEYE DISAGREED WITH HER ANALOGY, OBSERVING THAT THEY REMEMBERED EVENTS VERY DIFFERENTLY.
- BLACK WIDOW'S "WIDOW'S BITE" BRACELETS DELIVER POWERFUL ELECTRICAL SHOCKS TO OPPONENTS.

CAPTAIN AMERICA UPDATE

FIRST APPEARANCE:
Captain America: The First Avenger [2011]

When he woke from suspended animation, Steve Rogers quickly became disillusioned with the modern world he had sacrificed himself to save. However, he still went into action when S.H.I.E.L.D. Director Nick Fury approached him with a mission to recover the Tesseract, the artifact that had powered the war machines of Cap's archenemy, the Red Skull, during World War II, from the Asgardian trickster Loki. Cap was briefed by S.H.I.E.L.D. Agent Phil Coulson—who idolized Captain America, even asking Rogers to sign a set of vintage Captain America trading cards—and met Agent Natasha Romanoff and Bruce Banner, fellow candidates for S.H.I.E.L.D.'s Avengers Initiative. When Loki was spotted in Stuttgart, Germany, Cap fought him there, but was outmatched by the trickster. Before the fight could swing in Loki's favor, however, Iron Man intervened. Loki surrendered, but as he was being transported back to S.H.I.E.L.D., Loki's adoptive brother Thor took him from the S.H.I.E.L.D. transport to confront him for his actions and force him to face Asgardian justice. Iron Man and Thor came to blows over possession of Loki, but Cap defused the situation by blocking a strike from Thor's hammer with his shield, causing a massive shockwave that shocked the men out of their anger.

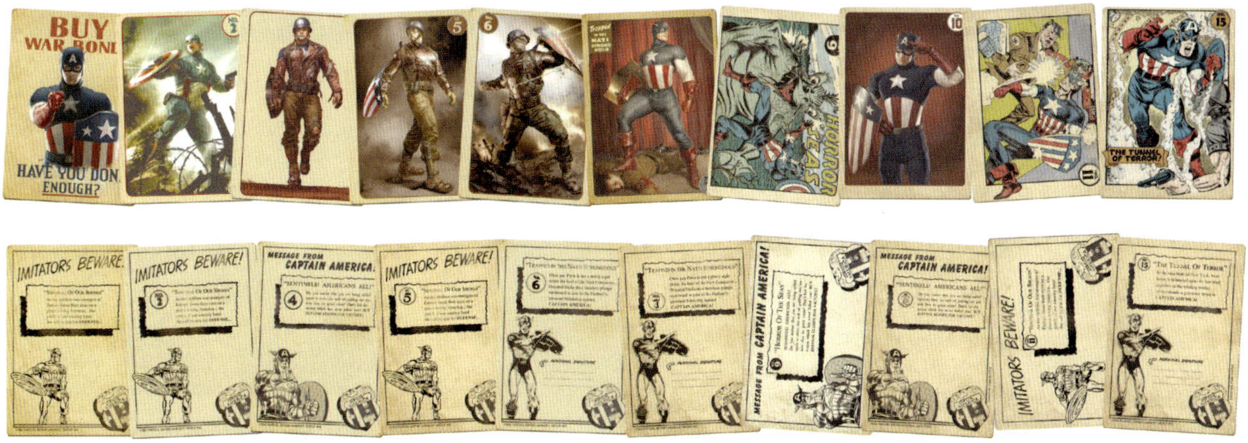

CAPTAIN AMERICA TRADING CARDS

With Loki finally in custody, Captain America clashed with the glib Stark, who found Cap to be comically old-fashioned. However, Stark voiced salient suspicions about S.H.I.E.L.D.'s true intentions for the Tesseract, prompting Rogers to privately investigate. He found a cache of Hydra weapons on the Helicarrier—part of S.H.I.E.L.D.'s plan to weaponize the Tesseract, as the Red Skull had decades before. Influenced by the mind-altering properties of Loki's scepter, the assembled group descended into infighting over Cap's discovery, but were interrupted when Loki's allies launched an attack on the Helicarrier. The initial assault damaged one of the Helicarrier's engines, threatening to crash the airship; Cap and Iron Man teamed up to restart the damaged engine, keeping the massive craft in the air. In the confusion, however, Loki escaped, killing Coulson in the process. Fury used Coulson's blood-stained trading cards to prompt Cap and the others to battle Loki and his allies.

When they arrived in New York City, Cap and his teammates found that Loki had used the Tesseract to open a portal to deep outer space, enabling an invading force of biomechanical Chitauri soldiers to attack the city. Cap quickly assumed the tactical leadership role, directing his teammates in handling the alien menace and emergency responders in protecting civilians. Cap also leapt into the fray himself, single-handedly saving a building full of hostages from a Chitauri grenade. Eventually, Iron Man hijacked a nuclear missile and directed it through the portal, destroying the Chitauri mothership and disabling the aliens on Earth—but leaving himself little time to escape back through the portal. Cap reluctantly ordered the portal closed; luckily, Iron Man fell through the portal at the last moment. After Thor took a captive Loki back to Asgard, Cap and the other victorious Avengers went their separate ways.

FACT SHEET

- CAP BET NICK FURY 10 DOLLARS THE S.H.I.E.L.D. DIRECTOR COULDN'T SURPRISE HIM WITH ANYTHING HE SHOWED HIM; AFTER SEEING THE MASSIVE HELICARRIER RISE INTO THE AIR, CAP SILENTLY GAVE FURY THE MONEY.
- S.H.I.E.L.D. PROVIDED CAP WITH A MODERNIZED VERSION OF HIS OLD UNIFORM; CAP SUPER-FAN AGENT PHIL COULSON HELPED WITH THE REDESIGN.
- WHEN THOR'S HAMMER MJOLNIR STRUCK CAP'S VIBRANIUM SHIELD, IT CAUSED A MASSIVE, TREE-FELLING SHOCKWAVE. CAP, HOWEVER, REMAINED UNHARMED.

IN THE COMICS

CAPTAIN AMERICA'S FROZEN form was discovered by the Avengers in one of their earliest adventures; once revived, he became a member of the team. Before long, the team's founding members retired from active duty, leaving Cap in charge of a team composed of himself and three reformed super villains—Hawkeye (Clint Barton), the Scarlet Witch (Wanda Maximoff), and Quicksilver (Pietro Maximoff). Over the years, Cap has been a steady presence on the team, his teammates even giving him retroactive founder status. Even now, with his superhuman abilities nullified, his true age restored, and his Captain America mantle passed to his former partner Sam Wilson (Falcon), Rogers leads the Avengers Unity Squad.

FIRST ACTIVE WITH THE AVENGERS:
AVENGERS #4 (1964)

CHITAURI

FIRST APPEARANCE: ***Marvel's The Avengers (2012)***

The Chitauri, an alien race of biomechanical warriors, were serving the mysterious alien Thanos when the vastly powerful Tesseract energy cube surfaced on Earth. Seeking this power, Thanos loaned control of a Chitauri army to the Asgardian Loki. In exchange, Loki stole the Tesseract from Project PEGASUS at the Joint Dark Energy Mission facility. Using mind control, he forced astrophysicist Dr. Erik Selvig to build a Tesseract harness device to generate a stable portal to Earth for a Chitauri invasion. Selvig activated the device on the top of New York City's Stark Tower, utilizing its Repulsor Tech Reactor to kick-start the Tesseract and open the portal above the city. Journeying through it, the Chitauri wreaked havoc, but found more opposition than expected in the form of the superhuman Avengers. When the World Security Council ordered a nuclear strike on Manhattan to contain the invasion, Iron Man co-opted the missile and steered it through the portal to Chitauri space where he directed it to destroy the Chitauri mothership, disabling the aliens on Earth. The Avenger Black Widow used Loki's scepter to destroy the Tesseract harness device and close the portal. Cut off from their collective, the Chitauri's invasion forces on Earth apparently died.

FACT SHEET

- THE CHITAURI ARE A TECHNOLOGICALLY ADVANCED EXTRATERRESTRIAL RACE UTILIZING ENERGY WEAPONS AND A HIVE-LIKE CONNECTION VIA THEIR MASSIVE MOTHERSHIP.
- THE CHITAURI USED THE GIANT ARMORED FLYING CREATURES KNOWN AS LEVIATHANS AS GROUND TROOP TRANSPORT. UNTIL DEPLOYMENT, SOLDIERS RESIDED INSIDE SCALES ALONG A LEVIATHAN'S ARMOR.
- THE CHITAURI'S FLYING CHARIOTS HAD A PILOT FUSED TO THE FRONT AND TWO GUNNERS IN THE BACK.

IN THE COMICS

IN THE ULTIMATE UNIVERSE, the shape-shifting Chitauri (translated as "Annakui" or "Skrull") were at war with the alien Kree. The Chitauri conquered worlds across the universe through infiltration and subterfuge. Aiding in the rise of Adolf Hitler and the Nazi Party, they almost conquered Earth during World War II, but seemingly perished at the end of the war following nuclear strikes on their Japanese bases. They rebuilt their ranks after the war and resumed the quiet infiltration of humanity. On the brink of losing the war against the Kree, the Chitauri fleet retreated to Earth and openly revealed themselves, thwarting their Earth agents' plans. Earth's military forces, S.H.I.E.L.D., and the Ultimates team destroyed the Chitauri fleet and ended the Chitauri invasion. Later, a truce between the Chitauri and Kree was formed to deal with the combined threat of the Gah Lak Tus swarm and the Marvel Universe's displaced world-devouring Galactus.

FIRST APPEARANCE:
THE ULTIMATES #8 (2002)

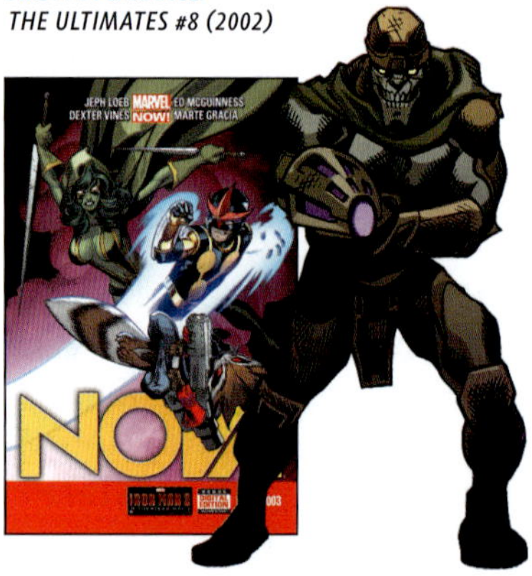

IN THE MARVEL UNIVERSE, the alien Chitauri constructed an Ultimate Nullifier, but were stopped from using it to destroy Earth by Nova (Sam Alexander). The Chitauri then vowed to leave Earth alone after Nova defeated the Chitauri warlord Warbringer. Some Chitauri served the living planet Kindun in a struggle against the nihilistic Thanos and the Guardian of the Galaxy Gamora.

FIRST APPEARANCE:
NOVA #3 (2013)

PHIL COULSON
UPDATE

FIRST APPEARANCE: ***Iron Man [2008]***

Following the Asgardian conflict in New Mexico, Agent Phil Coulson supervised S.H.I.E.L.D.'s recovery of the lethal Asgardian Destroyer weapon and its subsequent dismantling and re-engineering into a human-scale gun. As Agent Black Widow's handler, he assisted her infiltration of a massive Ten Rings arms operation. Later, when S.H.I.E.L.D.'s search to find the lost World War II hero Captain America proved fruitful, an elated Coulson kept tabs on the Captain's acclimation to modern times. Director Nick Fury assigned Coulson to the top-secret Project PEGASUS, part of a joint venture between S.H.I.E.L.D. and NASA billed as a "Joint Dark Energy Mission." The project was centered around the Tesseract artifact, an immense energy source. When the Tesseract activated itself during S.H.I.E.L.D.'s tests, Coulson assisted in the evacuation of personnel; during the confusion, the Asgardian Loki stole the Tesseract. When Loki's use of the Tesseract destroyed the base, Coulson barely escaped. Fury radioed to Coulson and Deputy Director Maria Hill that the Tesseract was out in the open, and they were at war.

Coulson tasked Black Widow with recruiting Dr. Bruce Banner to search for the Tesseract by tracking its gamma radiation output, then approached genius Tony Stark to also assist. After Fury recruited Captain America, Coulson transported Rogers to the Helicarrier and did his best to contain his excitement while briefing Rogers on Bruce Banner's Hulk alter ego, which was the result of an attempt to replicate the Super-Soldier formula that had empowered Cap. Coulson worked with Banner to locate the Tesseract by using spectrometers. Meanwhile, S.H.I.E.L.D. tracked Loki to Stuttgart, Germany, where the Asgardian was captured and imprisoned aboard the Helicarrier.

Loki's presence distracted the gathered heroes long enough for a brainwashed Hawkeye and a team of mercenaries to ambush the Helicarrier. Coulson grabbed the Destroyer gun and confronted Loki, who used illusions to distract Coulson long enough for the real Loki to stab Coulson through the chest with his scepter. Coulson crumpled to the ground, but managed to shoot Loki with the Destroyer gun, seeing the modified weapon's effects for the first time. Fury was with Coulson as he died, and passed on his last words expressing hope that his death would inspire the assembled remarkable individuals to form the Avengers.

DESTROYER GUN

FACT SHEET

- WHEN STARK TRIED TO IGNORE COULSON'S CALLS, THE AGENT OVERWROTE THE JARVIS A.I.'S PROGRAMMING AND HACKED STARK'S PERSONAL ELEVATOR TO GAIN THE INDUSTRIALIST'S ATTENTION.
- WHEN PEPPER POTTS ASKED COULSON ABOUT THE CELLIST HE HAD BEEN SEEING, COULSON TOLD HER SHE HAD RELOCATED TO PORTLAND. STARK OFFERED COULSON HIS JET TO VISIT HER AND "KEEP LOVE ALIVE."
- COULSON CONTRIBUTED TO THE REDESIGN OF CAPTAIN AMERICA'S UPDATED SUIT. HE ALSO HAD A NEAR-MINT SET OF CAPTAIN AMERICA VINTAGE TRADING CARDS THAT HE WANTED THE HERO TO SIGN.
- THE DESTROYER GUN'S STORAGE LOCKER REQUIRED A RETINAL SCAN FROM COULSON TO ACCESS IT.

NICK FURY UPDATE

FIRST APPEARANCE: ***Iron Man (2008)***

S.H.I.E.L.D. Director Nick Fury's hunt for the lost World War II legend Captain America was deemed a waste of resources by the World Security Council. The W.S.C. subsequently halted the search, including efforts to monitor the activities of Iron Man (Tony Stark) and track the gamma-irradiated Bruce Banner, and redistributed S.H.I.E.L.D.'s budget to the Tesseract research at Project PEGASUS. Knowing that centralizing S.H.I.E.L.D.'s focus would leave the spy organization vulnerable, Fury continued his projects in secret from the W.S.C.

Learning the miniature Repulsor Technology Arc Reactor in Stark's chest was killing him, Fury tried to contact the W.S.C., but they were preoccupied helping Gen. "Thunderbolt" Ross capture Banner and refused to answer. Over the following week, Fury supplied Stark with a S.H.I.E.L.D.-derived compound to slow the mini-reactor's poisoning, and reassigned Agent Phil Coulson from surveillance on Stark to an investigation of atmospheric disturbances in New Mexico. As Iron Man battled Whiplash at the Stark Expo, Fury ordered Agent Natasha Romanoff (Black Widow) to mine the databases of Stark Industries' rival Hammer Industries for anything worth taking, and then burn the rest. Fury then sent Romanoff to keep an eye on Banner at Culver University. After offering Stark a position as a S.H.I.E.L.D. consultant, Fury ordered Coulson to confiscate the defeated Asgardian Destroyer construct and learned that Gen. Ross had been working with the W.S.C. as their "sword" in conjunction with Fury's "shield." At the W.S.C.'s insistence, Fury changed S.H.I.E.L.D.'s focus from extraterrestrial enemies to defense and implemented the W.S.C.'s Phase 2 project: creating an arsenal powered by the extremely powerful Tesseract energy cube. Following Gen. Ross's botched attempt to capture Banner, Fury oversaw S.H.I.E.L.D.'s cleanup of Harlem. At the end of the week, he proposed a new S.H.I.E.L.D. budget to the W.S.C., revealing that because he ignored their order to stop his projects, S.H.I.E.L.D. now had several promising leads in Tesseract research. The W.S.C. approved Fury's expanded budget, but later shut down the Avengers Initiative, deeming it too unpredictable.

The W.S.C. approved Fury's expanded budget, but later shut down the Avengers Initiative, deeming it too unpredictable.

RETRIEVING TESSERACT

Over the following year, Fury recruited Dr. Erik Selvig to research the Tesseract and the Destroyer while S.H.I.E.L.D. researched Banner's erstwhile associate, the captured gamma-mutated Sam Sterns. S.H.I.E.L.D. found Captain America in the Arctic, verifying he was still alive but in a form of suspended animation. Simultaneously, unaware Selvig was under the Asgardian Loki's mental influence, Fury nonetheless felt the doctor was starting to act strangely and assigned Agent Clint "Hawkeye" Barton to keep an eye on Selvig at Project PEGASUS. Later, when Captain America was revived, Fury helped him acclimate to the modern day.

When the Tesseract activated itself, Fury attempted to destroy the Project PEGASUS facility to prevent the Tesseract from falling into enemy control. Using his scepter, Loki took complete mental control of Hawkeye and Selvig, and escaped with the Tesseract. Fury ordered agents Romanoff and Coulson to bring in Banner and Stark to find the Tesseract, and told the W.S.C. they needed to form a response team. Approaching Captain America during a workout, Fury told him they needed to retrieve the Tesseract to save the world.

Spearheading the Tesseract search from the S.H.I.E.L.D. Helicarrier, Fury sent Captain America and Black Widow after Loki when the Asgardian was spotted in Stuttgart, Germany. When Loki was captured, Fury caged him in a cell intended for the Hulk and threatened to kill him if he attempted escape. Suspecting Loki had intended to be in S.H.I.E.L.D. custody, Fury had Black Widow interrogate the Asgardian—during which time Captain America, Stark, and Banner confronted Fury over S.H.I.E.L.D.'s Hydra-based Phase 2 program. Too late, Black Widow learned Loki planned to provoke the Hulk to destroy the S.H.I.E.L.D. Helicarrier and the assembled taskforce. As Loki's scepter influenced the heroes to bicker among themselves, Hawkeye and a team of mercenaries attacked the Helicarrier. Fury and S.H.I.E.L.D. fought off Loki's henchmen during the ensuing siege, but Loki escaped, the heroes were scattered, and Coulson was killed. Afterward, Fury claimed that while S.H.I.E.L.D. was building weapons using the Tesseract, it was a last resort against superhuman powers. Fury instead hoped to form a team of extraordinary individuals that could handle the threats S.H.I.E.L.D. couldn't—but though Coulson died still believing in that idea, Fury now realized the group's

differing personalities wouldn't allow that to happen; he shrugged it off as an old-fashioned notion. S.H.I.E.L.D. Deputy Director Maria Hill later confronted Fury over using Coulson's death to manipulate the heroes, but Fury pointed out the group needed an extra push to form the Avengers.

When Loki used the Tesseract to open a portal over New York City for the alien Chitauri army to attack Earth, the W.S.C. ordered a nuclear strike to stop the invasion, planning to sacrifice one city to save the world. When Fury refused to follow the order, the W.S.C. stripped him of his S.H.I.E.L.D. command. Fury shot down one missile-carrying jet, but another made it past him and fired its missile. After Fury warned him of the impending strike, Iron Man forced the missile through the Tesseract's portal and destroyed the Chitauri mothership, disabling the Chitauri on Earth. Fury was relieved when Iron Man's plan worked, saving New York and the Avengers.

As New York started to recover from the alien invasion, Fury informed the W.S.C. that Loki and the Tesseract had both been handed over to Asgardian custody. The W.S.C. argued that Loki was a war criminal and should remain on Earth to be punished; Fury pointed out that Loki would be answering to Asgardian law for his crimes. The W.S.C. then expressed concern over the viability of the Avengers, considering them dangerous. Fury agreed—but countered that not just the world, but every world would recognize their might. With the Avengers, Earth would be protected—just not under S.H.I.E.L.D.'s direct control. When Hill later asked Fury how S.H.I.E.L.D. would contact the Avengers if they were needed, Fury said he had faith they would assemble when the need arose.

FACT SHEET

- THE W.S.C. PUT FURY ON DISCIPLINARY NOTICE TO ENSURE HE WOULD FOCUS ON TESSERACT RESEARCH.
- DURING THE SIEGE ON THE HELICARRIER, FURY ORDERED THE AGENTS TO FLY THE SHIP OVER WATER IN CASE IT CRASHED; WHEN THE NAVIGATION SYSTEMS FAILED, ONE AGENT CLAIMED HE COULD NOT FIND SOUTH, THE DIRECTION OF THE NEAREST LARGE BODY OF WATER. AN AGGRAVATED FURY POINTED OUT THAT SOUTH COULD EASILY BE FOUND USING THE SUN FOR NAVIGATION.
- FURY REFERRED TO COULSON AS HIS "ONE GOOD EYE."
- FURY WAS ARMED WITH A SMITH & WESSON M&P PISTOL AND WIELDED AN AIRTRONIC RPG-7 40MM ROCKET LAUNCHER AGAINST A S.H.I.E.L.D. LOCKHEED MARTIN F-35 JET FIGHTER.

HAWKEYE UPDATE

FIRST APPEARANCE: ***Thor* (2011)**

Following his assignment to help guard the Asgardian weapon Mjolnir in New Mexico, S.H.I.E.L.D. Agent Clint "Hawkeye" Barton was then assigned to Project PEGASUS to head the security detail guarding the Tesseract, a massive energy source used by Hydra terrorists to power weapons during World War II. Hawkeye summoned Director Nick Fury once the facility's researchers noticed unusual activity within the Tesseract. The rogue Asgardian Loki then appeared through a Tesseract-powered portal and killed or magically enthralled most of those present, including Hawkeye. Hawkeye shot Fury and led the others in helping Loki escape with the Tesseract. The mind-controlled Hawkeye set up a safehouse for Loki and recruited a number of mercenaries while Loki brought an alien Chitauri invasion force within striking distance of Earth using the Tesseract. Hawkeye led an insertion team to Stuttgart, Germany, where they stole a cache of iridium, an element needed to stabilize the Tesseract's energies. Loki allowed himself to be captured and taken aboard the Helicarrier, where he hoped to provoke the super-strong Hulk into destroying S.H.I.E.L.D. and its assembled allies. At the designated time, Hawkeye, using his customized arrows, and the mercenaries sabotaged the Helicarrier and freed Loki. Amidst the ensuing chaos, Hawkeye encountered and fought his longtime comrade Black Widow, but she gained the upper hand and, by striking Hawkeye's head against a steel pipe, broke Loki's sway over him before knocking him out.

Hawkeye took a rooftop position, where he acted as both sniper and lookout for the rest of the team.

After the Helicarrier was stabilized, Black Widow comforted Hawkeye over his ordeal and the deaths he had caused while under Loki's control. Collectively mourning the death of S.H.I.E.L.D. Agent

QUIVER ARROWHEAD ROTATOR

Phil Coulson, killed by Loki, the group began calling themselves the Avengers. Once Widow vouched that he was free of Loki's control, Captain America recruited Hawkeye to pilot a S.H.I.E.L.D. Quinjet to take him and Black Widow after Loki. Upon their arrival in New York City, Loki opened a massive portal over Stark Tower, letting loose an army of Chitauri soldiers and war machines. Hawkeye, Captain America, and Black Widow battled the hordes and protected the city's civilians alongside armored technologist Iron Man, Loki's heroic adoptive brother Thor, and the Hulk. At Captain America's direction, Hawkeye took a rooftop position, where he acted as both sniper and lookout for the rest of the team. During the battle, Hawkeye shot Loki's chariot with an explosive arrow, sending the Asgardian flying into Stark Tower where he was brutally pummeled by the Hulk. After the Chitauri were defeated and Loki captured, Hawkeye enjoyed a meal of shawarma with his teammates before watching Thor transport himself and the captive Loki to Asgard.

IN THE COMICS

HAWKEYE (CLINT BARTON) WAS originally recruited into the Avengers as part of a replacement roster for the team's founders, serving as a quarter of the "Kooky Quartet" alongside Captain America (Steve Rogers), Quicksilver (Pietro Maximoff), and Scarlet Witch (Wanda Maximoff). Hawkeye's cocky attitude initially caused great discord with his teammates, but his manner softened over time and he grew to become a mainstay of the team. Later, Hawkeye co-founded the Avengers' West Coast branch alongside his then-wife Mockingbird (Bobbi Morse) and led that team. Hawkeye also acted as mentor and leader to the Great Lakes Avengers and the Thunderbolts, and served in multiple incarnations of the Avengers and Secret Avengers.

FIRST ACTIVE WITH THE AVENGERS:
AVENGERS #16 (1965)

FACT SHEET

- BARTON USED A COLLAPSIBLE HOYT BUFFALO RECURVE BOW EQUIPPED WITH A LASER SIGHT AND CONTROLS FOR MECHANISMS IN HIS ARROW QUIVER THAT COULD AFFIX A VARIETY OF "TRICK" HEADS TO HIS ARROWS. THE ARROWHEADS INCLUDED IMPACT-TRIGGERED AND TIMED EXPLOSIVES, RAPPELLING LINES, AND AN ELECTRONIC JAMMING DEVICE.
- BARTON ALSO WIELDED A HECKLER & KOCH P30 HANDGUN AND A BUSSE COMBAT KNIFE.
- BLACK WIDOW AND HAWKEYE FORMED STRIKE TEAM: DELTA DURING A COVERT OPERATION IN ABIDJAN.

HELICARRIER 64

FIRST APPEARANCE:
Marvel's The Avengers (2012)

Helicarrier 64 is a large flight-capable vessel used by S.H.I.E.L.D. as a mobile headquarters and aircraft launch platform. Designed in both appearance and function as an aircraft carrier, the Helicarrier is capable of oceanic travel or sustained flight using a quartet of large turbines that can hold the ship aloft at 30,000 feet. The Helicarrier is equipped with holographic stealth technology that renders the ship's ventral bulkheads invisible while airborne. When deployed on water, the turbines are fully submerged, making the vessel appear as a conventional aircraft carrier.

Helicarrier 64 was used as a base of operations for many of S.H.I.E.L.D.'s endeavors, including Black Widow's missions in Russia, which Agent Phil Coulson directed from the ship. When the Asgardian Loki stole the Tesseract power source from S.H.I.E.L.D.'s Project PEGASUS research facility, Director Nick Fury coordinated the search for it from Helicarrier 64. To aid in the hunt, Fury recruited a response team consisting of Black Widow, former Strategic Scientific Reserve agent Captain America, and physicist Bruce Banner.

When Captain America, Black Widow, and Iron Man captured Loki, the Asgardian was placed in a prison cell designed to hold the Hulk, Banner's monstrous alter ego. A team led by mind-controlled S.H.I.E.L.D. Agent Clint "Hawkeye" Barton sabotaged the Helicarrier with explosives, disabling one of the turbines and provoking Banner to transform and rampage through the ship. Though Captain America and Iron Man were able to repair the engine, Loki escaped.

When Loki's extraterrestrial Chitauri army invaded New York City through a portal created with the Tesseract, the World Security Council ordered a S.H.I.E.L.D. pilot to launch from the Helicarrier and fire a nuclear missile at the city without Fury's authorization; Iron Man saved the city by steering the missile into the portal, destroying the Chitauri mothership and ending the invasion.

IN THE COMICS

THE S.H.I.E.L.D. HELICARRIER WAS designed as a self-sufficient airborne mobile headquarters by geniuses Iron Man (Tony Stark), Mr. Fantastic (Reed Richards), and mutant technologist Forge as part of a political compromise that no single nation would house the agency. S.H.I.E.L.D. typically fields a single primary Helicarrier, which has been destroyed and rebuilt several times, and a fleet of smaller Helicarriers for specialized units. Helicarriers have been used by other organizations, including Norman Osborn's corrupt enforcement agency H.A.M.M.E.R., the Howling Commandos private military corporation, and the Russian government.

FIRST APPEARANCE:
STRANGE TALES #135 (1965)

FACT SHEET

- THE PRISON CELL IN WHICH LOKI WAS CONFINED WAS EQUIPPED WITH A HATCH UNDERNEATH THAT WOULD DROP THE CELL, AND ANY OCCUPANT, THROUGH THE BOTTOM OF THE SHIP. THE CELL WAS ORIGINALLY DESIGNED TO CONTAIN THE HULK.
- HELICARRIER 64'S COMPLEMENT OF AIRCRAFT INCLUDED S.H.I.E.L.D. QUINJETS AND LOCKHEED-MARTIN F-35 FIGHTER JETS.
- A HIDDEN VAULT CONTAINED TESSERACT-POWERED DIRECTED-ENERGY WEAPONS USED BY HYDRA IN WORLD WAR II.

MARIA HILL

FIRST APPEARANCE:
Marvel's The Avengers [2012]

Deputy Director of S.H.I.E.L.D. Maria Hill accompanied Director Nick Fury to S.H.I.E.L.D.'s Project PEGASUS facility to investigate an energy surge issuing from the Tesseract, an alien artifact being studied there. The Tesseract unexpectedly opened a portal, bringing the Asgardian trickster Loki to Earth. Loki summarily mind-controlled several S.H.I.E.L.D. personnel and fled with the Tesseract—leaving behind a rift in space-time that threatened to consume the base. Hill chased the fleeing Loki in a jeep, but the rift collapsed, destroying the facility and trapping her in the rubble. Later, she manned the S.H.I.E.L.D. Helicarrier's bridge when Loki's henchmen attacked it to free their captive leader; she personally helped drive off a squad of mercenaries, but was injured by a grenade. When the stress of the attack prompted consultant Bruce Banner to transform into the monstrous Hulk, Hill coordinated an aerial attack that lured the rampaging creature off the Helicarrier. Loki escaped, however, and a number of S.H.I.E.L.D. agents were killed, including Phil Coulson. Fury used Coulson's blood-stained Captain America trading cards to motivate the Avengers to unite, but Hill privately noted that the cards had been in Coulson's locker at the time of his death.

After Loki used the Tesseract to open a portal in space to bring an alien Chitauri army to New York City, the World Security Council governing S.H.I.E.L.D. authorized a nuclear strike from the Helicarrier—even though the Avengers were dealing with the threat. Hill and Fury tried unsuccessfully to stop the launch, leaving Iron Man to hijack the missile and use it to defeat the Chitauri massing on the other side of the portal. After the victorious Avengers went their separate ways, Fury assured Hill that the heroes would reunite when they were needed again.

IN THE COMICS

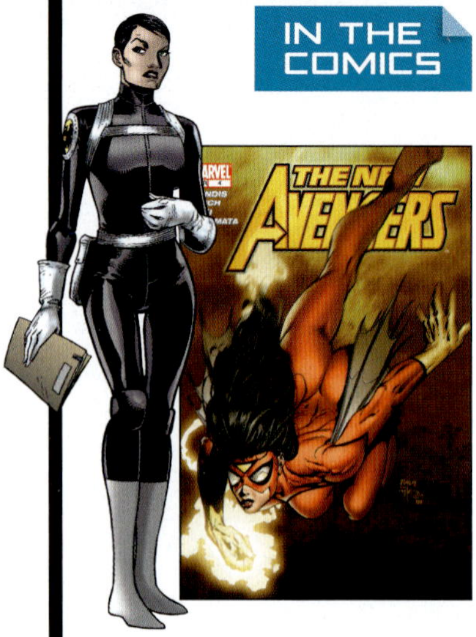

FOLLOWING SUCCESSFUL S.H.I.E.L.D. operations in crime-ridden Madripoor, Agent Maria Hill was assigned to command the organization after the previous director, World War II hero Nick Fury, waged a disastrous secret war against Latveria and went into hiding. Despite often working with Earth's super-powered heroes, Hill never overcame her suspicion of the superhuman community. Later, Tony Stark was promoted to direct S.H.I.E.L.D., leaving Hill as deputy director. However, S.H.I.E.L.D. had been thoroughly infiltrated by shape-shifting alien Skrulls; in the wake of that catastrophe, the organization was dissolved and replaced by Norman Osborn's H.A.M.M.E.R. Operating for a time as a fugitive, Hill was eventually reinstated as director of a reconstituted S.H.I.E.L.D. after Osborn's corrupt ways were revealed. For a time, Hill served as a leadership advisor for an Avengers squad.

FIRST APPEARANCE:
NEW AVENGERS #4 (2005)

FACT SHEET

- A SKILLED MARKSWOMAN, HILL CARRIED A GLOCK 19 PISTOL AS HER SIDEARM.
- HILL COMMANDED THE BRIDGE OF THE S.H.I.E.L.D. HELICARRIER.

HULK UPDATE

FIRST APPEARANCE: ***The Incredible Hulk (2008)***

Posing as a medical doctor in Kolkata, India, fugitive scientist Dr. Bruce Banner had gone over a year without transforming into his monstrous alter ego, the Hulk. S.H.I.E.L.D. dispatched Agent Natasha Romanoff to recruit Banner to track the low-level gamma-radiation signature emitted by the potentially world-killing Tesseract, which the Asgardian Loki had stolen. Trusting Agent Romanoff's word he wouldn't be imprisoned, Banner agreed to accompany her. Banner was uncomfortable with the massive military presence aboard S.H.I.E.L.D.'s Helicarrier, but agreed to help once Director Nick Fury said he could leave when the Tesseract was found. Learning Loki planned to use the Chitauri to invade Earth, Banner deduced the Tesseract was needed to open a portal for the extraterrestrial army.

Bonding through their passion for science, Banner and Tony Stark worked together to track the Tesseract.

Bonding through their passion for science, Banner and Tony Stark worked together to track the Tesseract using the Helicarrier's lab. Banner was impressed with Stark's portable technology. Stark, meanwhile, invited Banner to explore the stress-free environment of Stark Tower's Research and Development Department—then shocked him with a miniature electrical prod to evoke an angry reaction. Stark was amazed at Banner's control over his stress-induced transformations. Banner later surmised that both Loki and Fury had hidden agendas: Loki was targeting Stark Tower's self-sustaining power source, and Fury should have partnered with Stark earlier if S.H.I.E.L.D. truly intended to use the Tesseract as a clean energy source for mankind as Fury previously alleged. Although Banner insisted he was content to watch events unfold from the sidelines, Stark speculated Banner would

FACT SHEET

- BANNER REFERRED TO THE HULK AS THE "OTHER GUY."
- BANNER LEARNED FROM AGENT ROMANOFF THAT S.H.I.E.L.D. CONSTANTLY MONITORED HIS LOCATION, BUT MAINTAINED ITS DISTANCE—AND EVEN KEPT OTHER "INTERESTED PARTIES" AWAY BECAUSE DIRECTOR NICK FURY TRUSTED HIM.
- TONY STARK CLAIMED TO BE A HUGE FAN OF BANNER'S TRANSFORMATIONS INTO AN "ENORMOUS GREEN RAGE MONSTER."
- DEPRESSED AND DESPERATE TO END HIS TORMENT, BANNER ONCE ATTEMPTED SUICIDE BY SHOOTING HIMSELF IN THE MOUTH. THE HULK SPAT OUT THE BULLET. BECAUSE OF THIS, BANNER THEN FOCUSED ON HELPING OTHERS INSTEAD.
- BANNER STATED THE KEY TO CONTROLLING HIS TRANSFORMATIONS WAS TO ALWAYS REMAIN ANGRY.

TRANSFORMING INTO THE HULK

take part in the impending confrontation.

Discovering S.H.I.E.L.D. was developing Tesseract-powered weapons to battle prospective otherworldly and super-powered threats, Banner expressed his opinion that the superhumans assembled on the Helicarrier promoted chaos rather than teamwork. When Loki's mind-controlled human forces attempted to free him, Banner lost control and transformed. But before he destroyed the Helicarrier while battling the Asgardian Thor, the Hulk was lured outside by a S.H.I.E.L.D. fighter jet that attacked him; he wrecked the jet and plummeted to Earth. Instead of fleeing, Banner later reunited in Manhattan with the superhumans from the Helicarrier. As the Hulk, he helped defeat Loki and the Chitauri invasion. Subsequently, Banner left with Stark as the rest of the heroes went their separate ways.

IN THE COMICS

DUPED BY ASGARDIAN TRICKSTER god Loki into destroying a train trestle, the Hulk (Bruce Banner) was subsequently blamed and hunted. When the Hulk's teenage friend, Rick Jones, attempted to find aid for the fugitive Hulk, his radio transmission was heard by Iron Man (Tony Stark), Thor Odinson, Ant-Man (Hank Pym), and the Wasp (Janet Van Dyne). The heroes briefly battled the Hulk, eventually exposing and defeating Loki. The Hulk then helped them form the Avengers. Soon after, the extraterrestrial shape-shifting Space Phantom impersonated the Hulk and turned the Avengers against him. Although the Space Phantom's ruse was uncovered, the Hulk quit, feeling his teammates distrusted him. Since then, the Hulk has both allied with and fought against different Avengers incarnations; in modern times, the Hulk was convinced to rejoin the group to save Earth from cosmic threats such as the death-worshiping Thanos and a multiversal collapse.

FIRST ACTIVE WITH THE AVENGERS:
AVENGERS #1 (1963)

IRON MAN UPDATE

FIRST APPEARANCE: ***Iron Man (2008)***

Following Ivan Vanko's assault on the Stark Expo, Tony Stark (Iron Man) turned his attention to building New York City's Stark Tower, an Arc Reactor-powered skyscraper developed by his paramour Virginia "Pepper" Potts. As Stark and Potts celebrated the opening, S.H.I.E.L.D. Agent Phil Coulson arrived to seek Stark's aid recovering the Tesseract, an energy source stolen from S.H.I.E.L.D. by the Asgardian Loki.

Donning his Mark VI Iron Man armor, Stark flew to Stuttgart, Germany, and helped S.H.I.E.L.D. operatives Black Widow and Captain America capture Loki. En route to S.H.I.E.L.D.'s Helicarrier, Loki's adoptive brother Thor boarded their Quinjet and forcibly removed Loki. Stark pursued and came to blows with Thor, but Captain America's intervention ended the battle. Thor agreed to bring Loki back to S.H.I.E.L.D.

Aboard the Helicarrier, Stark aided physicist Bruce Banner in searching for the Tesseract, but not before planting a device that would allow him to hack S.H.I.E.L.D.'s computers. Stark and Banner learned of S.H.I.E.L.D.'s development of Tesseract-powered weapons, triggering an argument with Black Widow, Captain America, and S.H.I.E.L.D. Director Nick Fury that was intensified by Loki's mind-controlling scepter. When Loki's forces sabotaged one of the Helicarrier's engines, the group stopped arguing immediately. Iron Man repaired the turbine with Cap's aid, but escaping the restarted engine damaged his armor. Though the Helicarrier was stabilized, Loki killed Coulson and escaped.

IN THE COMICS

IRON MAN WAS ONE OF THE founding Avengers, as well as the team's financial benefactor for many years via the charitable Maria Stark Foundation. Stark's steadfast tenure with the team is only marred by a temporary descent into alcoholism, manipulation by the time-conqueror Kang, and public support of the since-repealed Superhuman Registration Act, which temporarily divided the Avengers.

FIRST ACTIVE WITH THE AVENGERS:
AVENGERS #1 (1963)

FACT SHEET

- NOT WANTING TO BE DISTURBED, STARK TRIED TO DODGE COULSON'S INCOMING PHONE CALL BY CLAIMING TO BE A LIFE MODEL DECOY.
- ON THE HELICARRIER'S BRIDGE, STARK CALLED OUT A CREWMAN FOR PLAYING THE ARCADE GAME GALAGA.
- STARK PROFESSED TO BE AN ADMIRER OF BANNER'S WORK, PARTICULARLY HIS RESEARCH INTO ANTI-ELECTRON COLLISIONS.
- STARK LIKENED BANNER'S TRANSFORMATIONS INTO THE HULK TO THE IMPLANTATION OF HIS R.T. REACTOR, A LIABILITY HE LEARNED TO MASTER AS AN ASSET.
- LOKI'S SCEPTER WAS UNABLE TO TAKE CONTROL OF STARK DUE TO THE R.T. MINI-REACTOR IMPLANTED IN HIS CHEST.
- THE MARK VI ARMOR WAS ABLE TO ABSORB LIGHTNING FROM THOR'S HAMMER MJOLNIR, OVERCHARGING THE SUIT'S POWER SUPPLY TO 400 PERCENT.
- THE MARK VII COULD BE COLLAPSED INTO A COMPACT POD AND WAS CAPABLE OF SELF-SUSTAINED FLIGHT IN THIS FORM. ONBOARD SENSORS TRACKED A PAIR OF METALLIC BRACELETS WORN BY STARK THAT ALLOWED THE SUIT TO FORM ONTO HIM.

Haunted by Coulson's death, Stark surmised Loki would seek a grandiose triumph; he immediately realized Stark Tower was the location from which Loki intended to bring forth a Chitauri invasion force with a Tesseract-powered portal. Along with Hawkeye—S.H.I.E.L.D. agent Clint Barton who was now freed from Loki's mind control—Iron Man, Captain America, and Black Widow flew to Stark Tower to confront Loki. After having his A.I. JARVIS rapidly ready his replacement Mark VII armor, Stark and Loki traded barbs in his penthouse before Loki hurled him out a window. The Mark VII flew to Stark and formed onto him in freefall; he then repulsor-blasted Loki in Coulson's name.

Loki's portal opened, allowing the Chitauri army to attack the city. Iron Man battled the invaders alongside Captain America, Hawkeye, Black Widow, Thor, and Banner (as his monstrous alter ego, the Hulk). Learning the World Security Council had launched a nuclear missile toward New York to sacrifice the city to destroy the Chitauri, Iron Man steered the missile into the portal, destroying the Chitauri mothership. Doing so depleted his power reserves and life support, however, causing him to fall unconscious through the portal toward Earth. The Hulk caught him before impact, and the assembled heroes recaptured Loki; the Chitauri on Earth were disabled by their mothership's destruction. After a meal of shawarma with his colleagues—dubbed "the Avengers" by Stark and the world at large—Stark watched Thor return to Asgard with Loki, drove Banner to parts unknown, and then met with Potts to begin redesigning Stark Tower into Avengers Tower.

LOKI UPDATE

FIRST APPEARANCE:
Thor (2011)

Left adrift in space after battling his adoptive brother Thor, Loki was discovered by the alien Other and his enigmatic master Thanos. They armed the Asgardian trickster with a powerful scepter, gave him command of an army of biomechanical Chitauri, and tasked him with a mission he was eager to accomplish: the conquest of Earth. Thanos sought the massively powerful Tesseract, which had come into S.H.I.E.L.D.'s possession. Loki swayed the actions of scientist Dr. Erik Selvig, who was studying the extraterrestrial artifact, to give Loki access to S.H.I.E.L.D.'s Project PEGASUS. Loki used his scepter to control the minds of Selvig and S.H.I.E.L.D. Agent Clint "Hawkeye" Barton, and escaped the facility with them and the Tesseract in tow. Loki intended to use the Tesseract to create a portal large enough to bring the full Chitauri force to Earth, but required specific materials to build a device to harness its energies. In Stuttgart, Germany, he attacked Dr. Heinrich Schäfer at a museum gala to gain access to his institution's iridium supply. Demonstrating his power, he then ordered the assembled crowd to kneel before him. A lone, elderly man refused. As Loki prepared to make an example of him, Captain America arrived on the scene. Unable to contend with both Captain America and the late-arriving Iron Man, Loki surrendered.

Learning of Loki's activities, Thor returned to Earth to retrieve his wayward adopted brother, abducting him from Iron Man and Captain America's Quinjet. Loki watched as Thor and Iron Man brawled over his custody, but Captain America soon defused the conflict. They then imprisoned Loki aboard a S.H.I.E.L.D. Helicarrier in a cell intended to contain the monstrous, gamma-powered Hulk. Meanwhile, the Hulk's human alter ego, Bruce Banner, had been brought aboard himself to help search for the Tesseract along with Tony Stark—genius/billionaire/playboy/philanthropist (a.k.a. Iron Man). Much to Loki's amusement, Hawkeye's colleague Black Widow came to him in an apparent attempt to bargain for her friend's life—a ploy to lead Loki to reveal his plan to

IN S.H.I.E.L.D. CAPTIVITY

unleash the Hulk within the Helicarrier. Before she could stop him, Hawkeye and a team of mercenaries attacked; Loki killed S.H.I.E.L.D. Agent Phil Coulson, and trapped Thor in the Hulk's cell, ejecting it from the ship. Loki and the surviving mercenaries escaped in the chaos of the enraged Hulk's rampage and headed for New York City's Stark Tower, where Selvig had begun using the Repulsor Technology Arc Reactor to jumpstart the Tesseract and open the portal to Chitauri space. The death of the well-liked Coulson galvanized the heroes—now including the vengeful Hawkeye, freed from Loki's control.

At Stark Tower, Stark confronted Loki. When Loki tried to control him with his staff, he was prevented from doing so by Stark's chest-mounted Repulsor Technology mini-reactor; Loki settled for tossing him out the skyscraper's window. Stark was saved by his armor—but Selvig's portal opened before he could confront Loki, unleashing the Chitauri on the city. While Iron Man, Captain America, Hawkeye and Black Widow engaged the invaders, Thor attacked Loki, who fled after stabbing his brother. Loki took to the skies in a Chitauri chariot, directing the battle himself. Hawkeye destroyed the craft with an exploding arrow that hurled Loki back to Stark Tower, where he was brutally beaten by the Hulk. Helpless, Loki surrendered to the assembled Avengers, and Thor returned him to Asgard to face justice.

IN THE COMICS

SEEKING TO MANIPULATE HIS HATED adoptive brother, Thor Odinson, into battling the Hulk (Bruce Banner), Loki diverted a Hulk-related distress call to Thor. Ultimately, his actions resulted in the first gathering of Hulk, Thor, Iron Man (Tony Stark), the Wasp (Janet Van Dyne), and Ant-Man (Hank Pym). After stopping Loki, the group stayed together as the Avengers, which eventually became Earth's mightiest assemblage of superhumans — much to Loki's great anger and regret.

UNWILLINGLY HELPED FORM THE AVENGERS:
AVENGERS #1 (1963)

STEALING HEINRICH SCHAFER'S EYE

FACT SHEET

- LOKI'S REFLEXES ARE SO QUICK HE CAN CATCH AN ARROW IN MID-FLIGHT.
- LOKI'S BODY IS DURABLE ENOUGH TO WITHSTAND BEING PUMMELED BY THE HULK.
- TO ACCESS THE IRIDIUM, LOKI'S MEN NEEDED TO PASS A RETINAL SCAN—AND SO LOKI STOLE DR. SCHÄFER'S EYEBALL.
- AFTER HE WAS CAPTURED BY THOR, LOKI'S MOUTH WAS SEALED WITH A METAL MUZZLE.

S.H.I.E.L.D.

FIRST APPEARANCE: ***Iron Man [2008]***

Born out of the World War II-era Strategic Scientific Reserve, S.H.I.E.L.D. (Strategic Homeland Intervention and Enforcement Logistics Division) was a world government-funded operation most recently headed by Director Nicholas J. Fury, Deputy Director Maria Hill, and committed senior agent Phil Coulson. The organization was dedicated to the investigation and counteracting of potential threats to the safety of mankind. Overseen by the World Security Council, S.H.I.E.L.D. was tasked with research, development, and exploration of advanced technology from Earth or other worlds.

Operating in secret, S.H.I.E.L.D. began the Avengers Initiative, an effort to recruit a superhuman operative squad. Toward this goal, Fury slowed potential recruit Tony Stark (Iron Man)'s palladium poisoning from the mini-R.T. Reactor implanted in his chest, had Agent Coulson forge an alliance with the Asgardian Thor in New Mexico, and helped restore order in Harlem after the gamma-empowered Hulk's brawl with the similarly strong Abomination largely destroyed it.

The World Security Council ordered Fury to change focus from "wasteful" programs like the Avengers Initiative to Phase 2, weaponizing the extremely powerful Tesseract artifact into an arsenal based on the terrorist Hydra's WWII-era technology. Fury was resistant to these orders, but complied.

S.H.I.E.L.D. created a joint effort with NASA, the Joint Dark Energy Mission, comprising Project PEGASUS, a S.H.I.E.L.D. Accelerator Test Facility, and a NASA Space Radiation Facility, to further study the Tesseract. During Dr. Erik Selvig's research, the Tesseract activated itself, causing highly unstable energy fluctuations. As the base was evacuated, a portal opened, bringing the malevolent Asgardian Loki to Earth. In an attempt to stop Loki, Fury self-destructed the base, but Loki fled with the Tesseract. Gathering former superhuman Avengers Initiative candidates on the Helicarrier, Fury oversaw the mission to retrieve the Tesseract.

Re-tasking wireless communication devices across the globe, S.H.I.E.L.D. tracked Loki to Stuttgart, Germany. With the assistance of Iron Man, Captain America, and Black Widow, S.H.I.E.L.D. apprehended the Asgardian and held him prisoner on the Helicarrier. An ambush by Loki's minions, including mind-controlled S.H.I.E.L.D. agents, severely crippled the Helicarrier and allowed Loki's escape, during which Loki impaled Coulson with his scepter; Coulson's death served to strengthen the resolve of the Initiative candidates to stop Loki.

IN THE COMICS

S.H.I.E.L.D. (SUPREME HEADQUARTERS International Espionage Law-Enforcement Division), created to battle threats both international and extraterrestrial, was secretly run by the S.H.I.E.L.D. executive council and publicly directed by Rick Stoner and later Nick Fury. When Fury learned the terrorist organization Hydra had infiltrated S.H.I.E.L.D., he dismantled and re-formed S.H.I.E.L.D. (Strategic Homeland Intervention, Espionage and Logistics Directorate) without the council. After Fury waged a disastrous secret war in Latveria and went into hiding, Maria Hill was appointed the agency's new director before Tony Stark was given the position. Following the alien Skrulls' secret invasion of Earth, S.H.I.E.L.D. was disbanded and replaced by H.A.M.M.E.R. under corrupt businessman Norman Osborn's leadership. When Osborn was deposed, S.H.I.E.L.D. was re-formed (Strategic Homeland Intervention, Enforcement and Logistics Division) with Steve Rogers as director. After Rogers stepped down to resume his responsibilities as Captain America, Daisy Johnson (Quake) briefly directed S.H.I.E.L.D. before Maria Hill resumed command. S.H.I.E.L.D. remains a primary line of defense for Earth and humanity.

FIRST APPEARANCE:
STRANGE TALES #135 (1965)

TECHNOLOGY

As Earth's premier peacekeeping agency and advanced technology research organization, S.H.I.E.L.D. has access to some of the most cutting-edge vehicles known to man.

QUINJET

With the final components of the Tesseract harness device in place atop Manhattan's Stark Tower, Loki opened a portal allowing the alien Chitauri army access to New York City. As the Initiative candidates, now calling themselves the Avengers, responded to the violent invasion, S.H.I.E.L.D. provided tactical support. However, the World Security Council decided to sacrifice one city to save the world and ordered a nuclear missile to destroy Manhattan and the Chitauri threat. Warned by Fury, Iron Man redirected the missile through the portal, where it destroyed the Chitauri mother ship in space, disabling the alien foot soldiers in New York City.

The portal destroyed and the Avengers victorious, S.H.I.E.L.D. allowed Thor to return the Tesseract and Loki to Asgard, much to the dismay of the World Security Council. After the Battle of New York, the general public became aware of the existence of extraterrestrial life, the Avengers, and of organizations like S.H.I.E.L.D., which had been operating in the shadows until then.

FACT SHEET

- S.H.I.E.L.D. IS COMMONLY PERCEIVED AS A SPY ORGANIZATION; MANY OF THEIR OPERATIONS ARE CLASSIFIED IN THE INTEREST OF SECURITY.
- IN THE SAME FACILITY THAT THE ASGARDIAN DESTROYER WAS TURNED INTO A HANDHELD WEAPON, GAMMA-MUTATED DR. SAMUEL STERNS WAS HELD IN CAPTIVITY AND OBSERVED UNDER THE CODENAME PROJECT: MR. BLUE.
- S.H.I.E.L.D. IDENTIFIED THE TESSERACT'S DOMINANT ELEMENTS TO BE CARBON, NITROGEN, AND OXYGEN.

THOR UPDATE

FIRST APPEARANCE: ***Thor [2011]***

When Odin discovered Loki, who was believed dead, on Earth, he sent Thor to retrieve his adoptive brother and recover the stolen energy source, the Tesseract. Thor arrived to find the fugitive Asgardian in the custody of Iron Man, Captain America, and Black Widow, under orders from S.H.I.E.L.D. Forcibly boarding their aircraft, Thor seized Loki and flew to the ground where he tried to coerce Loki to give him the Tesseract's location. Thor appealed to Loki's childhood memories, but Loki remembered only living in Thor's shadow and instead declared his intention to rule the Earth. The talk was cut short when Iron Man attacked Thor, telling him that S.H.I.E.L.D. would maintain custody of Loki until they had retrieved the Tesseract. Thor retaliated, instigating a violent brawl between the two. Captain America intervened, calling for both of them to put down their weapons. An enraged Thor struck at Cap with his hammer Mjolnir, but Cap blocked the blow with his shield, unleashing a shockwave that diffused the conflict. After calming down, Thor agreed to join the others in bringing Loki to S.H.I.E.L.D. for interrogation.

On S.H.I.E.L.D.'s Helicarrier, Thor informed the others of Loki's alliance with the alien Chitauri, whom he believed would help Loki conquer Earth in exchange for the Tesseract. Physicist Bruce Banner (also the monstrous Hulk) told Thor that astrophysicist Erik Selvig had been mentally enthralled by Loki. Thor's fears that

the presence of Asgardians on Earth might have been harmful to humanity were confirmed by the discovery that S.H.I.E.L.D. had used the Tesseract to develop weapons, which Director Nick Fury justified as a need for protection from otherworldly threats like Thor's previous battle with the Destroyer automaton in New Mexico. An attack by mind-controlled S.H.I.E.L.D. Agent Clint "Hawkeye" Barton and other Loki pawns blew out one of the Helicarrier's engines, creating havoc on the ship and prompting Banner to become the Hulk. While Captain America and Iron Man repaired the engines, Thor battled the Hulk to keep the brute occupied until Thor went to Loki's confinement cage to prevent his brother from escaping. However, Loki tricked Thor into the cage, which Loki ejected from the ship. Thor broke free just before the cage struck the ground and was destroyed.

Loki then used the Tesseract to open a portal in space, allowing the Chitauri army to invade New York City. Thor arrived and demanded Loki close it. Loki refused and stabbed Thor in the side before fleeing. Thor joined the other heroes, now calling themselves the Avengers, in battling the Chitauri. They contained the damage to a few city blocks until Iron Man used a nuclear missile aimed at New York by the World Security Council to destroy the Chitauri mothership, and Black Widow shut down the portal with Loki's scepter. Later, Thor took both Loki and the Tesseract back to Asgard for containment.

IN THE COMICS

AFTER HIS ADOPTED BROTHER LOKI attempted to trick him into battling the Hulk (Bruce Banner), a group of superhumans were gathered in conflict. However, when Loki's deception was discovered, Thor and Hulk, along with Iron Man (Tony Stark), Ant-Man (Henry Pym) and the Wasp (Janet Van Dyne) agreed to band together as the Avengers, Earth's mightiest heroes. Since then, Thor has been a frequent member of the ever-changing roster. Much of Thor's time away from his cherished allies has been due to incidents in Asgard or other events that draw him away from Earth.

FIRST ACTIVE WITH THE AVENGERS:
AVENGERS #1 (1963)

FACT SHEET

- WHEN THOR FIRST CONFRONTED LOKI ABOUT THE LOCATION OF THE TESSERACT, THEY WERE OBSERVED BY ODIN'S RAVENS, HUGIN AND MUNIN.
- DESPITE THE SEVERITY OF THEIR CONFLICTS, THOR AND ALL OF ASGARD MOURNED WHEN THEY BELIEVED LOKI DEAD.
- TO PROTECT HER FROM LOKI, AND TO THOR'S RELIEF, S.H.I.E.L.D. OFFERED THOR'S CLOSE FRIEND JANE FOSTER A HIGH-PAYING CONSULTING JOB IN TROMSO, NORWAY AS A MEANS OF RELOCATING HER SAFELY.

WORLD SECURITY COUNCIL

FIRST APPEARANCE:
Marvel's The Avengers (2012)

Comprising politicians from various nations, the World Security Council established S.H.I.E.L.D.'s objectives and budget, mainly communicating with the spy organization's director, Nick Fury. Growing impatient with Fury's sense of priorities, the Council ordered him to stop searching for the lost Captain America, keeping an eye on Iron Man's activities, and tracking the gamma-irradiated Bruce Banner; instead, they wanted Fury to focus on research of the vastly powerful Tesseract object and reallocated his budget accordingly. When Fury objected, the Council put him on disciplinary notice. Meanwhile, the Council granted Gen. Thaddeus "Thunderbolt" Ross clearance to use an experimental Weapons Plus Super-Soldier serum and access to the S.H.I.E.L.D. database in his quest to capture Banner.

Later, Fury proposed a new S.H.I.E.L.D. budget, revealing that because he ignored the Council's previous order to stop his projects, S.H.I.E.L.D. had several promising leads in Tesseract research and reminded the Council of their role in Ross' actions that almost destroyed Harlem. The Council approved Fury's expanded budget. Wanting to protect Earth from potential extraterrestrial threats such as the Asgardians, the Council implemented Phase 2, a program to develop Tesseract-powered weapons. Later, the Council shut down the Avengers Initiative, feeling it was too unpredictable.

When the Asgardian Loki stole the Tesseract from S.H.I.E.L.D.'s Project PEGASUS, effectively nullifying the Phase 2 plans, the Council reluctantly authorized Fury to assemble a response team: the Avengers. As Loki used the Tesseract to open a portal for the extraterrestrial Chitauri army to attack Earth, the Council ordered a nuclear strike against Manhattan, willing to sacrifice one city to save the world. Fury refused, so the Council removed Fury from command and sent a missile anyway. After the Avengers stopped the alien invasion and the nuclear strike, Fury told the Council that the Tesseract had been returned to the Asgardians, but the world now has the Avengers to protect it.

IN THE COMICS

WHEN TONY STARK CONVINCED world politicians and businesspeople to fund S.H.I.E.L.D., the United Nations-authorized, multinational peacekeeping taskforce was run by the anonymous S.H.I.E.L.D. executive council, comprising representatives of national and corporate sponsors of the agency. Over the years, Hydra slowly infiltrated S.H.I.E.L.D., replacing the council and other high-ranking members with Life Model Decoys under their control. When Nick Fury discovered how far-reaching the corruption had become, he defeated the plot and disbanded S.H.I.E.L.D., including the council. Fury eventually re-formed S.H.I.E.L.D., but he did so without the executive council.

FIRST APPEARANCE:
NICK FURY VS. S.H.I.E.L.D. #1 (1988)

FACT SHEET

- THE WORLD SECURITY COUNCIL COMMUNICATED WITH FURY THROUGH ENCRYPTED VIDEO CHANNELS.
- UNDER THE COUNCIL'S ORDERS, S.H.I.E.L.D. TOLD PEOPLE THAT TESSERACT RESEARCH WAS TO ATTAIN A RENEWABLE ENERGY SOURCE, INSTEAD OF A WEAPONS PROJECT. THE PHASE 2 WEAPONRY WAS BASED ON THE EQUIPMENT OF WORLD WAR II TERRORIST GROUP HYDRA, WHICH HAD UTILIZED TESSERACT-EMPOWERED WEAPONS DURING THE WAR.
- WHEN THE COUNCIL REMOVED THE S.H.I.E.L.D. DIRECTORSHIP FROM FURY, OVERRIDE CODE "SEVEN ALPHA ONE ONE" WAS USED.

JARVIS UPDATE

FIRST APPEARANCE:
Iron Man [2008]

Tony Stark (Iron Man)'s artificial-intelligence program JARVIS was transferred to Stark's New York City Stark Tower, a self-sustaining complex powered by a Repulsor Technology Arc Reactor. When Stark ignored S.H.I.E.L.D. Agent Phil Coulson's attempts to contact him, Coulson overrode JARVIS's protocols to gain Stark's attention. Coulson told Stark the Asgardian Loki had stolen the Tesseract, an alien object of great power. After deducing Loki planned to use the Tesseract at Stark Tower to open a portal for the invading Chitauri, Stark had JARVIS turn off the building's power. But it was too late: JARVIS determined Loki's portal device was already self-sustaining and surrounded by an impenetrable force field. While Stark distracted Loki with bravado, JARVIS finalized construction of the Mark VII Iron Man armor, completing it in time to save Stark after Loki threw the industrialist out a window.

During the Chitauri invasion, JARVIS provided Iron Man with alerts to incoming threats while also attempting to scan the aliens for weaknesses. When the World Security Council launched a nuclear missile at New York City to stop the invasion, JARVIS, not waiting for Iron Man's order, transferred all the suit's available power to its thrusters to meet the missile in mid-air so Stark could redirect it into the portal. JARVIS offered to call Iron Man's girlfriend, Pepper Potts, so Stark could say goodbye before his potentially fatal course of action. Surviving the nuclear blast that destroyed the Chitauri mothership in space, Stark used JARVIS to begin planning renovations to the damaged Stark Tower.

FACT SHEET

- JARVIS IS ABLE TO PERFORM MULTIPLE FUNCTIONS SIMULTANEOUSLY AND PRIORITIZE COMMANDS.

GEORGI LUCHKOV

FIRST APPEARANCE:
Marvel's The Avengers [2012]

During an uncover sting, illegal exporter Georgi Luchkov recognized S.H.I.E.L.D. Agent Natasha Romanoff as the Black Widow; unsure who hired her, he had his two henchmen bring her to 1-14 Silensky Plaza, where he intended to forcibly extract information from her. Romanoff feigned ignorance during the interrogation, prompting Luchkov to inadvertently reveal information about his operation. However, before she could capitalize on this confession, a henchman's phone rang with a call from Agent Phil Coulson. Coulson threatened Luchkov until he handed Romanoff the phone, then informed her that her longtime S.H.I.E.L.D. partner Hawkeye had been compromised by the Asgardian trickster Loki. Luchkov was distraught to hear Romanoff tell Coulson she was manipulating Luchkov into telling her what she wanted to know. When Luchkov retrieved the phone, Romanoff took down Luchkov's men, broke free, and incapacitated Luchkov by roughly stringing him up by a chain wrapped around his ankle.

FACT SHEET

- LUCHKOV TOLD ROMANOFF THAT TORTURING HER FOR INFORMATION WAS NOT WHAT HE HAD INTENDED FOR THEIR EVENING. UNDERSTANDING WHAT HE MEANT, ROMANOFF RESPONDED THAT TORTURE WAS BETTER.
- LUCHKOV LET ROMANOFF SPEAK WITH COULSON AFTER COULSON REVEALED HE KNEW LUCHKOV'S EXACT LOCATION, AND AN F-22 FIGHTER JET WAS READY TO DESTROY THE BLOCK BEFORE LUCHKOV COULD GET AWAY.

IN THE COMICS

GEORGI LUCHKOV WAS A KGB INFORMANT who turned in numerous dissidents before the Soviet Union collapsed. After relocating to the United States and becoming a food cart vendor, Luchkov began murdering relatives of those he had turned in, fearing now-public records of his misdeeds would lead them to seek retribution against him. When confronted by the Black Widow (Natasha Romanoff), Luchkov tried to distract her by threatening an infant, but he was still captured and taken into custody for his crimes.

FIRST APPEARANCE:
MARVEL COMICS PRESENTS #135 (1993)

OTHER

FIRST APPEARANCE:
Marvel's The Avengers [2012]

The grotesque Other is the loyal servant of Thanos. His sights set on obtaining the Tesseract, a vast extraterrestrial energy source, Thanos provided the Asgardian Loki with a powerful scepter and an alien army and directed him to invade Earth, the planet where the Tesseract was located. When the Tesseract activated, the Other informed Thanos that Loki was ready to lead the Chitauri to acquire it for him. After stealing the Tesseract from the Project PEGASUS Joint Dark Energy Mission, Loki telepathically contacted the Other, who told the Asgardian that the Chitauri were growing restless. The Other became angry when Loki questioned the Chitauri's might and the gifts Thanos had provided. Aggravated by the Asgardian's childish ambitions and his insinuation he might not hand over the Tesseract when the time came, the Other threatened Loki, then forcefully sent his telepathic avatar back to Earth. After the heroic Avengers defeated the Chitauri, the Other informed Thanos of Loki's failure, and that the Tesseract and Loki both had been returned to Asgard. The humans, he said, were not as defenseless as Loki had promised. When the Other compared challenging humanity to courting death, Thanos turned and smiled.

FACT SHEET

- THE OTHER POSSESSES SIX DIGITS ON EACH HAND, INCLUDING TWO OPPOSABLE THUMBS.
- THE OTHER CAN CONVERSE WITH ANOTHER'S SPIRIT FORM AND INFLUENCE THEM REMOTELY.

SCEPTER

FIRST APPEARANCE:
Marvel's The Avengers [2012]

When Loki formed an alliance with the Other and the alien Chitauri, he was given a powerful golden scepter adorned with a glowing blue gem encircled by silver blades. Loki raided S.H.I.E.L.D.'s Project PEGASUS facility, using the scepter to fire energy beams at agents and take over the minds of Clint "Hawkeye" Barton, Dr. Erik Selvig, and others. After escaping with the Tesseract and his mind-controlled victims, Loki allowed himself to be captured during a heist at Germany's Stuttgart Museum, giving Tony Stark and Bruce Banner time to examine the scepter aboard a S.H.I.E.L.D. Helicarrier. While Selvig used the Tesseract to build a portal to Earth for the Chitauri, the scepter subtly influenced the S.H.I.E.L.D.-gathered heroes' misgivings about each other, distracting them with arguments while Hawkeye and Loki's mind-controlled soldiers attacked the Helicarrier. Loki escaped captivity, and impaled Agent Phil Coulson in the back with his scepter, killing him. With the portal activated atop Stark Tower in New York City, the Chitauri invaded Earth and battled the Avengers. During the battle, Loki's attempt to mind-control Stark failed due to the miniature Repulsor Technology unit in Stark's chest. However, Loki successfully blasted the Quinjet carrying Hawkeye and Black Widow out of the sky. After the monstrous Hulk defeated Loki, Selvig, now freed from Loki's control, revealed he had designed the scepter as a safety to cut off the portal's power. Black Widow closed the portal to the Chitauri, and the scepter was left with S.H.I.E.L.D.

FACT SHEET

- AT THE STUTTGART MUSEUM, LOKI DISGUISED THE SCEPTER AS A CANE.
- BANNER'S ANALYSIS OF THE SCEPTER REVEALED SIMILARITIES TO THE TESSERACT.
- DURING AN ARGUMENT AMONG THE FUTURE AVENGERS, BRUCE BANNER WAS INFLUENCED TO PICK UP THE SCEPTER, BUT WAS DISTRACTED BY AN ATTACK ON THE HELICARRIER BEFORE IT COULD FORCE HIM TO DO LOKI'S BIDDING.
- LOKI'S CONTROL OF HAWKEYE WAS BROKEN BY REPEATED BLOWS TO THE HEAD FROM THE BLACK WIDOW.

ERIK SELVIG UPDATE

FIRST APPEARANCE: ***Thor [2011]***

Following the events in New Mexico, while under the Asgardian Loki's subtle influence, Dr. Erik Selvig weaponized the captured Destroyer automaton for S.H.I.E.L.D. Because Selvig began acting strangely, Nick Fury assigned Agent Clint "Hawkeye" Barton to watch over Selvig's research at Project PEGASUS. When the Tesseract's energy levels spiked, Selvig proved unable to stop it and Loki arrived on Earth via a Tesseract-created portal. Needing Selvig's knowledge to open a larger portal for the alien Chitauri invasion, Loki used his scepter to completely corrupt Selvig into working on a Tesseract harness device using iridium as a stabilizer. While Selvig installed iridium onto the harness, he subconsciously created a failsafe to close the portal using Loki's scepter. Meanwhile, Loki allowed himself to be captured by S.H.I.E.L.D. to disrupt their plans to assemble heroes against him. Upon Loki's escape, the corrupted Selvig installed and activated the Tesseract harness atop Stark Tower, giving the invading Chitauri access to Earth. Selvig was subsequently knocked unconscious by a shock wave generated when Iron Man, unaware of the Tesseract's energy barrier, tried to blast the Tesseract harness device. Awakening with his mental faculties restored, Selvig realized what he had been forced to do and aided Black Widow in shutting down the Tesseract portal using Loki's scepter.

FACT SHEET

- BEFORE TESTING THE TESSERACT, SELVIG WAS REQUIRED TO GET APPROVAL FROM NASA.
- WHILE WORKING WITH S.H.I.E.L.D., SELVIG WAS NOT ALLOWED ANY CONTACTS OR INSTANT MESSAGES WITH THE OUTSIDE WORLD.
- WHEN LOKI ARRIVED FROM THE TESSERACT PORTAL AND INTRODUCED HIMSELF, SELVIG IMMEDIATELY RECOGNIZED THE NAME AS THOR'S BROTHER.

JASPER SITWELL UPDATE

FIRST APPEARANCE: ***Thor [2011]***

Tasked with keeping tabs on Dr. Bruce Banner, S.H.I.E.L.D. agent Jasper Sitwell periodically reported back to Nick Fury on Banner's status before the Asgardian events in Puente Antiguo, New Mexico. Following New Mexico, Sitwell was stationed aboard a flying S.H.I.E.L.D. Helicarrier and was tasked with searching for signs of the Asgardian Loki, who had escaped S.H.I.E.L.D. forces with the massively powerful Tesseract artifact by corrupting the minds of Agent Clint "Hawkeye" Barton and Dr. Erik Selvig with a mind-controlling scepter provided to Loki by extraterrestrial allies. Believing he'd located Loki in Stuttgart, Germany, Sitwell expanded his search to confirm his location. Sitwell interrupted a conversation between Agent Phil Coulson and Captain America to report his findings. Commenting that Loki was not exactly hiding, Sitwell watched as Fury sent Captain America to deal with the situation. Later, during an attack on the Helicarrier by Hawkeye and Loki's forces, Sitwell witnessed Hawkeye's shutdown of the Helicarrier's computer and engine systems, and attempted to get them back online.

FACT SHEET

- SITWELL SEARCHED FOR LOKI BY RUNNING FACIAL RECOGNITION SOFTWARE AND RE-TASKING WIRELESS COMMUNICATION DEVICES ACROSS THE GLOBE, WHICH ULTIMATELY HELPED SITWELL LOCATE THE ASGARDIAN.
- SITWELL'S SEARCH FOR LOKI IDENTIFIED LOKI'S STUTTGART LOCATION AS 28 KÖNIGSTRASSE.

MARVEL'S IRON MAN 3

GUIDEBOOK TO THE MARVEL CINEMATIC UNIVERSE

MARVEL

IRON MAN 3™

MARVEL STUDIOS PRESENTS IN ASSOCIATION WITH PARAMOUNT PICTURES AND DMG ENTERTAINMENT A MARVEL STUDIOS PRODUCTION ROBERT DOWNEY JR. "IRON MAN 3" GWYNETH PALTROW DON CHEADLE GUY PEARCE REBECCA HALL STEPHANIE SZOSTAK JAMES BADGE DALE WITH JON FAVREAU AND BEN KINGSLEY CASTING BY SARAH HALLEY FINN, C.S.A. MUSIC BY BRIAN TYLER MUSIC SUPERVISOR DAVE JORDAN VISUAL EFFECTS SUPERVISOR CHRISTOPHER TOWNSEND COSTUME DESIGNER LOUISE FROGLEY EDITED BY JEFFREY FORD, A.C.E. PETER S. ELLIOT PRODUCTION DESIGN BILL BRZESKI DIRECTOR OF PHOTOGRAPHY JOHN TOLL, ASC EXECUTIVE PRODUCERS STAN LEE DAN MINTZ EXECUTIVE PRODUCER ALAN FINE EXECUTIVE PRODUCERS CHARLES NEWIRTH VICTORIA ALONSO STEPHEN BROUSSARD EXECUTIVE PRODUCER LOUIS D'ESPOSITO EXECUTIVE PRODUCER JON FAVREAU PRODUCED BY KEVIN FEIGE SCREENPLAY BY DREW PEARCE & SHANE BLACK DIRECTED BY SHANE BLACK

Collecting information from *Marvel's Iron Man 3 (2013)* and *Iron Man 3 Prelude (2013)*.

HEAD WRITER/COORDINATOR: **MIKE O'SULLIVAN**

COORDINATION: **DARON JENSEN**

WRITERS: **ANTHONY COTILLETTA**, **PATRICK DUKE**, **MIKE FICHERA**, **DARON JENSEN**, **ROB LONDON**, **CHRIS MCCARVER**, **MARKUS RAYMOND**, AND **KEVIN WASSER**

ARTISTS: **MARK BRIGHT**, **JOHN BUSCEMA**, **MIKE DEODATO**, **DON DRAKE**, **RODNEY FUENTEBELLA**, **ADI GRANOV**, **JACKSON GUICE**, **PAUL GULACY**, **KEVIN HOPGOOD**, **JACK KIRBY**, **SALVADOR LARROCCA**, **RON LIM**, **DAVID MARQUEZ**, **RYAN MEINERDING**, **LIAM SHARP**, AND **GUS VASQUEZ**

COVER ARTIST: **MARCOS MARTIN**

SPECIAL THANKS TO DAVE ALTHOFF, SHAWN "KEEBLER" BYERS, JEFF CHRISTIANSEN, MATT DELMANOWSKI, ERIKA DENTON, TIM DILLON, PERCIVAL LANUZA, JACQUE PORTE, RYAN POTTER, AND DR. DAVE UNANDER

IRON MAN CREATED BY STAN LEE, LARRY LIEBER, DON HECK, AND JACK KIRBY

EXTREMIS SOLDIERS

FIRST APPEARANCE: ***Iron Man 3 (2013)***

Advanced Idea Mechanics (A.I.M.) CEO Aldrich Killian recruited crippled military veterans including Ellen Brandt, Chad Davis, Drew Grey, David Samuels, Eric Savin, and Jack Taggart to take the next step in human evolution by taking Maya Hansen's Extremis biotechnology. The first illegal test injections on June 25, 2009, showed its effectiveness when it regenerated Brandt's left arm, but also its instability when another soldier's body rejected Extremis and exploded. A.I.M. tried to keep the Extremis subjects stable with regular injections while working to fix the flaw. After Sgt. Chad Davis exploded in his hometown of Rose Hill, Tennessee, killing himself and five others, Killian secretly hired an actor to play the part of the Mandarin, an international terrorist who took credit for eight more subjects' explosions.

Following an Extremis soldier's explosion in Kuwait's Ali Al Salem Air Base's chapel, U.S. President Ellis sent Lt. Col. James Rhodes in the Iron Patriot armor after the Mandarin. Suspicious of Savin after encountering him at Stark Industries, Stark Head of Security Happy Hogan confronted Savin at Hollywood's Chinese Theater where Savin had just met with Taggart. However, Taggart's body rejected Extremis, violently exploding, leaving Hogan gravely injured. Believing the explosion to be another terrorist attack, Tony Stark challenged the Mandarin on live TV. Savin, having survived the Hollywood explosion, led an attack on Stark's home, and after destroying it, accompanied Brandt to Tennessee to retrieve Davis'

SAVIN

BRANDT

FACT SHEET

- EXTREMIS SOLDIERS POSSESS SUPERHUMAN STRENGTH, DURABILITY, ENHANCED SPEED, AND IMMUNITY TO PAIN. THEY CAN REGENERATE MISSING LIMBS AND HEAL MOST WOUNDS WITHIN SECONDS.
- THEY CAN CHANNEL MASSIVE HEAT THROUGH THEIR SKIN, GENERATING TEMPERATURES HIGH ENOUGH TO MELT MOST METALS.
- WHEN A SUBJECT'S BODY REJECTED EXTREMIS OR THE WRONG DOSAGE WAS INJECTED, THEY WOULD EXPLODE, CAUSING TEMPERATURES OF 3000°F, WHICH WOULD INCINERATE ANY OTHER LIFE FORM WITHIN A FEW DOZEN FEET.

TAGGART

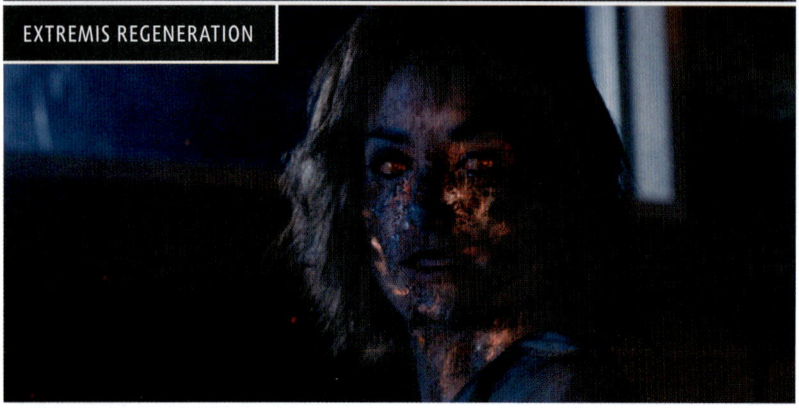

EXTREMIS REGENERATION

A.I.M. personnel file from his mother. Posing as a Department of Homeland Security agent, Brandt encountered Stark, who had also journeyed to Tennessee to investigate the Davis incident. She tried abducting him, but when local authorities intervened, she was distracted by attacking them, allowing Stark to escape. Catching up with him in a nearby diner, Brandt apparently died in a gas explosion caused by Stark. After incapacitating Savin, Stark left Tennessee with Davis' file.

In Afghanistan, a female Extremis soldier captured Iron Patriot in a trap set up in a sweatshop and brought him to Killian in Florida. Tracking the "Mandarin" to Florida, Stark learned he was actually actor Trevor Slattery; during this discovery, Savin captured Stark and delivered him to Killian before departing in Iron Patriot's armor to infiltrate *Air Force One*. Savin abducted President Matthew Ellis by placing him in the Patriot armor and sending it to Killian. After which, Savin was killed by an escaped Stark, who fired a repulsor blast through Savin's chest via a remote-controlled Iron Man armor. Locating Ellis at the derelict Roxxon oil tanker *Norco*, Stark and Rhodes rescued him before Killian could execute him, so A.I.M. supporter Vice President Rodriguez could ascend to the presidency. During a massive battle at the *Norco*, the remaining Extremis soldiers apparently perished fighting the JARVIS-controlled Iron Legion (dozens of Iron Man armors) and Killian was apparently killed in battle against Iron Man and a temporarily Extremis-powered Pepper Potts.

IN THE COMICS

EXTREMIS-ENHANCED SUBJECT

INVENTED BY MAYA HANSEN while she sought to mimic the Captain America-creating Super-Soldier serum, Extremis could hack the brain's repair center and completely rewrite a subject's genome. Though the process was painful, it could grant the injected specimen not only improved organs, but also superhuman levels of healing, strength, speed, durability, and the power to breathe fire.

FIRST APPEARANCE:
IRON MAN #1 (2005)

FEELING NEGLECTED BY HER husband, scientist Ted Sallis, pregnant Ellen Brandt betrayed him to Advanced Idea Mechanics, who wanted his work on recreating the Super-Soldier serum. Sallis injected himself with the serum, involuntarily becoming the monstrous Man-Thing. Instinctively lashing out, Man-Thing unintentionally left Brandt horribly scarred; Brandt gave up their newborn son for adoption. Years later, Brandt and Man-Thing mystically merged as the Nexus of Realities.

FIRST APPEARANCE:
SAVAGE TALES #1 (1971)

MERCENARY JACK TAGGERT piloted the government-sanctioned Firepower armor created by industrialist Edwin Cord, whom he aided in bankrupting Stark Enterprises. Iron Man saved Taggert's life when the damaged Firepower armor malfunctioned.

FIRST APPEARANCE:
IRON MAN #230 (1988)

LT. COL. ERIC SAVIN WAS forcefully turned into the cyborg Coldblood after a mine explosion during investigations of Project: Ultra-Tech's illegal activities. Aided by scientist Gina Dyson, he broke free of Ultra-Tech's control and became a mercenary. Imprisoned for opposing the Superhuman Registration Act (SHRA), he vanished after a mass breakout from the SHRA's Prison 42.

FIRST APPEARANCE:
MARVEL COMICS PRESENTS #26 (1989)

COVER SHOWN: *DEATHLOK #20 (1993)*

MAYA HANSEN

FIRST APPEARANCE: ***Iron Man 3* (2013)**

Biogeneticist Maya Hansen created Extremis, a genetic treatment designed to enhance the immune system and rapidly speed healing. Attending the Bern Tech Summit on New Year's Eve 1999, Maya Hansen connected with genius inventor Tony Stark, hoping to show him Extremis. The couple was approached by Aldrich Killian, who sought for them to join his start-up think tank, Advanced Idea Mechanics. Stark rudely dismissed Killian, but Hansen expressed interest. After Hansen showed Stark her Extremis research, the two spent the night together; Stark was gone by morning, but left a note with some suggestions for improving her work. Wanting to see her work help mankind, but also realizing Stark had no more interest in her than as a one-night stand, Hansen turned to Killian and joined A.I.M. as a biological DNA coder.

Years later, when a programming glitch resulted in illegal human Extremis test subjects violently exploding, A.I.M. secretly hired an actor to play the part of the Mandarin, an international terrorist who claimed responsibility for the "bombings." Following Stark's public threats against the Mandarin, Hansen approached Stark at his Malibu estate to ask him to help fine-tune Extremis. Before they could talk, the house was attacked by Extremis troops reporting to Killian, separating Stark from her and Stark Industrialist CEO Pepper Potts. Later, after feigning friendship with Potts, Hansen handed her over to Killian, suggesting they use Potts to blackmail Stark into working for them.

When Stark was later captured by A.I.M., Hansen pleaded with him to help fix the volatile Extremis, but Stark dismissed Hansen, questioning her morality. When Killian revealed he was injecting Extremis into Potts to force Stark's cooperation, Hansen demanded Killian let Stark go, threatening to inject herself with a lethal dose of Extremis and leave her work incomplete. Angered by this betrayal and dismissive of the consequences, Killian shot and killed Hansen.

IN THE COMICS

MAYA HANSEN WORKED alongside scientist Aldrich Killian to develop Extremis, an attempt to create super-soldiers by genetically rewriting the body's healing ability. To generate military contractor interest, Hansen secretly allowed the serum to fall into the hands of terrorists, who weaponized it. When Iron Man (Tony Stark) was later injured in battle with the Extremis-enhanced terrorist Mallen, Hansen injected Stark with Extremis, healing him; Stark then defeated Mallen. Hansen was imprisoned when her part in releasing Extremis to terrorists was revealed. Stark, now director of S.H.I.E.L.D., eventually released Hansen from prison to help when he started experiencing Extremis-induced hallucinations. Later, Hansen was kidnapped by A.I.M. and forced to create a new Extremis strain, but was killed while trying to escape.

FIRST APPEARANCE:
IRON MAN #1 (2004)

FACT SHEET

- HANSEN ATTENDED THE MASSACHUSETTS INSTITUTE OF TECHNOLOGY, WHERE HER RESEARCH GAINED NOTORIETY IN SCIENTIFIC CIRCLES AND GAINED KILLIAN'S INITIAL INTEREST.
- HANSEN'S FIRST EXTREMIS TEST SUBJECTS WERE PLANTS, ONE OF WHICH EXPLODED AFTER STARK'S BODYGUARD HAPPY HOGAN PULLED OFF A BRANCH.
- HANSEN COMPARED HERSELF TO WERNHER VON BRAUN, THE GERMAN AEROSPACE ENGINEER WHO DREAMED OF SPACE TRAVEL BUT ENDED UP BUILDING MISSILES FOR THE NAZIS.

IRON MAN
UPDATE

FIRST APPEARANCE:
Iron Man (2008)

Tony Stark developed acute post-traumatic stress following the Avengers' battle with the extraterrestrial Chitauri in New York, which manifested in insomnia, anxiety attacks, and a compulsion to build new Iron Man armors, a veritable "Iron Legion" of 35 additional suits, many of which were stored in a bunker beneath his wine cellar. Stark rebuffed any overtures of help, even from friend and military liaison Lt. Col. James Rhodes and romantic partner Pepper Potts, who moved in with him sometime after the events in New York.

Stark dismissed the concerns of Happy Hogan, now Stark Industries' security chief, over Potts' meeting with

Advanced Idea Mechanics head Aldrich Killian, who Stark had callously rebuffed at a 1999 conference in Switzerland. When Potts returned home, she was irritated when she learned the armor she believed Stark was in was being remotely operated while Stark was working in his shop. Though Stark assured her that his distractions would not affect their relationship, the Mark XLII, triggered by Stark's nightmares, threatened Potts as she slept. Despite Stark waking and stopping the armor, Potts was further infuriated.

When a suspicious Hogan was gravely injured while shadowing Killian's henchman Eric Savin, a vengeful Stark publicly challenged international terrorist the Mandarin, who claimed culpability in the explosion that injured Hogan. Stark began to research the Mandarin's activities, finding a suicide bombing similar to the one that injured Hogan in Rose Hill, Tennessee, but before he could act on this, a trio of helicopters destroyed the Estate. Though Stark, using the Mark XLII, saved Potts and the visiting biogeneticist Maya Hansen, the Estate toppled into the ocean with Stark inside. Though believed killed, Stark's artificial intelligence JARVIS saved Stark and flew him to Rose Hill, but the armor's low power reserves caused him to crash outside town.

Stark dragged the inert armor into the garage of young gadgeteer Harley Keener, who allowed Stark to recharge the armor there. After Keener told Stark about Rose Hill's suicide bomber, a local war hero, Stark met with the vet's mother, who gave him a file on A.I.M.'s Extremis, a serum that enhanced the human body's healing, strength and durability, but Savin and A.I.M. operative Ellen Brandt, both empowered by Extremis, attacked him. Stark killed Brandt and subdued Savin before leaving Rose Hill in Savin's car, telling Keener to safeguard the Mark XLII.

With the help of Rhodes and a TV news cameraman, Stark hacked into A.I.M.'s mainframe to learn more about Killian's Extremis experiments, then called Keener, who, with JARVIS' help, pinpointed the Mandarin's broadcast location as Killian's Miami mansion. Armed with improvised weapons, Stark broke into the mansion and discovered the Mandarin was actually troubled actor Trevor Slattery, hired by A.I.M. to pose as the Mandarin. Savin subdued and captured Stark, then Killian taunted Stark by showing a video of Potts, captured with the help of Hansen, Killian's secret compatriot, being injected with Extremis. When Hansen threatened to kill herself to stop Killian, he shot Hansen dead. Stark summoned the Mark XLII to his location and fought his way out of the mansion, but could not prevent Savin from using the captured Iron Patriot armor to abduct U.S. President Matthew Ellis from *Air Force One*. Though Savin sent Ellis to Killian in the Iron Patriot armor, Stark, remotely controlling the Mark XLII, killed Savin and rescued the passengers and crew that had fallen into open sky through a rupture in the plane's fuselage.

Aided by Rhodes (who rescued President Ellis) and dozens of JARVIS-controlled Iron Man armors (the "Iron Legion"), Stark combated Killian's Extremis-powered soldiers and Killian himself, whom he encased in the Mark XLII and ordered JARVIS to detonate with Killian inside. Though Killian survived due to his Extremis abilities, Potts killed him with one of the armors' repulsors. As a gesture for Potts that he was setting aside distractions to focus on health, Stark ordered JARVIS to initiate his "clean slate" protocol, which caused all of the armors to self-destruct. Later, Stark had the shrapnel surgically removed from his chest, rewarded Keener with a well-equipped upgrade to his garage, then relayed recent events to fellow Avenger Bruce Banner (a.k.a. the Hulk).

FACT SHEET

- STARK INTRODUCED HIMSELF TO KEENER AS "THE MECHANIC."
- STARK CONTINUALLY DEFLECTED MENTIONS OF THE EVENTS IN NEW YORK OR THE WORMHOLE THROUGH WHICH HE FLEW TO DESTROY THE CHITAURI INVADERS, ALL OF WHICH TRIGGERED ANXIETY ATTACKS.
- BRANDT TAUNTED STARK FOR EMPLOYING A "CHEAP TRICK AND A CHEESY ONE-LINER" AGAINST HER; STARK QUIPPED THAT COULD BE THE TITLE OF HIS AUTOBIOGRAPHY.
- THE STARK ESTATE WAS LOCATED AT 10880 MALIBU POINT.

IRON MAN'S ARMORS UPDATE

FIRST APPEARANCE: [Mark VIII-XLII] ***Iron Man 3* (2013)**

As a means of working through the post-traumatic stress he suffered during the Avengers' battle against the Chitauri armada, Tony Stark developed nearly three dozen new Iron Man armors, some of them simple improvements of the standard armor and others geared for specific mission profiles or hostile environments. The most recent armor Stark developed prior to the destruction of the Stark Estate was the Mark XLII, which, thanks to microchips implanted in his arms and miniature propulsion systems throughout the armor, could form onto Stark piece-by-piece without the Suit-Up Gantry; Stark could also command the armor to form itself onto another person. Additionally, the Mark XLII could be operated remotely via an augmented cognition headset; however, the suit was a fragile prototype that could easily fly apart on impact, even during the suit-up process.

The Mark XLII became a bone of contention between Stark and Pepper Potts on two separate occasions, the first when Stark interacted with Potts remotely through the armor without Potts knowing Stark was physically elsewhere, and the second when the armor grabbed Potts as she slept, mistaking her for a threat while Stark experienced a nightmare. When Aldrich Killian, the biogenetically enhanced head of Advanced Idea Mechanics, arranged a helicopter attack on the Stark Estate, Stark formed the Mark XLII armor onto Pepper to protect her long enough for her to escape, then formed the armor onto himself to attack the helicopters, but the collapsing Estate dragged Stark into the ocean. Stark's artificial intelligence, JARVIS, freed Stark from the rubble and engaged the armor's flight systems to escape, but the armor crash-landed when the armor's minimal power supply was exhausted.

Stark dragged the Mark XLII to the garage of pre-teen tinkerer Harley Keener, who provided Stark with materials needed to repair and recharge the armor. While the suit replenished its power reserves, Stark snuck into Killian's mansion but was captured. Stark was able to summon the armor from Keener's garage and escape, then used the armor via telepresence to attempt to stop Killian's lieutenant Eric Savin from abducting U.S. President Matthew Ellis from *Air Force One*. Though unable to stop the kidnapping, Stark saved the passengers that had fallen out of the plane. Once back on the ground, the suit was hit by a truck and shattered.

Ellis was taken to the abandoned Roxxon tanker *Norco* by Killian and his biogenetically enhanced soldiers. Stark had JARVIS initiate his "house party" protocol, deploying all of the Iron Man armors (the "Iron Legion") that had survived the Estate's destruction to aid him and Lt. Col. James Rhodes in combating Killian and his subordinates. The armors, either autonomously or personally piloted by Stark, waylaid Killian's soldiers, and Stark encased Killian in the returning Mark XLII before ordering JARVIS to detonate the suit's self-destruct mechanism. Though Killian survived the blast, Potts, whom Killian had abducted and infused with Extremis, killed him using a repulsor blast from an armor's gauntlet. As a gesture to show Potts his renewed sense of purpose, Stark ordered JARVIS to initiate his "clean slate" protocol, which detonated self-destruct explosives in the remaining armors, destroying them all.

THE IRON LEGION

MARK
VIII

MARK
IX

MARK
X

MARK
XI

MARK
XII

MARK
XIII

MARK
XIV

MARK
XV

"SNEAKY" —
STEALTH SUIT

MARK
XVI

"NIGHTCLUB" —
BLACK STEALTH SUIT

MARK
XVII

"HEARTBREAKER" —
ARTILLERY-LEVEL RT SUIT

MARK
XVIII

"CASANOVA" — STEALTH
ARTILLERY-LEVEL RT SUIT

MARK
XIX

"TIGER" — HIGH-VELOCITY
PROTOTYPE SUIT

MARK
XX

"PYTHON" —
LONG-DISTANCE SUIT

IN THE COMICS

WHEN TONY STARK SUFFERED debilitating nerve damage that left him paralyzed from the neck down, he developed the Model 12 Iron Man armor, which could be operated remotely via a neuromimetic telepresence headset. Though Stark regained his mobility, he continued to use variations on the telepresence system to remotely control his armor, sometimes multiple suits at once; over the years, Stark has developed numerous versions of his armor, in recent times operating Mark 52.

FIRST APPEARANCE:
(MODEL 12 ARMOR) *IRON MAN #290 (1993)*; (MODEL 52 ARMOR) *INVINCIBLE IRON MAN #1 (2015)*

FACT SHEET

- STARK BEGAN ASSIGNING NICKNAMES FOR HIS LATER SUITS, INCLUDING "HEARTBREAKER" (MARK XVII), "RED SNAPPER" (MARK XXXV), AND "IGOR" (MARK XXXVIII).
- STARK STORED THE MARK VIII THROUGH MARK XLI ARMORS IN A REINFORCED UNDERGROUND ARMORY THAT ALLOWED THEM TO SURVIVE THE ESTATE'S DESTRUCTION. THE MARK I THROUGH VII ARMORS, KEPT IN STARK'S GARAGE GALLERY, WERE DESTROYED WITH THE ESTATE.

THE IRON LEGION

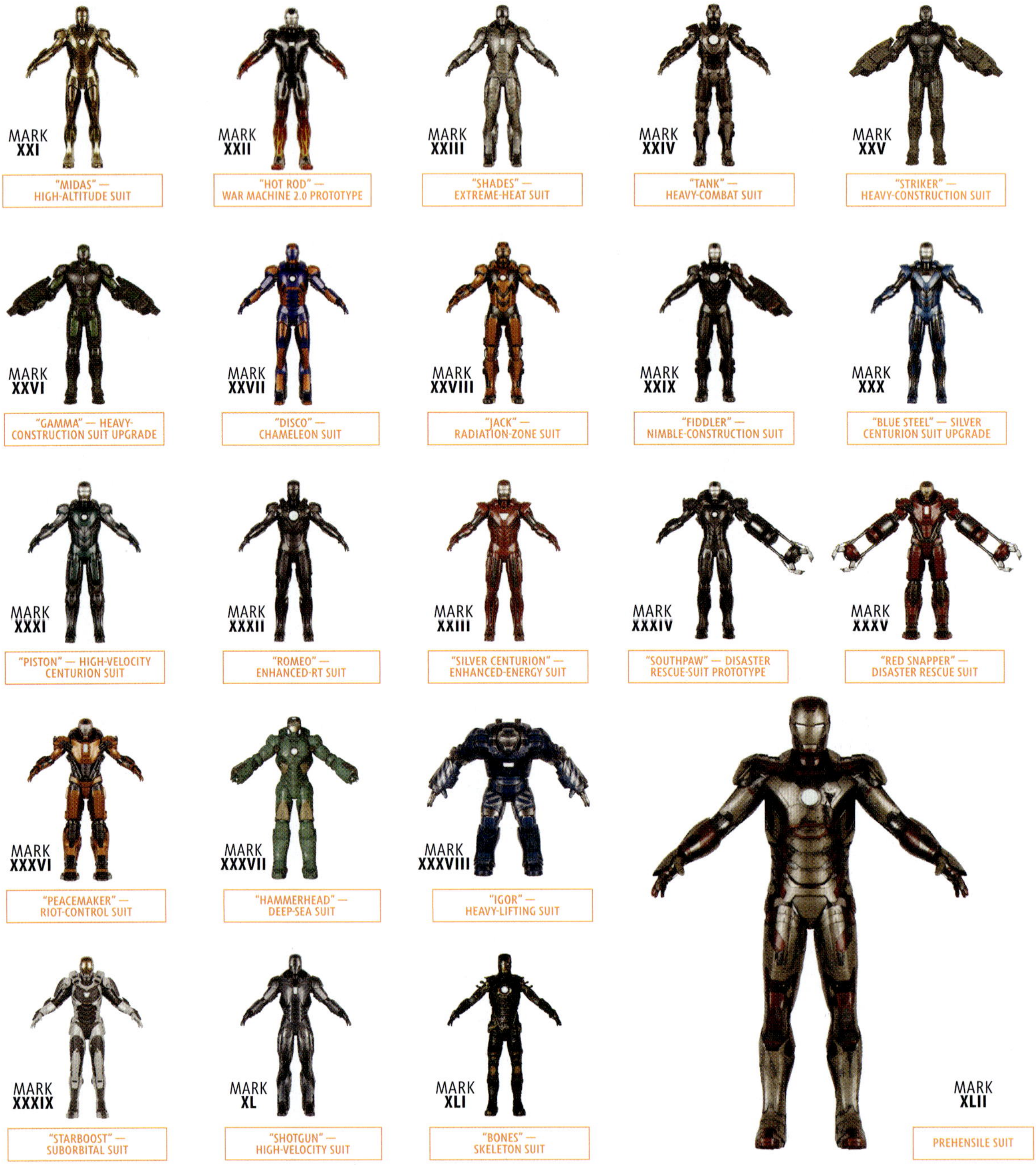

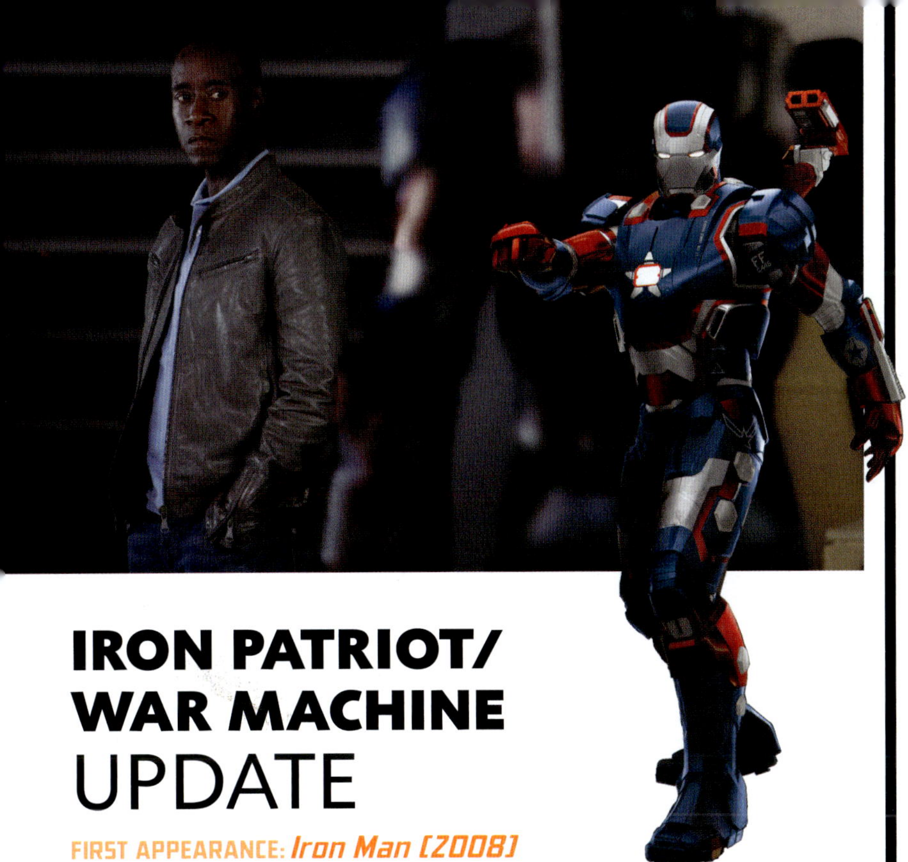

IN THE COMICS

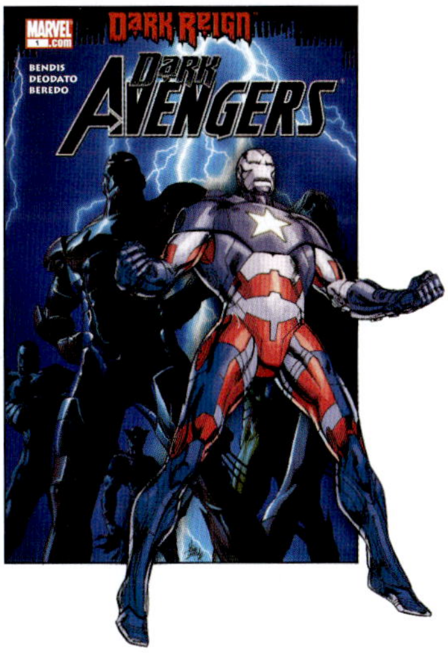

THE IRON PATRIOT ARMOR WAS A suit of Iron Man armor modified and piloted by Norman Osborn (a.k.a. the villainous Green Goblin), who was installed as director of the intelligence agency H.A.M.M.E.R., following the decommissioning of its predecessor, S.H.I.E.L.D. The corrupt Osborn wore the suit while leading his personal team of Avengers, which was comprised primarily of disguised costumed criminals.

After Osborn and H.A.M.M.E.R. were toppled by Earth's heroes during Osborn's siege of Asgard, the Iron Patriot armor was re-engineered by the U.S. Department of Defense as a drone, which A.I.M. stole and mass-replicated. James Rhodes proved able to appeal to the drones' artificial intelligence due to their familiarity with him; the drones accepted Rhodes as their leader and provided him an Iron Patriot armor to pilot. Rhodes operated as Iron Patriot for a short period before re-assuming his previous armored identity of War Machine.

FIRST APPEARANCE:
(IRON PATRIOT ARMOR)
DARK AVENGERS #1 (2009)

IRON PATRIOT/ WAR MACHINE UPDATE

FIRST APPEARANCE: ***Iron Man [2008]***

Following the Stark Expo, Tony Stark gave Lt. Col. James "Rhodey" Rhodes a new War Machine (armor to replace his Hammer-modified Mark II Iron Man armor) so Stark could reclaim the Mark II and allow Rhodes to continue operating as War Machine for government missions. Rhodes was primarily assigned to act against the Ten Rings; one such mission in Hong Kong prevented Rhodes from aiding Stark and the Avengers from repelling the extraterrestrial Chitauri attack on New York City. At the government's behest, Rhodes had his War Machine armor modified by Advanced Idea Mechanics, including a red-white-and-blue repaint, and his codename changed to "Iron Patriot." Rhodes told Stark about the rebranding at a restaurant, saying "War Machine" was deemed too aggressive. Rhodes expressed concern over Stark's haggard demeanor just before Stark suffered an anxiety attack upon seeing a child's drawing of the Chitauri portal and abruptly left.

During Rhodes' raid on a terrorist cell, Stark contacted Rhodes to request his login information for A.I.M.'s computer system in order to investigate a potential link between international terrorist-warlord the Mandarin and A.I.M. CEO Aldrich Killian. Later, Rhodes was dispatched to a possible location of the Mandarin only to find a sweatshop. There, one of Killian's Extremis-enhanced operatives, posing as a worker, immobilized Rhodes' armor and captured him.

At Killian's Miami mansion, Killian forced Rhodes out of the armor by using his Extremis abilities to heat the suit's exterior. Killian's operative Eric Savin used the armor to attack *Air Force One* and kidnap U.S. President Matthew Ellis by putting him in the Iron Patriot armor and sending it back to Florida. Savin was killed in a subsequent battle with Iron Man on *Air Force One*. Aboard the *Norco*, a former Roxxon tanker vessel, Killian intended to publicly execute Ellis. Stark and Rhodes infiltrated the *Norco*, and, as Stark and dozens of remote-controlled Iron Man armors (the "Iron Legion") fought Killian and his soldiers, Rhodes rescued Ellis, reclaimed his armor, and flew the president to safety. After foiling Killian's plot, Rhodes observed the arrest of Killian's White House mole, Vice President Rodriguez, and later observed Stark's surgery to finally remove the shrapnel from his chest.

FACT SHEET

- STARK BUILT THE NEW WAR MACHINE ARMOR SO RHODES WOULD HAVE A SUIT CONTAINING ONLY STARK TECHNOLOGY, BEREFT OF JUSTIN HAMMER'S MODIFICATIONS TO THE MARK II.
- RHODES' A.I.M. LOGIN AND PASSWORD WERE, RESPECTIVELY, "WARMACHINE68" AND "WARMACHINEROX."
- RHODES WAS PROMOTED TO A FULL COLONEL FOLLOWING HIS RESCUE OF PRESIDENT ELLIS.

ALDRICH KILLIAN

FIRST APPEARANCE: ***Iron Man 3* (2013)**

Disabled scientist Aldrich Killian approached Tony Stark at a conference in Bern, Switzerland, on New Year's Eve 1999 and tried to sell the industrialist on his think tank, Advanced Idea Mechanics. To get rid of him, Stark promised to meet Killian atop the hotel roof, but never showed up. After contemplating suicide, Killian realized how anonymous he was, and decided to turn that into a strength, believing he could manipulate the world from the shadows. Partnering with Stark's ex-lover Maya Hansen, Killian helped her develop Extremis, a serum that could superhumanly enhance the body's strength, durability, and healing, and could even regrow limbs. Illegally testing it on injured soldiers, Killian soon learned that Extremis-enhanced subjects were massively powerful but unstable, and could violently explode if subjected to the wrong dosage. To exploit this, Killian hired actor Trevor Slattery to pose as the Mandarin, a terrorist who claimed responsibility for the "bombings;" the spike in terrorism would then drive sales of A.I.M.'s weapons. Killian plotted with U.S. Vice President Rodriguez to exchange Extremis to restore his daughter's missing limb for lucrative defense contracts. Killian also enhanced himself with Extremis, eliminating his physical defects, and created plans to assassinate U.S. President Matthew Ellis so the now A.I.M.-loyal Rodriguez could rise to power.

Killian reached out to Stark's romantic partner, Pepper Potts, now CEO of Stark Industries, to partner with A.I.M., but she refused, believing Extremis too easily weaponizable. After Stark publicly threatened the Mandarin, Killian had his army destroy Stark's house; Stark survived and began to piece together Killian's plan while evading A.I.M.'s Extremis-enhanced agents. Killian then abducted Potts and had her injected with Extremis; Killian had hoped that Stark would help them stabilize the Extremis formula to save Pepper, but Stark refused. Believing her work was being abused, Hansen betrayed her employer, provoking Killian to shoot and kill her. After kidnapping President Ellis, Killian prepared to kill him on the decommissioned Roxxon oil tanker *Norco*, where he had also kept the Extremis-enhanced Potts as a trophy. While Stark attacked the Extremis soldiers with an army of Iron Man armors, Rhodes rescued the president. Killian battled Stark and soon gained the upper hand, but Stark trapped him in an Iron Man suit and self-destructed it. Killian survived, but was promptly blown to pieces by Potts, who used an Iron Man repulsor blaster against him.

IN THE COMICS

A SCIENTIST AT FUTUREPHARM, and about to lose funding for his research, Dr. Aldrich Killian worked with his research partner Maya Hansen to steal a sample of the bio-electronic human enhancement solution Extremis from the company's vaults and sell it to domestic terrorists, hoping the world would see its potential. Remorseful for what he had unleashed on the world, Killian composed a confession, then committed suicide.

FIRST APPEARANCE:
IRON MAN #1 (2004)

FACT SHEET

- PRIOR TO HIS EXTREMIS ENHANCEMENT, THE PHYSICALLY WEAK KILLIAN NEEDED GLASSES AND WALKED WITH A CANE.
- KILLIAN COULD REGENERATE LOST LIMBS, SUPERHEAT HIS BODY, AND EVEN BREATHE FIRE.
- KILLIAN REFERRED TO HIMSELF AS THE REAL MANDARIN, AND HAD SEVERAL LARGE DRAGON TATTOOS ON HIS TORSO.

MANDARIN
TREVOR SLATTERY

FIRST APPEARANCE: ***Iron Man 3* (2013)**

Drug-addicted former British stage actor Trevor Slattery was hired off the street by Advanced Idea Mechanics to play the Mandarin, an international terrorist claiming responsibility for explosions that killed numerous innocents; in actuality, the explosions were caused when test subjects of A.I.M.'s illegal, unstable biotechnology Extremis overloaded and violently detonated. Provided a wealthy lifestyle in a heavily guarded Miami mansion and a constant supply of drugs and women, Slattery played the role of the Ten Rings' enigmatic leader in front of a green screen and was never trusted with real guns during the filmings.

In a video aired across the U.S. via hijacked TV signals, the Mandarin took credit for a church bombing on the Ali Al Salem Air Base in Kuwait and called it a lesson for the United States and U.S. President Matthew Ellis. After Extremis test subject Jack Taggart exploded in front of Hollywood's Chinese Theatre, the Mandarin took credit for the "bombing," calling it the destruction of another cheap American knock-off. Tony Stark, whose friend Happy Hogan was heavily injured during the Hollywood explosion, threatened the Mandarin on live TV, providing his home address on the airwaves. When A.I.M.'s Extremis soldiers attacked Stark's home, Stark escaped the destruction as Iron Man. The Mandarin later apparently executed Roxxon Oil Corporation accountant Thomas Richards during a live broadcast, despite President Ellis complying with the Mandarin's demands to call him. Stark tracked down the broadcast signal and confronted the terrorist leader in Miami, Florida, only to learn from a drunken, unstable Slattery that the Mandarin was merely an A.I.M.-created fiction. When A.I.M. operative Eric Savin knocked Stark out and reprimanded Slattery for not pressing the panic button, Slattery told Savin he had everything under control. After escaping A.I.M. custody, Stark called the authorities to arrest Slattery. As he was brought into custody, the actor relished in his newfound fame and the gathered press.

FACT SHEET

- SLATTERY'S PORTRAYAL OF KING LEAR WAS THE TOAST OF CROYDON, LONDON.
- SLATTERY WENT THROUGH PLASTIC SURGERY FOR THE MANDARIN ROLE.
- A.I.M. CREATED THE MANDARIN COSTUMES AND WROTE THE MANDARIN SCRIPTS, WHICH WERE FILLED WITH HISTORICAL FACTS AND MANIPULATION OF WESTERN ICONOGRAPHY.

IN THE COMICS

THE MANDARIN WAS THE WEALTHY son of a Chinese businessman and a British noblewoman who used 10 powerful rings found in an alien spaceship in numerous attempts to conquer China and restore it to its former glory. Clashing numerous times with American heroes including Iron Man (Tony Stark), he fell into a coma after a disastrous defeat. Mandarin's son Temujin continued his legacy until Mandarin reawakened to terrorize the world anew using the biogenetic Extremis serum and armored villains. Despite the aid of former lover Justine Hammer and their daughter Sasha, Mandarin was repeatedly stopped by Iron Man. Stark rival Ezekiel Stane apparently slew Mandarin for enslaving him during a plot against Iron Man.

FIRST APPEARANCE:
TALES OF SUSPENSE #50 (1964)

PEPPER POTTS UPDATE

FIRST APPEARANCE: ***Iron Man [2008]***

Years before her involvement with Stark Industries, Virginia "Pepper" Potts worked with the disabled Aldrich Killian, who had an unrequited crush on her. Years later, now the CEO of Stark Enterprises, Potts met Killian again, now head of Advanced Idea Mechanics, who presented a proposal to help back Extremis, a biotechnological program that could chemically recode human DNA, a serum Killian used on himself to reach a pinnacle of human health. Despite Killian's impressive demonstration, she rejected the proposal, feeling Extremis could be easily weaponized.

After the meeting, Potts went to the mansion she shared with Tony Stark, who probingly mentioned her encounter with Killian, having been informed of the meeting by security head Harold "Happy" Hogan. Stark then admitted to her his growing anxiety since the alien invasion in New York months before, anxiety which later fueled nightmares. One such dream caused Stark to inadvertently summon his latest cybernetically controlled Iron Man armor, which threatened Potts before Stark woke up and deactivated it.

When Stark publicly threatened international terrorist the Mandarin for his attacks on the innocent, he offered his home address so the Mandarin could bring the fight to him. Potts subsequently packed bags so they could go into hiding just as Maya Hansen, a scientific acquaintance of Stark's, arrived seemingly to tell Stark she suspected her boss, Killian, was working for the Mandarin. As Stark refused to go, a missile struck the mansion; Stark ordered his armor to form around Potts to protect her. After Potts used the armor to get Hansen outside the collapsing mansion, Stark summoned it back to himself to battle their attackers. Potts watched as the mansion collapsed into the sea with Stark still inside, only learning he survived when she donned an earlier armor's helmet and heard a message he'd left her from a payphone.

While hiding from Mandarin's men, Hansen told Potts of Killian's Extremis experiments, which resulted in fiery explosions of many of its illegal subjects. However, Killian arrived and Hansen revealed she was working with him; the two took Potts prisoner. Killian later injected her with Extremis to use as leverage against Stark and to be a "trophy" of Killian's victory. When Stark attempted to rescue her, the ensuing battle caused Potts to fall from a crane into a raging inferno. However, Potts survived the fall, thanks to Extremis' superhuman enhancements, which she used to battle Killian before using a repulsor blaster from one of Stark's Iron Man armors to kill Killian. Stark later reversed the Extremis effects on Potts; she then watched as Stark finally had the shrapnel removed from his chest.

EXTREMIS EMPOWERED

FACT SHEET

- ALTHOUGH CLOSE WITH HOGAN, POTTS FOUND HIS OVER-EAGERNESS AFTER HIS PROMOTION TO STARK INDUSTRIES' HEAD OF SECURITY TO BE IRRITATING.
- STARK'S CHRISTMAS PRESENT TO POTTS WAS AN ENORMOUS STUFFED RABBIT. SHE TOLD STARK SHE APPRECIATED THE THOUGHT.
- AFFECTED BY EXTREMIS, POTTS DISPLAYED SUPERHUMAN STRENGTH AND DURABILITY, AND THE ABILITY TO GENERATE GREAT HEAT.

ADVANCED IDEA MECHANICS

FIRST APPEARANCE:
***Iron Man 3* (2013)**

Scientist Aldrich Killian founded Advanced Idea Mechanics (A.I.M.) as a privately funded think tank, but after a drunken rejection by Tony Stark, Killian bitterly realized that his anonymity was a strength and turned A.I.M.'s focus to weapons manufacturing. Recruiting scientist Maya Hansen into A.I.M., Killian helped Hansen develop her Extremis project, an unstable biological enhancement treatment that could re-grow lost limbs. Illegally testing Extremis on wounded soldiers, A.I.M. found Extremis also granted superhuman strength, durability, healing, and heat-based powers to the recipients, but improper dosage caused the test subjects to explode, killing any nearby. Using the explosions to A.I.M.'s benefit, Killian hired failed actor Trevor Slattery to act as international terrorist the Mandarin, and claim responsibility for the "bombings;" fear of future attacks spiked sales for A.I.M.'s weapons. When Killian tried to force Stark to help stabilize Extremis, Stark refused and used his Iron Man armors to eventually defeat Killian and his enhanced army, which also prevented A.I.M.'s plans to assassinate the U.S. President Matthew Ellis.

FACT SHEET

- FOLLOWING STARK'S REJECTION, KILLIAN CHANGED A.I.M.'S FOCUS FROM PUBLIC TO COVERT ACTIVITIES AFTER BRIEFLY CONTEMPLATING SUICIDE.
- KILLIAN USED A REFINED VERSION OF EXTREMIS TO CURE HIMSELF OF HIS PHYSICAL AILMENTS.
- A.I.M. RECEIVED LUCRATIVE DEFENSE CONTRACTS AFTER KILLIAN PROMISED TO USE EXTREMIS TO RESTORE THE MISSING LIMB OF U.S. VICE PRESIDENT RODRIGUEZ'S DAUGHTER.

IN THE COMICS

A.I.M. (ADVANCED IDEA MECHANICS) is a scientific organization dedicated to toppling world governments through technology. Originally the science division of the terrorist group Hydra, A.I.M. became its own entity led by their elected leader, the Scientist Supreme, eventually going public as an arms manufacturer to further its agenda of acquiring world power. After the Avengers' Sunspot (Roberto Da Costa) staged a hostile takeover of A.I.M., he turned their efforts toward benevolent causes rather than world domination.

FIRST APPEARANCE:
TALES OF SUSPENSE #75 (1966)

HAPPY HOGAN
UPDATE

FIRST APPEARANCE: *Iron Man* (2008)

On New Year's Eve 1999, Harold "Happy" Hogan was inventor Tony Stark's bodyguard while Stark attended a convention in Bern, Switzerland. Hogan followed Stark to scientist Maya Hansen's hotel room where Hogan ignored Hansen's request not to touch her plant and snapped off a piece, unaware it was an Extremis experiment. The plant exploded, but no one present was harmed. In modern times, Hogan became head of security at Stark Industries, and took his job very seriously. When Advanced Idea Mechanics CEO Aldrich Killian came to visit now-S.I. CEO Pepper Potts to propose his latest technological innovation, a suspicious Hogan alerted Stark while keeping an eye on Killian's disrespectful associate Eric Savin. Hogan later followed Savin to Hollywood's Chinese Theatre, where Savin provided Extremis subject Jack Taggart with a case of Extremis injections. Hogan bumped into Taggart and swiped an injector. After Hogan and Savin exchanged punches, Savin violently threw Hogan across the plaza. Taggart's body exploded, leaving Hogan comatose and gravely wounded. A Killian-hired actor posing as international terrorist Mandarin claimed responsibility for the explosion, and Stark publicly swore vengeance. Reviewing crime scene scans, Stark noticed Hogan's hand pointing to Taggart's dog tags, revealing his name and a military connection. This led Stark to a similar recent explosion in Tennessee, and ultimately to Killian, who was trying to subversively claim control of the U.S. presidency. Sometime after Killian's defeat, Hogan awoke from his coma.

FACT SHEET

- WHEN THE PLANT EXPLODED, HOGAN LEAPT ATOP STARK ASSUMING A Y2K ERROR WAS THE CAUSE.
- HOGAN COULDN'T UNDERSTAND HOW TO REVERSE HIS TABLET'S FORWARD-FACING CAMERA.
- HOGAN WAS GENUINELY PROUD THAT HIS SECURITY METHODS CAUSED S.I. STAFF COMPLAINTS TO RISE BY 300 PERCENT, INCORRECTLY BELIEVING THIS PROVED THAT WRONGDOINGS WERE BEING STOPPED.

HARLEY KEENER

FIRST APPEARANCE: ***Iron Man 3* (2013)**

When his armor ran out of energy, Tony Stark crash-landed in Tennessee and dragged the armor into a garage. Found there by potato-gun-wielding pre-teen Harley Keener, Stark revealed who he was and engaged in conversation with Keener, who suggested Stark create a stealth Iron Man suit. In exchange for a device that could protect him from a school bully, Keener agreed to help Stark gather materials he needed to repair his armor and show him the site of an apparent terrorist bombing that Stark wanted to investigate. When Stark was attacked by biotechnologically enhanced soldiers reporting to terrorist mastermind Aldrich Killian, Keener used a snowball to throw off Eric Savin's aim when he tried to shoot Stark. Savin used Keener as a hostage, but Keener used the anti-bully device to escape so Stark could defeat Savin. Later, after Stark left Tennessee, Keener calmed him down over the telephone when Stark had a panic attack. After Stark defeated Killian, he outfitted Keener's garage with advanced technology and equipment to thank him.

FACT SHEET

- KEENER HAS A BURGEONING, SHARP SCIENTIFIC MIND.
- KEENER'S INQUISITIVENESS GOT HIM IN TROUBLE WHEN HE PRIED AT IRON MAN'S HAND AND BROKE A FINGER OFF THE ARMOR.
- KEENER TRIED TO GUILT STARK INTO STAYING IN TOWN BY REFERRING TO HIS FATHER'S ABANDONMENT OF HIS FAMILY SIX YEARS BEFORE. WHEN CALLED ON IT BY STARK, KEENER SHRUGGED AND SAID, "IT WAS WORTH A SHOT."
- WHEN STARK ASKED KEENER FOR A WATCH TO USE FOR REPAIRS, HE PROVIDED HIS 6-YEAR-OLD SISTER'S TOY-THEMED WATCH ABOUT WHICH STARK RAZZED KEENER.

MATTHEW ELLIS

FIRST APPEARANCE: ***Iron Man 3* (2013)**

After an explosion at Kuwait's Ali Al Salam air base, the international terrorist the Mandarin challenged U.S. President Matthew Ellis on national television, insinuating Ellis wouldn't find him or predict his next target. The attacks were secretly the work of Aldrich Killian who hoped to usurp power over the U.S. presidency and had hired an actor to play the Mandarin to hide his Extremis experiments. Ellis responded by publicly re-introducing War Machine in newly re-painted, re-christened "Iron Patriot" armor. Ellis was ridiculed by the press for suggesting an armor's paint job could defeat the Mandarin. The Mandarin later threatened to kill Roxxon Oil accountant Thomas Richards on live television if Ellis did not call the Mandarin on a number implanted into Ellis' phone; despite being advised not to negotiate with terrorists, Ellis complied. However, the Mandarin executed Richards and told a shocked Ellis he was next. Ellis was later kidnapped from *Air Force One* by an Extremis-enhanced soldier using the Iron Patriot armor. The president was slated for public execution aboard the Roxxon *Norco* oil tanker, but Lt. Col. James Rhodes and Tony Stark infiltrated the *Norco* and used Stark's Iron Legion to fight Extremis-enhanced soldiers. Rhodes saved Ellis and flew him to safety with the recovered Iron Patriot armor.

FACT SHEET

- ELLIS BELIEVED THE MANDARIN HACKED HIS CELL PHONE WHEN IT WAS POTENTIALLY VICE PRESIDENT RODRIGUEZ, SECRETLY WORKING WITH KILLIAN IN EXCHANGE FOR THE RESTORATION OF HIS DAUGHTER'S MISSING LIMB WITH EXTREMIS BIOTECHNOLOGY.
- TWO YEARS PRIOR TO ELLIS' KIDNAPPING, ELLIS HELPED ROXXON OIL CORPORATION'S EXECUTIVES AVOID LEGAL RAMIFICATIONS WHEN THE *NORCO* SPILLED ONE MILLION GALLONS OFF PENSACOLA, FLORIDA; AN ACT KILLIAN THOUGHT WOULD PLAY WELL IN ELLIS' EXECUTION.

MARVEL'S *THOR: THE DARK WORLD*

GUIDEBOOK TO THE MARVEL CINEMATIC UNIVERSE

MARVEL

THOR: THE DARK WORLD

MARVEL STUDIOS PRESENTS CHRIS HEMSWORTH NATALIE PORTMAN TOM HIDDLESTON AND ANTHONY HOPKINS AS ODIN "THOR: THE DARK WORLD" STELLAN SKARSGÅRD IDRIS ELBA CHRISTOPHER ECCLESTON ADEWALE AKINNUOYE-AGBAJE KAT DENNINGS RAY STEVENSON ZACHARY LEVI TADANOBU ASANO JAIMIE ALEXANDER WITH RENE RUSSO CASTING BY SARAH HALLEY FINN, C.S.A. MUSIC BY BRIAN TYLER MUSIC SUPERVISOR DAVE JORDAN VISUAL EFFECTS SUPERVISOR JAKE MORRISON COSTUME DESIGNER WENDY PARTRIDGE EDITED BY DAN LEBENTAL, A.C.E. WYATT SMITH PRODUCTION DESIGN CHARLES WOOD DIRECTOR OF PHOTOGRAPHY KRAMER MORGENTHAU, ASC EXECUTIVE PRODUCERS NIGEL GOSTELOW STAN LEE EXECUTIVE PRODUCER ALAN FINE EXECUTIVE PRODUCERS VICTORIA ALONSO CRAIG KYLE EXECUTIVE PRODUCER LOUIS D'ESPOSITO PRODUCED BY KEVIN FEIGE, p.g.a. STORY BY DON PAYNE AND ROBERT RODAT SCREENPLAY BY CHRISTOPHER L. YOST AND CHRISTOPHER MARKUS & STEPHEN McFEELY DIRECTED BY ALAN TAYLOR

MARVEL

Collecting information from *Thor: The Dark World* (2013) and *Marvel's Thor: The Dark World Prelude* #1-2 (2013).

HEAD WRITER/COORDINATOR: **MIKE O'SULLIVAN**

COORDINATION: **DARON JENSEN**

WRITERS: **ROB BOCK**, **ANTHONY COTILLETTA**, **PATRICK DUKE**, **MIKE FICHERA**, **DARON JENSEN**, **ROB LONDON**, **CHRIS MCCARVER**, **MARKUS RAYMOND**, AND **JACOB ROUGEMONT**

ARTISTS: **BOB CHESHIRE**, **OLIVIER COIPEL**, **VERONICA FISH**, **JACK KIRBY**, **ANDY KUBERT**, AND **WALT SIMONSON**

COVER ARTIST: **MARCOS MARTIN**

SPECIAL THANKS TO DAVE ALTHOFF, STEVEN BOYD, SHAWN "KEEBLER" BYERS, JEFF CHRISTIANSEN, CAROLYN CLARKSON, MATT DELMANOWSKI, ERIKA DENTON, TIM DILLON, PERCIVAL LANUZA, AMANDA NALLEY, JACQUE PORTE, AND RYAN POTTER.

THOR CREATED BY STAN LEE, LARRY LIEBER, AND JACK KIRBY

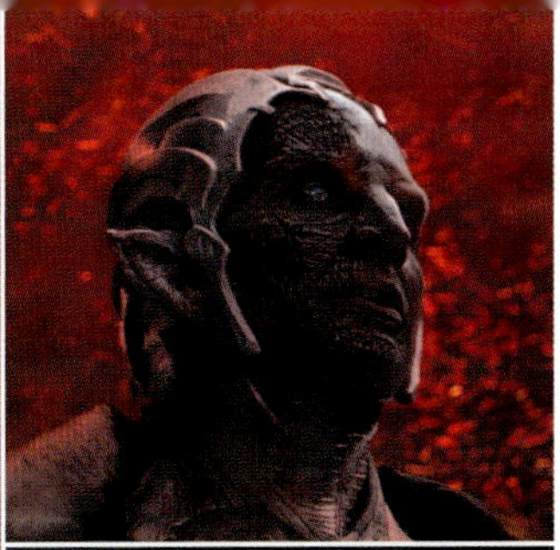

MALEKITH EMPOWERED BY THE AETHER

AETHER

FIRST APPEARANCE: ***Thor: The Dark World [2013]***

Five thousand years ago, during a Convergence of the Nine Realms, the Dark Elf Malekith sought to return the universe to eternal night by releasing the ancient, destructive force of the Aether. Asgardian King Bor and his armies opposed the Dark Elves, defeating Malekith and hiding the Aether. In modern times, another Convergence weakened the borders between realms, allowing human scientist Jane Foster to stumble upon—and become host to—the Aether. Taking note of these events, Malekith attacked Asgard seeking the Aether, but was driven back by Thor and Asgard's army. Thor took Foster to Svartalfheim, where he intended to destroy the Aether, but failed. Malekith seized the Aether and brought it to Earth to release during the Convergence and destroy the universe. After a prolonged battle between Malekith and Thor, Foster used Dr. Erik Selvig's gravimetric spikes to teleport the Dark Elf back to Svartalfheim, where his Ark starship crushed him when it fell through another portal. Asgard reclaimed the Aether, entrusting it to the Collector for safekeeping in his vast archive.

FACT SHEET

- WHEN IT PERCEIVED THREATS AGAINST ITS HOST, THE AETHER WOULD LASH OUT WITH A VIOLENT RELEASE OF DARK ENERGY.
- ASGARDIAN HISTORY BOOKS STATE THE AETHER PREDATES THE UNIVERSE, IS FLUID THOUGH ITS FELLOW RELICS ARE STONE, CHANGES MATTER TO DARK MATTER, AND DRAWS STRENGTH FROM A HOST'S LIFE FORCE.
- THE AETHER'S ENERGIES MANIFEST AS SMOKEY TENDRILS PROTRUDING FROM THE HOST AND CAN CHANGE THE COLOR OF ITS HOST'S EYES TO SOLID BLACK OR RED.
- AFTER THOR HIT THE AETHER WITH LIGHTNING, IT SHATTERED INTO RED CRYSTALS. WHEN MALEKITH MYSTICALLY GATHERED THESE TOGETHER, THE AETHER RESUMED ITS STANDARD FLUID ENERGY FORM.

AETHER UNLEASHED IN LONDON

ALIGNMENT OF WORLDS

FANDRAL

FIRST APPEARANCE: ***Thor (2011)***

Asgardian swordsman Fandral is Thor's longtime ally. Together, he and his companions, Volstagg and Hogun, are known as the Warriors Three. Against King Odin's orders, Fandral accompanied Thor to Jotunheim to confront the Frost Giants following their infiltration of Asgard. Afterward, Odin banished Thor to Earth for his disobedience. When Odin fell into his rejuvenating Odinsleep and the untrustworthy trickster Loki assumed Asgard's throne, Fandral journeyed with Volstagg, Hogun, and Sif to Earth to find Thor. There, they helped him battle the Destroyer construct, sent by Loki to kill Thor. When they returned to Asgard, Thor confronted Loki, and Odin reclaimed the throne.

During the next two years, Fandral was among the Asgardian warriors who defended the Nine Realms from invading marauders. Following a battle in Vanaheim, Fandral enjoyed a celebration in Asgard. Fandral and Volstagg later brought captured enemies to Asgard for imprisonment—unaware one among their number was the Dark Elf Algrim, sent to infiltrate the dungeon and cause a distraction by transforming into the seemingly unstoppable Kurse. When Kurse freed his fellow prisoners, Fandral and Asgard's forces fought the escapees while Dark Elves invaded Asgard to capture Jane Foster, inadvertent host to the Aether. To stop Dark Elf Malekith's plans for the Aether, Fandral and his companions conspired to sneak Foster out of Asgard against Odin's wishes. During their flight from the city, Thor, Loki, and Foster abandoned a captured Dark Elf Harrow ship and boarded a flying skiff manned by Fandral, while Odin's soldiers continued after the Dark Elf vessel. When the soldiers caught up with the skiff, Fandral boarded the pursuing ship and fought them while his friends escaped. Fandral told the soldiers it wasn't personal as he beat them.

IN THE COMICS

FANDRAL THE DASHING IS A swashbuckling member of Asgard's Warriors Three, a band of adventurers often allied with Thor. He, Hogun, and Volstagg are a tight-knit group of companions, seldom not at one another's side. One of Asgard's most capable swordsmen, Fandral is dashing, charming, daring, optimistic, and a known womanizer; he often encourages his allies into great adventures.

FIRST APPEARANCE:
JOURNEY INTO MYSTERY #119 (1965)

FACT SHEET

- A CHARMING ROGUE, FANDRAL IS STYLISH IN ALL HE DOES, INCLUDING BATTLE—HE OFTEN JOYOUSLY LAUGHS DURING CONFLICT.
- WHEN CELEBRATING ASGARD'S VICTORIES, HE WAS SEEN ENTERTAINING MORE THAN ONE WOMAN.
- FANDRAL SERVED AS ONE OF ODIN'S ADVISORS WHEN DISCUSSING THE DARK ELVES' ATTACK.
- FANDRAL IS A MASTERFUL AND AGILE SWORDSMAN; WHEN S.H.I.E.L.D. AGENTS FIRST ENCOUNTERED HIM, THEY REFERRED TO HIM AS "ROBIN HOOD."

JANE FOSTER
UPDATE

FIRST APPEARANCE: ***Thor [2011]***

Dr. Jane Foster was distressed when a year passed with no word from Thor, but persisted in trying to re-open the Bifrost, ignorant of its destruction. When Loki later attempted to conquer Earth, S.H.I.E.L.D. relocated Foster to Norway for her safekeeping. Foster was doubly hurt when she saw footage of Thor battling Loki in New York, unaware that Thor's access to Earth required use of Dark Energy that nearly killed him. During the subsequent second year of no contact, Foster abandoned hope for their relationship. Unable to leave Asgard, Thor kept watch over Foster through the all-seeing Heimdall.

Living in London with Erik Selvig and Darcy Lewis, Foster contemplated finally seeing other people, but cut short a date with a man named Richard when Lewis showed her spatial anomaly readings similar to Thor's first arrival on Earth. While exploring these disruptions of Earth's physical laws in isolated spots around the city, Foster inadvertently passed through an interdimensional portal and became a host for the Aether. Alarmed by Heimdall's inability to see Foster while she was off-Earth, Thor used the rebuilt Bifrost to reunite with Foster, who was initially angry with Thor until he explained Bifrost's destruction and Asgard's isolation. When the Aether perceived policemen trying to arrest Foster for trespassing as a threat, it explosively repelled them. Startled, Thor took Foster to Asgard for examination.

Thor's father Odin recognized the Aether and explained its origins, but had no knowledge of how to extract it. When the Aether's previous owners, the Dark Elves, invaded Asgard to retrieve it and finish their eons-old plan to plunge the Nine Realms into eternal darkness, Thor's mother Frigga took Foster under her protection, but was killed by the beastly Kurse on Dark Elf leader Malekith's orders. Against Odinvs commands and with the help of Loki, Thor took Foster off Asgard to lure Malekith into a trap—but when Malekith drew the Aether out of Foster, Thor's attempt to destroy it failed, allowing Malekith to claim it and leave for Earth. Following him through an interdimensional portal, Thor battled Malekith until Foster and Selvig used gravimetric devices to open portals to Svartalfheim, sending both Malekith and the Ark, his massive starship, home; the ship apparently crushed Malekith upon landing. After facing Odin to atone for his treasonous actions, Thor returned to Earth and was joyously reunited with Foster.

DISCOVERING THE AETHER

FACT SHEET

- WHEN THOR AND FOSTER WERE FIRST REUNITED, SHE SLAPPED HIM TWICE—ONCE TO MAKE SURE HE WAS REAL, AND AGAIN FOR FAILING TO RETURN TO HER AS PROMISED.
- FOSTER STRUCK LOKI IN THE FACE UPON THEIR FIRST MEETING, STATING IT WAS "FOR NEW YORK."
- FOSTER IMPRESSED ONE OF THE ASGARDIAN PHYSICIANS WITH HER UNDERSTANDING OF A MYSTIC SOUL FORGE, WHICH FOSTER CORRECTLY RECOGNIZED AS A QUANTUM-FIELD GENERATOR.

FRIGGA UPDATE

FIRST APPEARANCE: ***Thor (2011)***

Queen Frigga never abandoned hope that her son Loki survived falling from the shattered Bifrost; however, one year later, she mystically detected him in Chitauri space. She projected her astral form to meet him, but Loki quickly dissipated her ghostly shape with his newly acquired scepter. Both Odin and Thor doubted Frigga's discovery, believing Loki's body was scattered across the universe after plummeting into a space warp, but Frigga insisted Loki was alive and planning something involving the Tesseract energy cube. Eventually traveling to Earth, Loki stole the Tesseract from S.H.I.E.L.D. in a ploy to rule the planet, but he was defeated by Earth's Avengers and returned home to face Asgardian justice. Frigga welcomed Loki with an affectionate embrace, pleading with him not to further provoke Odin's wrath; Odin claimed it was only Frigga's love that saved Loki from execution.

Odin sentenced Loki to eternal imprisonment and prohibited Frigga from seeing him, but she secretly visited in astral form and had furnishings and books brought to his cell. When Loki blamed Odin for unfairly incarcerating him, Frigga challenged Loki to take responsibility for his actions as a true king would, but Loki lashed out at her, reminding her that Odin was not his true father. When asked, Loki gently admitted he did not consider Frigga his true mother. Saddened, Frigga stated that she wished Loki's powers of perception extended to others as well as himself, then vanished.

After the Aether claimed Jane Foster as its host, Thor brought her to Asgard, and Frigga pleasantly greeted her. When the Dark Elves attacked Asgard to reclaim the Aether, Frigga fiercely guarded Foster, easily besting the Dark Elf leader Malekith in swordplay. Malekith's protector, Kurse, restrained Frigga as Malekith attempted to seize Foster—only to discover her appearance was an illusion created by Frigga's magic. Malekith ordered Frigga to disclose the Aether's location, but she defiantly refused, and Kurse slew her at Malekith's command moments before Thor and Odin arrived. Later, all of Asgard's citizens mourned and attended Frigga's funeral. When Loki heard the news, he was overcome with grief and anger, and later helped Thor attack Malekith, seeking vengeance for Frigga's death.

FACT SHEET

- THOR INITIALLY LEARNED OF THE DARK ELVES IN HIS CHILDHOOD WHEN FRIGGA TOLD HIM STORIES ABOUT THEM.
- FRIGGA ALWAYS KNEW WHEN ODIN LIED TO HER SO SHE WOULD NOT WORRY FOR HIS WELL-BEING, BUT SHE STILL DID. DESPITE ALL ODIN HAD BEEN THROUGH IN HIS LIFETIME, FRIGGA CLAIMED IF NOT FOR HER WORRYING, HE MIGHT NOT HAVE SURVIVED IT ALL.
- FRIGGA NURTURED LOKI'S APTITUDE FOR MAGIC THROUGHOUT HIS LIFE.

ALGRIM

KURSE

FIRST APPEARANCE: ***Thor: The Dark World* (2013)**

Five millennia ago, Algrim—one of the most loyal of Svartalfheim's Dark Elf army—fought alongside Dark Elf leader Malekith during a Convergence, an alignment of the Nine Realms. After failing in his attempt to use the Aether to plunge the universe in darkness, Malekith sacrificed much of the Dark Elf race in a last-ditch effort to destroy the Asgardian army during his escape attempt. Believing the Elves obliterated, Asgardian monarch Bor ordered the Aether hidden. Malekith took Algrim along with the few remaining Dark Elves into deep space, where they remained in suspended animation.

In modern times, the Aether was accidentally rediscovered and absorbed into the body of Jane Foster. Reawakened by the Aether's activity, Malekith vowed to reclaim it. For Malekith's plans to prevail, Algrim needed to infiltrate Asgard, where Thor had taken Foster, and disable their defenses so Malekith could capture her. To assist him, Malekith granted Algrim the power to become the last of the Kursed: Dark Elf warriors transformed and empowered by pure darkness. Algrim affirmed his loyalty without hesitation, allowing Malekith to cut open his abdomen and hide a Kurse stone inside.

Disguised among a group of marauders captured by Asgardian forces, Algrim was imprisoned in the Asgardian palace dungeons. Algrim retrieved the hidden stone from his body and activated its power, becoming the monstrous Kurse. Now immensely powerful, Kurse broke free of his cell and led an army of prisoners in revolt while the forces of Malekith's Dark Elf army began their siege on the Asgardian palace. When Kurse destroyed the palace's shield generator, Malekith's ship crashed through the palace walls. Finding Malekith mid-battle with the Asgardian queen Frigga, Kurse murdered Frigga with her own sword when she refused to reveal Foster's location. Thor arrived as his mother was killed, but Kurse escaped with Malekith.

Later, Thor and Loki took Foster to Svartalfheim as bait, but Thor's plan to destroy the Aether while Malekith drew it out of Foster failed. After absorbing the Aether's power, Malekith boarded his ship as Kurse battled Thor. During the struggle, Loki impaled Kurse with his sword, which failed to slow the monster. Instead, Kurse pulled Loki against his own body, stabbing the trickster. Despite his injury, Loki activated one of Kurse's black-hole grenades, killing him.

FACT SHEET

- KURSE LEARNED THE LOCATION OF THE PALACE SHIELD GENERATOR FROM THE MISCHIEVOUS LOKI, WHO WAS ALSO IMPRISONED IN ASGARD'S DUNGEON AT THE TIME.
- IN ADDITION TO HIS GREAT STRENGTH, KURSE WAS ARMED WITH GRENADES THAT CREATED MINIATURE BLACK HOLES THAT CAUSED PEOPLE AND OBJECTS TO IMPLODE.
- KURSE WAS STRONG ENOUGH TO EASILY WITHSTAND BLOWS FROM THOR'S HAMMER MJOLNIR; HE PUMMELED THOR INTO SUBMISSION DURING THEIR FIGHT ON SVARTALFHEIM.

IN THE COMICS

THE STRONGEST DARK ELF IN the realm of Svartalfheim, Algrim the Strong was ordered by his ruler, Malekith the Accursed, to fight Thor. During the battle, Malekith also attempted to kill Thor. However, Thor escaped, and Algrim was gravely injured by Malekith's actions. Amnesiac after the battle, Algrim remembered only his hatred for Thor, and was later transformed by cosmic entity the Beyonder into the massively powerful Kurse. During a subsequent battle with Thor, Kurse's memories were restored, and his animosity turned to Malekith, who Kurse killed. Later, a resurrected Kurse sacrificed himself protecting Asgard's children during the latest Ragnarok, the "twilight of the gods."

FIRST APPEARANCE:
(ALGRIM THE STRONG) THOR #347 (1984); (KURSE) SECRET WARS II #4 (1985)

LOKI UPDATE

FIRST APPEARANCE: ***Thor (2011)***

For his crimes against both Asgard and Earth, Loki was sentenced to spend eternity in Asgard's dungeon. While he resented his father Odin and brother Thor for this, Loki maintained his affection for his mother, Frigga, who continued to visit him. When Thor's mortal love, Jane Foster, inadvertently became the host of the Aether, the Dark Elf Algrim infiltrated the prison in order to create a distraction for the Dark Elves to invade Asgard. Algrim transformed into the monstrous Kurse and freed numerous prisoners, but left Loki in his cell, despite Loki giving Kurse directions to leave the dungeon; later, Loki learned that Kurse and his leader Malekith had murdered Frigga. Soon, Thor came to Loki with a proposition; he needed to smuggle Foster out of Asgard, as part of a plan for Malekith to extract the Aether so Thor could destroy it. Loki agreed, and successfully led Thor and Foster to a hidden portal to Svartalfheim, the ancient Dark Elf homeworld.

In front of the Dark Elves, Loki and Thor engaged in a showy mock battle that ended with Loki apparently severing Thor's hand. Loki handed Foster over to Malekith, who extracted the Aether—but when Thor blasted it with lightning, it quickly reconstituted itself and was absorbed by Malekith, who departed, leaving Kurse and a company of Dark Elves to battle the two Asgardians. Loki defeated the Elves, and saved Thor by stabbing Kurse—only for Kurse to, in turn, mortally wound Loki. However, Loki killed Kurse by activating one of the Dark Elf's grenades, then apparently died. Loki survived, however, and returned to Asgard disguised as one of Odin's soldiers — then somehow secretly replaced Odin. In this guise, he counseled Thor on his decision to refuse the throne of Asgard, and gave his "son" his tacit approval, leaving Loki the king he always longed to be.

FACT SHEET

- UPON LEARNING OF HIS MOTHER'S DEATH, LOKI BECAME ENRAGED, MAGICALLY LASHING OUT, DESTROYING MUCH OF HIS CELL.
- WHEN THOR VISITED LOKI IN THE DUNGEON, LOKI INITIALLY MAINTAINED A MAGICAL FAÇADE OF COMPOSURE, BUT QUICKLY LET IT DROP TO LET THOR SEE THE DISHEVELED STATE HE WAS TRULY IN.
- DURING HIS ESCAPE FROM CAPTIVITY, LOKI TOOK ON THE APPEARANCE OF THOR'S FELLOW AVENGER CAPTAIN AMERICA AND ENJOYED THE EXPERIENCE, CLAIMING TO FEEL RIGHTEOUSNESS SURGING WITHIN HIM.
- MUCH LIKE ODIN, LOKI WAS DISMISSIVE OF THOR'S ROMANCE WITH JANE FOSTER, CITING THE SHORT LIFE SPANS OF HUMANS COMPARED TO ASGARDIANS.

MALEKITH

FIRST APPEARANCE: ***Thor: The Dark World (2013)***

Five millennia ago, Malekith led the Dark Elves of Svartalfheim in a campaign to return the universe to eternal darkness by releasing the Aether during a rare Convergence of the Nine Realms. Asgardian King Bor and his armies prevented this, taking the Aether from Malekith. To escape, Malekith dropped all but one Ark ship on the Asgardian army, sacrificing most of his people in the process. Boarding the last Ark, Malekith and his remaining army waited in suspended animation for another chance to plunge the universe into darkness.

In modern times, at the beginning of another Convergence, Malekith and his army awakened when Jane Foster accidentally absorbed the Aether. Swearing revenge on Asgard and wanting to reclaim the Aether, Malekith sent his warrior Algrim to infiltrate Asgard as a prisoner. When Algrim transformed into Kurse and caused a prison break as a distraction, Malekith attacked Asgard with Harrow ships. Unable to reclaim the Aether because Odin's wife Frigga hid Foster from him, Kurse slew Frigga on Malekith's order. Thor struck Malekith with lightning in retaliation, severely burning, scarring, and blackening the right side of his face, but Kurse saved Malekith and took him back to the Ark. While Malekith healed, Thor and Loki brought Foster to Svartalfheim to lure the Dark Elves there, where Thor planned to destroy the Aether when Malekith took it from Foster. However, Malekith absorbed the Aether and journeyed to Earth, planning on releasing it during the Convergence. Thor battled Malekith, ultimately using Dr. Erik Selvig's gravimetric spikes to teleport Malekith back to Svartalfheim where he was crushed by his own Ark ship after it fell through another portal at the conclusion of the Convergence.

IN THE COMICS

MALEKITH THE ACCURSED WAS sold by his impoverished mother at a young age and became a sorcerer after a lengthy tutelage under a Dark Elf wizard. After his master turned half his skin black for betraying him, Malekith returned home to feed his mother to her hounds. When a war against Asgard ended in defeat, Odin banished Malekith to a limbo of endless night. In recent years, the fire demon Surtur freed Malekith, who found new allies and enemies in the modern era. He also found imprisonment on numerous occasions and death at the hands of his vengeful ally Kurse. Escaping Hel, he eventually became Svartalfheim's king once again in a brutal campaign against his own kind.

FIRST APPEARANCE:
THOR #344 (1984)

FACT SHEET

- EMPOWERED BY THE AETHER, MALEKITH POSSESSED TELEKINETIC POWERS AND VAST DURABILITY.
- MALEKITH'S ARK CARRIER HOUSED THE LAST OF HIS KIND AND AN ARMADA OF HARROW SHIPS.

ODIN UPDATE

FIRST APPEARANCE: ***Thor [2011]***

After the Bifrost bridge's destruction, Asgardians were limited in their efforts to keep peace in the Nine Realms, which fell into chaos. Odin ordered the Bifrost repaired but after a year, the complicated mechanism still was not completed. When Frigga discovered Loki alive, she told Odin their adopted son was planning something on Earth involving the Tesseract. Knowing the Tesseract could be used to quickly repair the Bifrost, Odin used Dark Energy to send Thor to Earth, but the process almost killed Odin. Loki subsequently attempted to conquer Earth and killed thousands of humans in the process, but was eventually defeated by Thor and the Avengers. After Thor brought Loki to Asgard for imprisonment, and returned the Tesseract to Asgard, Heimdall used it to rebuild the Bifrost. This enabled Thor and Asgardian forces to restore peace in the Nine Realms while Odin recovered.

As Asgard celebrated peace across the Nine Realms, Odin took a melancholy Thor aside and, knowing he still pined for the human Jane Foster, recommended Thor take an Asgardian lover, heavily insinuating it be Sif. When Thor did not respond favorably, Odin directed Thor to at least celebrate his recent victories.

When Foster inadvertently became host for the ancient Aether energy, Thor brought her to Asgard. Initially upset by Thor bringing her there, Odin recognized the Aether and told its history as a weapon of the Dark Elves in millennia past until it was believed destroyed by Odin's father Bor. When the Dark Elves attacked Asgard to reclaim the Aether, Foster was protected by Odin's wife Frigga, but Frigga was killed while doing so. In his grief, Odin ordered the Bifrost closed and refused to listen to Thor's alternate plan to take Foster away from Asgard and destroy the Aether; Odin declared war against the Dark Elves and their leader, Malekith. Needing his help to leave Asgard, Thor freed Loki and left Asgard with Foster, disobeying Odin. When Odin learned of this, he ordered his guards to stop Thor at any cost. Later, Odin listened to a guard report he found Loki dead on Svartalfheim, unaware the guard was secretly Loki in disguise. When Thor returned to Asgard to report his defeat of Malekith, he remained ignorant that he was actually reporting to Loki, who had magically disguised himself as Odin and claimed the throne; Odin's whereabouts remain unrevealed.

FACT SHEET

- ODIN KEPT TRACK OF THOR'S PROGRESS RESTORING ORDER TO THE NINE REALMS VIA REPORTS FROM HIS RAVENS, HUGIN AND MUNIN.
- OUT OF RESPECT FOR FRIGGA, ODIN ONLY IMPRISONED LOKI INSTEAD OF KILLING HIM.
- POSING AS ODIN, LOKI DID NOT DISCOURAGE THOR FROM TURNING DOWN THE THRONE SO LOKI COULD KEEP IT FOR HIMSELF.

THOR UPDATE

FIRST APPEARANCE:
Thor (2011)

After the Bifrost was destroyed, the Nine Realms fell into chaos. As Asgard's mightiest warrior, Thor was charged with bringing order—and preventing the foretold twilight of the gods, Ragnarok. Thor traveled to Earth via Odin's dark magic, which nearly killed both men, and he and the Avengers defeated Loki's attempt to conquer humanity. Thor brought Loki and the Tesseract back to Asgard, where the latter was used to rebuild the Bifrost. Thor then led Asgard's forces on a number of successful campaigns, defeating marauders across the realms. But despite his successes, Thor still pined for Jane Foster, and frequently visited the all-seeing Heimdall to learn of her whereabouts and activities. After bringing peace to Vanaheim, Thor returned to Asgard; struck by melancholy, he left the celebratory feast to visit Heimdall, who was startled when Foster had disappeared from his sight after she inadvertently stumbled through a spatial anomaly created by the impending Convergence of the Nine Realms. During the unintentional trip, Foster became the unwilling host of the Aether, an ancient and destructive energy source weaponized by the violent Dark Elves five thousand years before.

Thor went to Earth to find Foster, who had returned five hours after disappearing, disarming her anger over not contacting her for two years by explaining the fallout of the Bifrost's destruction. However, Thor realized something was amiss when the Aether violently flared after a police officer grabbed Foster; he took her to Asgard for examination. Shortly after, Asgard was beset by Dark Elves seeking the Aether, which they planned to unleash during the Convergence to return the universe to primordial darkness. Thor did his best to

PILOTING A CAPTURED HARROW SHIP

drive them back, but he was unable to save his mother, Frigga, who died defending Foster. Thor vengefully scarred the Dark Elves' leader, Malekith, with lightning, and forced him to retreat. Thor suggested to a mourning Odin that Foster should leave Asgard, but Odin refused, and ordered the Bifrost closed. Undaunted, Thor enlisted the help of Heimdall, Sif, the Warriors Three, and even the imprisoned Loki to sneak Foster out. While the others caused distractions, Thor freed Loki; the pair fled Asgard with Foster to the Dark Elf homeworld, Svartalfheim, through a secret portal of which only Loki knew. There, Thor hoped to destroy the Aether at the moment Malekith extracted it from Foster, ending its threat.

On Svartalfheim, Loki appeared to betray Thor—severing his hand—and offered Foster to Malekith, who extracted the Aether. His wound revealed as an illusion, Thor struck the Aether with lightning, but it quickly reconstituted and bonded to Malekith. The Dark Elf set out for Earth, leaving the monstrous Kurse to deal with the two Asgardians. While Thor battled Kurse, Loki stabbed the monster from behind, but Kurse shrugged off the wound and impaled Loki. Apparently mortally wounded, Loki activated one of Kurse's grenades, which destroyed the monster. Believing Loki dead, Foster and Thor located a Convergence portal and returned to Earth, leaving Loki's body behind. The two strategized with their friend Erik Selvig, who had built gravimetric devices to control the portals.

Learning that Greenwich would be the focal point of the Convergence, Thor and his human companions journeyed there. As the Convergence began, Thor battled Malekith, their struggle taking them through portals to Svartalfheim, Vanaheim, Jotunheim, and back to Earth. When Malekith prepared to release the Aether, Thor used Selvig's devices to transport Malekith back to Svartalfheim, saving the Nine Realms. Selvig then sent Malekith's massive, toppling Ark starship to Svartalfheim, as well, where it killed Malekith when it fell on him. Thor returned to Asgard, where he told Odin he did not want the throne, but promised he'd always defend the realm. Unaware he had been speaking to a disguised Loki, who had somehow replaced Odin after surviving his apparent death, Thor returned to Earth and reunited with Foster, unintentionally leaving Loki on the throne.

FACT SHEET

- ON VANAHEIM, THOR SHATTERED THE KRONAN STONE-MAN, A GIANT ROCK CREATURE, WITH A SINGLE BLOW, PROMPTING ITS MARAUDING COMPATRIOTS TO SURRENDER.
- DURING THEIR ESCAPE FROM ASGARD, LOKI BRIEFLY DISGUISED THOR AS SIF, MUCH TO HIS DISPLEASURE.
- WHILE BATTLING MALEKITH, THOR WAS SEPARATED FROM MJOLNIR; HE HAD TO TAKE PUBLIC TRANSPORTATION TO RESUME THE FIGHT.

IAN BOOTHBY

FIRST APPEARANCE:
Thor: The Dark World (2013)

Ian Boothby was an unpaid intern for Darcy Lewis, who herself was an intern for Jane Foster. While Lewis searched for the missing Foster and their colleague Dr. Erik Selvig, Boothby noticed Selvig on the TV news—after he was arrested for running amok at Stonehenge, in the nude, having apparently gone mad. Boothby posed as Selvig's son to release him from police custody. Outside, Boothby observed starlings flying in a murmuration vanish from the sky and reappear beneath them, proving Selvig's theory of an interdimensional Convergence. When Foster and Thor returned from Asgard, Boothby joined their efforts to prevent the Dark Elf Malekith from releasing the power of the Aether during the Convergence and destroying the universe. Boothby helped Lewis hammer Selvig's gravimetric spikes into the ground at the focal point of the Convergence in Greenwich, England, while Thor fought Malekith. During the chaos caused by the Convergence, Boothby saved Lewis' life by crushing several Dark Elves with a gravity-defying car. Lewis rewarded Boothby with a passionate kiss. After Malekith was defeated, Lewis kissed him again. Boothby and Lewis kept Foster company while she waited for Thor to return from Asgard.

FACT SHEET

- INITIALLY, LEWIS CALLED BOOTHBY "THE INTERN" DESPITE HIS REQUESTS TO BE CALLED IAN.
- PLAYING WITH AN ANOMALY THE SCIENTISTS DISCOVERED, BOOTHBY UNINTENTIONALLY THREW THEIR CAR'S KEYS INTO A ONE-WAY PORTAL TO SVARTALFHEIM.
- BOOTHBY USED TO GO BIRDWATCHING WITH HIS FATHER AS A CHILD.

BOR

FIRST APPEARANCE:
Thor: The Dark World (2013)

Five thousand years ago, King Bor fearlessly led Asgard's armies against Svartalfheim's Dark Elves during the previous Convergence of the Nine Realms. When the Dark Elves' malevolent leader, Malekith, attempted to shroud the universe in eternal darkness using the Aether, Bor and his warriors seized the ancient power and defeated the Elves. Seeking to annihilate the Asgardians, Malekith ordered his soldiers to crash their ships into their own home planet, Svartalfheim, but Bor survived. Knowing the Aether was too powerful to be destroyed, Bor entrusted an Asgardian warrior to hide it where it would never be found. It was later written that Bor's victory ushered in peace for thousands of years.

FACT SHEET

- BOR WIELDED THE SPEAR GUNGNIR BEFORE IT WAS PASSED TO HIS SON, ODIN.
- DUE TO HIS INEXPERIENCE FLYING A DARK ELF HARROW AIRSHIP, THOR ACCIDENTALLY DESTROYED A STATUE OF BOR. LOKI CHIDED THOR FOR DECAPITATING HIS OWN GRANDFATHER.

IN THE COMICS

ASGARDIAN KING BOR WAS AMONG the gods who created the universe. His son, Odin, sought to forge a legacy for himself on Earth and created humankind—which greatly displeased Bor, who unleashed brutal punishments upon the mortal race. Amidst war with the Frost Giants, a time-traveling Loki trapped Bor's spirit within the snow; rather than save him, Odin chose to ascend to Asgard's throne and rule undisputed. Loki restored Bor centuries later, but magically altered his perception so he only perceived demons. Bor threatened to destroy Earth, so his grandson, Thor, reluctantly killed the grandfather he had never met.

FIRST APPEARANCE:
JOURNEY INTO MYSTERY #97 (1963)

HEIMDALL UPDATE

FIRST APPEARANCE: ***Thor (2011)***

The all-seeing Heimdall resumed his role as guardian of the Bifrost after its power was restored using the Tesseract, a device claimed by Thor after the Avengers' Battle of New York. Heimdall was often visited by Thor, who—unable to visit her due to his peacekeeping duties—was concerned about Jane Foster's welfare. When Heimdall lost sight of her after she inadvertently traveled to the hiding place of the Aether energy, he transported Thor to Earth to investigate, then brought both Thor and Foster to Asgard once Thor discovered the Aether had taken root within Foster's body.

Later, Heimdall was the first to detect one of the Dark Elves' cloaked Harrow warships approaching Asgard in their search for the Aether; though he destroyed the ship, Heimdall could only watch as other Dark Elf ships uncloaked and attacked the city. Heimdall activated the royal palace's protective energy dome, but the Dark Elf Kurse, having infiltrated the palace dungeons, destroyed the dome's power source, leaving Asgard unprotected. Though the Dark Elves were routed, Heimdall was disheartened by the Elves' murder of Queen Frigga and his own inability to defend Asgard. With the Bifrost closed at Odin's order, Heimdall conspired with Thor, Sif, and the Warriors Three to transport Foster off-world, hoping the Dark Elves' leader, Malekith, would follow. As Thor and his allies escaped with Foster, Heimdall requested Odin's presence in his observatory, where he surrendered himself for his act of treason.

FACT SHEET

- HEIMDALL'S SWORD CAN ACTIVATE A DOME-SHAPED ENERGY SHIELD AROUND THE ASGARDIAN ROYAL PALACE.
- THOUGH HEIMDALL UNDERSTOOD THAT THE CONVERGENCE—THE ALIGNMENT OF THE NINE REALMS THAT OCCURS EVERY FIVE THOUSAND YEARS—HAD GREAT DESTRUCTIVE POTENTIAL, HE ALSO CONSIDERED THE EVENT BEAUTIFUL.

HOGUN UPDATE

FIRST APPEARANCE: ***Thor (2011)***

Following the destruction of the Bifrost, the rainbow bridge that connected Asgard to the Nine Realms, Hogun and the Warriors Three aided Thor and the Asgardian armies in maintaining peace among the realms, often resorting to warfare to accomplish that goal. They also fought to slow the progression toward Ragnarok, the prophesied twilight of the gods of Asgardian legend. When marauders threatened Vanaheim, Hogun's homeworld, he assisted Sif and Asgardian forces in battling them. After Thor's timely arrival and defeat of the marauders' massive stone warrior, the invaders surrendered. Later, at Thor's friendly urging, Hogun remained in Vanaheim to be with his people.

FACT SHEET

- DESPITE HIS NORMALLY HUMORLESS DEMEANOR, HOGUN WAS PLEASED TO BE ABLE TO REMAIN IN HIS HOMELAND, AND EXPRESSED GRATITUDE TO THOR FOR MAKING IT HAPPEN.
- WHEN INTERSPACIAL PORTALS WERE RANDOMLY OPENED BETWEEN THE NINE REALMS DUE TO THE CONVERGENCE, AN ALIGNMENT OF THE NINE WORLDS THAT OCCURS ONCE EVERY FIVE THOUSAND YEARS, HOGUN WITNESSED THE CURIOUS SIGHT OF BRITISH FIGHTER JETS FLYING ACROSS THE VANAHEIM SKY.

DARCY LEWIS UPDATE

FIRST APPEARANCE: ***Thor [2011]***

Still an unpaid intern for Jane Foster, Darcy Lewis worked out of a laboratory in Foster's mother's London home; Lewis even took on her own intern, Ian Boothby. Lewis interrupted Foster during a date because one of Foster's devices had detected readings similar to when they first encountered Thor. Lewis, Foster and Boothby investigated the location, there finding the laws of physics suspended. While exploring this, Foster was pulled through an interdimensional portal, returning unintentionally imbued with the ancient Aether energy. After Thor took Foster to Asgard to seek a cure, Lewis fruitlessly attempted to locate their friend, Dr. Erik Selvig, ultimately finding him in police custody, apparently insane. After observing evidence that Selvig's theory of a Nine Realm Convergence was true, Lewis worked with Selvig, Foster, Boothby, and Thor in preventing the Dark Elf Malekith from destroying the universe by unleashing the Aether, which he had reclaimed from Foster. While Thor and Malekith battled, Lewis and Boothby hammered Selvig's gravitational spikes into the ground as directed. After Boothby saved Lewis by smashing Dark Elves with a gravitationally affected car, she responded by passionately kissing him; once Malekith was defeated, she kissed him again. Later, Lewis kept Foster company while she waited for Thor to return to Earth.

FACT SHEET

- LEWIS WAS SHAMELESS WHEN INTERRUPTING A TENDER MOMENT BETWEEN THOR AND FOSTER.
- LEWIS STILL PROVED UNABLE TO PRONOUNCE THOR'S HAMMER, AGAIN CALLING IT "MYEU-MUH" INSTEAD OF MJOLNIR.

ERIK SELVIG UPDATE

FIRST APPEARANCE: ***Thor [2011]***

Mentally unbalanced by Loki's mental control preceding the Chitauri invasion of New York, astrophysicist Erik Selvig became obsessed with the Convergence of the Nine Realms, which he believed foreshadowed a coming universal cataclysm. Determined to prove his theory, Selvig arrived at Stonehenge with a series of gravimetric spikes of his own design to detect the spatial disruptions caused by the Convergence, but his choice to completely disrobe disturbed the monument's visitors, and police confined him to a psychiatric ward.

Seeking Selvig's help after Jane Foster unintentionally absorbed the Aether, Darcy Lewis and Ian Boothby arranged his release. Upon Thor and Foster's return from Asgard, the pair met with Selvig, Lewis, and Boothby to devise a plan to stop the Dark Elf Malekith from using the Aether, which he had claimed from Foster, to cast the Nine Realms into eternal darkness. Selvig's research allowed him to identify Greenwich as the location where Malekith would unleash the Aether. With Selvig's gravimetric spikes modified to create interspatial portals within the Convergence, the four scientists occupied Malekith's forces while Thor fought their leader. After Malekith's defeat, Selvig was present when Thor returned from Asgard, fulfilling his promise to reunite with Foster.

FACT SHEET

- SELVIG PRESENTED AN EDUCATIONAL LECTURE ON THE CONVERGENCE TO THE OTHER PATIENTS IN THE PSYCHIATRIC WARD AS THOUGH THEY WERE HIS STUDENTS.
- SELVIG THREW AWAY HIS PSYCHIATRIC MEDICATIONS UPON LEARNING HIS CONVERGENCE THEORIES WERE NOT THE PRODUCT OF MADNESS.
- WHEN THOR SPOKE OF LOKI'S DEATH, SELVIG EXPRESSED ILL-TIMED RELIEF.